Dr. Dennis

Psychological Behavior in Sport

R. B. ALDERMAN

**Faculty of Physical Education,
University of Alberta,
Edmonton, Alberta**

W. B. SAUNDERS COMPANY

PHILADELPHIA • LONDON • TORONTO

W. B. Saunders Company: West Washington Square
Philadelphia, PA 19105

1 St. Anne's Road
Eastbourne, East Sussex BN21 3UN, England

1 Goldthorne Avenue
Toronto, Ontario M8Z 5T9, Canada

Psychological Behavior in Sport   ISBN 0-7216-1089-7

Last digit is the print number: 9   8   7   6   5

To
FRANKLIN M. HENRY

*. . . who, during those years at Berkeley,
taught us all to think clearly and to realize
and appreciate that ". . . words have meaning."*

PREFACE

The purpose of this book is to explore the behavior of individuals participating in play, games, and sports. Its focus is on *why* people behave the way they do in various athletic and physical activity settings and its scope encompasses what I consider to be the major psychological dimensions underlying such behavior. The principal objective of this approach is to provide the reader with an understanding of, and insight into, these important psychological systems. The book, I hope, will provide answers to questions and problems of a psychological nature as they pertain to the handling, coaching, and understanding of the young participant in sport. The general context of the book is directed toward a logical and careful analysis of the background knowledge required for understanding the behavioral dimensions of sport. This is essentially a phenomenological approach, in which intuitive understanding, rather than precise explanation, is the main goal, and in which some attempt is made to present diverse theoretical positions in such a manner that the reader can integrate for himself some kind of *holistic* or total understanding of the content.

Because of the incredible expansion of knowledge occurring in all disciplines, it is impossible to include all those concepts having a bearing on behavior in athletics and physical activity. To do so would necessitate, at best, only a cursory or superficial treatment of constructs that are deeply rooted in behavior. Rather, the intention here has been to carefully select those broad dimensions which exert the major influences on individual behavior in sport and examine, in depth, their structure and dynamic functioning. A serious attempt has been made to cover the major theories in each of these areas, especially in terms of their relevance for physical activity and sport, but again it is a dialectical choice at best. Unfortunately, research in physical activity and sport has, to date, been mainly concerned with performance rather than behavior; we know much about *how* a person performs but little about *why* he performs. This lack of direct research information has necessitated an approach which is more intuitive and speculative than empirical. There is nothing wrong with this kind of knowledge acquisition as long as the reader is aware that many of the observations, interpretations, and implications in this book are presented in such a context.

This book is directed toward the senior undergraduate student and the graduate student who has had some psychology and sociology somewhere in his educational past. It is also a book designed to supplement the psychological insight of professional teachers and coaches already aware of the myriad psychological problems in physical activity and sport. Everyone is an amateur psychologist, and nowhere is this more evident than in sport, where it seems everyone always has an explanation for some particular instance of behavior. This book is an attempt to provide a framework for integrating these scattered pieces of knowledge in such a way that we can better understand and help the young participant.

The book is thinly structured into three broad sections. The first four chapters deal with the structure and functioning of play, games, and competitive sport in Western society. This is an attempt to place the terms "sport" and "physical activity" into a context which will provide a common basis for discourse. The next three chapters deal with the concept of "personality" and its usefulness in helping us to understand behavior in sport. The last four chapters are concerned with the major *motivational* dimensions of behavior and the relevance they have for increasing our insight into why people behave the way they do in various athletic and physical activity situations. This is a "person-oriented" book. It is written on a "need to know" basis—that is, it is imperative that we begin to understand why children and adults behave the way they do in sport if we are to help them realize the fun and enjoyment they are seeking.

RICHARD B. ALDERMAN

ACKNOWLEDGMENTS

I wish to acknowledge myself, without whose help my graduate students would never have been able to write this book.

*** *** ***

I would like to express particular thanks to my industrious secretaries, Mrs. Ellen Winchester and Miss Laurel Ozarko, and to my freely critical graduate students Doctors Wankel, Orlick, Davey, Scott, Klavora, Danielson, and Paddick.

My profound thanks go to my lovely wife Dorothy and to my long-suffering editor, Wally Pennington.

RICHARD B. ALDERMAN

CONTENTS

3

4

5

6

THE PERSONALITY TRAIT STRUCTURE OF ATHLETES

7

THE DYNAMICS OF PERSONALITY IN SPORT

11

INTRODUCTION

Traditionally, the psychological area in physical education and sport has been concerned with motor performance, motor learning, and sport skill acquisition. This emphasis has been the result of the training and interests of psychologists, mainly trained in experimental psychology, who have switched over to and worked in physical education. McCloy, Brace, Henry, and Slater-Hammel were scientists of this type, and their students have mostly carried on this approach down through the 1950's and 1960's. Recently, however, the psychological area in physical education has undergone considerable modification in terms of emphasis. There is now evident a large swing toward a looser, more phenomenological approach to the psychology of physical activity and sport, and this is exemplified by an increasing interest in the *behavior* of the participant rather than in his *performance*, per se. The emphasis in this book on the underlying dimensions of behavior rather than on the indices of performance is consistent with this general change.

Behavior can be defined as the *total aggregate of human responses that the person makes to both internal and external stimuli.* Though very much a stimulus-response viewpoint, this definition is useful in that it places a behavioral approach to the psychology of sport in a context in which everything that the participant does, thinks, and feels should be examined. *Performance*, on the other hand, is usually interpreted as that *relatively short-term aspect of behavior which is marked by activity toward the execution of an observable, identifiable discrete task.* Individual behavior in physical activity and sport thus becomes all-encompassing in scope within which individual performance is only one aspect.

A behavioral analysis of the psychology of sport is thus concerned, in general terms, with the broad psychological, social, and emotional aspects of the individual in a context of physical activity and athletics. This is an emphasis directed toward dealing with the needs, interests, attitudes, dispositions, and motivations of the young participant rather than just focusing on an analysis of his performances. The primary intent of such an approach is to understand *why* an individual behaves the way he does in sports situations. Motor and athletic performances are viewed only in terms of how they are influenced by the behavior of the individual. A recent trend in the motor performance area serves to delineate this difference. Human performance theory, as outlined by Fitts and Posner (1967) and sometimes known as "information theory," generally discusses the limits of man's ability to sense, attend to, process, store, and transmit information. This strongly mechanistic approach to man's ability to perform skilled tasks, though quite important for students and scholars of physical activity and sport, differs dramatically from the broader analysis of behavior as covered in this book.

The attempt is made in this book to identify the *substantive* nature of physical activity and sport, to "get at" the real or essential nature of the psychology of sport. Here the attempt is made at describing and explaining what Cratty (1968) calls the "behavioral supports" underlying final performance. With this in mind, the dimensions of behavior covered in this book are factors such as self-actualization, tension seeking, need for achievement, level of aspiration, internal conflict, affiliation, aggression, and competitiveness, etc. It is through such "nebulous intangibles" that the real nature of behavior in sport can be understood in a realistic context.

One can also view the distinction between an emphasis on performance as contrasted to an emphasis on behavior in terms of the way the *dependent* variable is handled in experimental research in physical education. In the motor or human performance area one is primarily concerned with the dependent variable of performance, how it varies, what influences it, and how it can be better understood. The independent variables operating in this kind of experimentation are important only in the way in which they can better improve insight into performance. So one varies these independent variables to find out what happens to the dependent variable of performance. In a behavioral approach to the psychology of sport, however, it is the independent variables that receive all the attention. The contention here is simply that understanding a construct such as anxiety is more important *in and of itself* than just understanding its effects on performance of a skilled task. In order to receive valid information on the latter, one must thoroughly understand the former first. This has not generally been the case in the past, thus reducing the value of information gathered from strictly performance research.

If one can assume that the general approach in the motor performance area is *experimental* and in the behavioral area *clinical,* then another distinction can be made between the two. This distinction emanates from tradition. Experimental psychologists such as Helmholtz, Pavlov, Thorndike, and Wundt derived their inspiration and values from the natural sciences, combining technical skill with the rigor and precision of delimited investigation in controlled laboratory situations in what was considered to be the only proper way to do research. The clinical tradition arising from the work of Freud, Jung, and McDougall, however, was more concerned with intuitive feelings and insights directed toward a more creative reconstruction of human behavior. These psychologists tended to scorn the trappings of science with its restrictions upon the imagination. Such a functionalistic orientation was mainly concerned with man's adjustment to his environment. A similar functional orientation can be found in the psychology of sport, where the main issues investigated should have immediate practical importance for the teacher and coach. Issues such as identifying the causes of underachievement in physical education classes and athletic performance, the psychological coaching of young athletes, and the examination of the play behavior of young children are only a few examples of human adjustment in a physical activity and sports milieu. It is issues of these types that assume major importance in this book. In fact, such a functional approach holds considerable attractiveness for the teacher and coach in that behavioral problems are usually harder to diagnose and correct than are performance problems. The field worker also wants answers immediately and wants to solve the problems himself rather than be constantly waiting for "experts" to help him. He cannot afford to wait for carefully controlled experimentation to provide answers for him. He wants immediate insight into everyday problems, and a functional approach to the psychology of sport can go a long way toward providing him with this basic understanding.

A psychological theory should consist of a set of assumptions concerning human behavior, together with rules for relating these assumptions, and definitions to permit their interaction with empirical or observable events. A psychological theory in physical education and sport is useful only in terms of its success in relating assumptions to empirical or observable events in physical activity and sport. Some types of theories lend themselves better to accomplishing this objective. *General* behavioral theories, for example, though academically contentious, actually do deal with the adjustment of the individual in real behavioral situations. Why one child learns to swim more easily than another, why one person is more aggressive than another, why emotional stability is so important in outstanding athletic performance, are behavioral issues that can be understood only in the context of general theories such as personality theories. *Single-domain* theories, on the other hand, restrict their focus to certain *classes* of events by delimiting their intent to behavior as it occurs under certain carefully prescribed conditions.

Motor performance theory, for example, can be seen as generally fitting into this context in that it implicitly professes a focused interest on performance that can be carefully analyzed. Theories of personality and motivation are clearly general theories and are of importance in the psychology of sport. Such theories, in a sense, accept the challenge of accounting for or incorporating extremely varied events so long as they contain demonstrable functional significance for the individual. Such *looseness* is both a strength and a weakness. On one hand, the psychology of sport content can be directed toward any behavior that can be seen to have functional significance, whereas, on the other hand, such an approach can be seen to lack a coherent, scientific basis for the reliability and content validity of its information. How useful such intuitive information is at this point remains to be seen. At any rate, such an approach is a direct attempt to provide the practitioner with essential insight into why people behave the way they do in physical activity and sport.

THE UNDERLYING DIMENSIONS OF ATHLETIC PERFORMANCE

The performance of a champion athlete is always impressive. When Nicklaus slashes a 300 yard drive down the middle of the fairway, or Laver hits a pin-point volley with a power most players wish they could get on their serve, or O.J. Simpson runs 40 yards off tackle through some of the biggest and most aggressive humans in sports history, one may ask: What are the dimensions underlying such outstanding athletic ability? Not only are these performances, and others like them, successful, but they are invariably executed with a seemingly effortless smoothness, speed, and coolness that make it look easy. A veteran baseball observer once said of Willie Mays that "... he is so good that he makes the hard ones look easy—the hallmark of a true champion." Other examples, of course, come immediately to mind: Orr in hockey, Pele in soccer, Namath in football, Spitz in swimming, and countless numbers of other great performers in the world of sport. The list, however, is not endless. At any one time, the group of best athletes in the world is a finite population consisting of only a very few individuals in each sport. In various levels below these select groups exist thousands upon thousands of other participants; some good, some not so good, and some in between. Because of the obvious differences that exist between these participants in terms of the quality of their performances, one can become interested in exactly what factors contribute to this differentiation.

Cratty (1968) suggests that factors at three levels contribute to a person's final motor or athletic performance: (1) the basic behavioral supports underlying all performance, (2) the person's physical ability traits, and (3) the specific skills required in the relevant task. It is his contention that the three levels are mutually dependent on each other in that a person's success or failure in a particular task "feeds back" into the basic behavioral supports to raise or lower such psychological dimensions as his need for achievement or his level of aspiration. This psychological effect, in turn, affects his persistence in continuing to participate, and this influences the further perfection of his physical ability traits which, in turn, contribute to a greater command of the required skill specifics. Cratty describes the basic supports of behavior as being such qualities as level of aspiration, need for approval, need for achievement, emotional stability, and other various components of a person's personality and motivational structure.

Such an approach is consistent with Davey's (1972) analysis of the main factors that are necessary for athletic excellence. Davey feels that skill, physical fitness, and *attitude* are the three major components of performance. He contends, in his evaluation of several hundred outstanding Australian athletes, that a differentially weighted formula consisting of varying degrees of each of these factors can be constructed which will provide a predictive basis for judging a person's potential for both motor and athletic performance. Singer (1972) indirectly presents a more sophisticated picture by structuring the basic dimensions of athletic performance into: (1) growth and development factors, (2) personality factors, (3) personal factors, (4) social factors, (5) practice factors, (6) learning factors, and (7) training factors. An extremely simplified synthesis of these viewpoints could express athletic performance as being mainly dependent on four major groups of factors: (1) the natural ability, capacity, and physical endowment an individual receives via genetic inheritance, (2) the acquisition of the specific skills required for excellence in a particular task or sport, (3) the specific type and level of physical fitness mandatory for that task or sport, and (4) the general psychological makeup of the person in terms of his personality, motivational, and emotional strengths (Diagram 1).

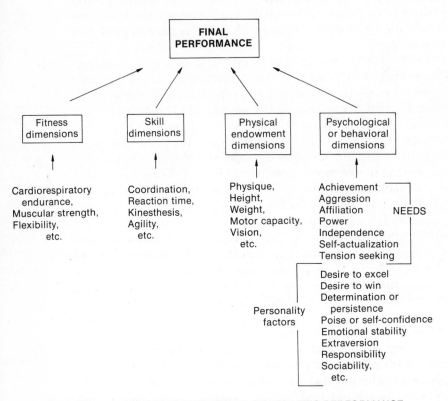

DIAGRAM 1. UNDERLYING DIMENSIONS OF ATHLETIC PERFORMANCE.

All motor performance, regardless of a person's ability level, is a function of the meshing of these four dimensions. These factors, and the performances resulting from an interaction of them, are also very definitely influenced by the general environment in which the person lives and the specific conditions under which the situation is occurring. This rather simple representation, then, applies not only to outstanding athletic performance, but also to the performances of people ranging all the way down to the beginner level. It is a paradigm that could be applied just as easily to children first learning the rudiments of a motor task as it could to adolescents learning how to play competitive basketball in high school. These different levels of ability become a straight function of the amount and quality of each one of these factors in the individual. Generally speaking, when each one of these groups of factors is at an optimum level in the person, his or her performance will also be optimal. One can thus look into these factor groups for the explanations of why particular individuals are failing to achieve their potential.

One essential point which can be stressed when viewing athletic performance in this manner is that regardless of how much ability, skill, or fitness a person possesses for a particular task or sport, the success or quality of his performance will, in the final analysis, probably depend on his particular psychological makeup. It will depend, to a large extent, on his personality structure, how motivated he is to succeed, and how much emotional control he possesses. The converse, of course, is also true. Even with a perfect psychological makeup for sport, an athlete will not be able to reach his potential for high performance unless he has acquired the specific skills required for his sport, has the proper physical attributes, and is in good physical condition. It is generally with the psychological makeup of the participant in physical activity and sport that this book is concerned. The premise here is that without an understanding of the behavioral structure of the individual, the teacher or coach cannot help him or her to achieve those basic objectives which impel the boy or girl to participate in recreative physical activity or competitive sport. Before developing this premise, a brief overview of several related concepts is necessary.

THE EXISTENCE OF INDIVIDUAL DIFFERENCES

Overlaid on the aforementioned four major dimensions underlying sport and physical activity is the existence of individual differences in each one. The investigation of individual differences is primarily concerned with the description and explanation of the causes and relationships among the many varieties of individual differences. Some degree of initial awareness of their existence in the makeup of people participating in sport is of obvious importance.

Probably the most interesting facet of individual differences in the area of sport is the challenging problem of their origins — are they genetically or environmentally determined? Whether or not there is factual evidence to justify the statement that "natural athletes are born not made," there still exists the realization that differences not inherited from one's parents are, to a large extent, the result of variations in diet, climate, early childhood interests and training, parental pressures, schooling, and myriad other social and cultural influences. The issue is a complex one as is demonstrated by the assessment of even the simplest physical characteristics. Take height for example. Though tall parents normally produce tall children, the relationship between the height of fathers and sons is not a perfect one. The *average* height of the sons of tall fathers tends to be less than the average height of the fathers; and the average height of sons of small fathers tends to be *greater* than the average height of the fathers. This predisposition of children's height to be closer to the mean or average height of the population was discovered by the British scientist, Galton, and designated by him as *filial regression*. Even though positive relationships exist between parental and offspring characteristics, heredity cannot account for all the individual differences that occur. Some variability results from diet, exercise, and other environmental influences, and if such variability operates with a simple characteristic like height, consider what happens to the more complex physical characteristics such as coordination, speed, and agility? And athletic ability or athletic behavior, the composites of numberless physical, social, and psychological variables, are even more difficult to assess in terms of the variability of individual differences as a function of either heredity or environment.

Another source of interest is the degree to which individual differences are a function of sex, race, and culture. In terms of performance, men tend to be superior to women in athletics, but whether or not this is caused by biological differences or is due to the extremely different environmental conditions and cultural roles presented to boys and girls in our society remains to be seen. With relation to racial differences, very little objective evidence exists regarding the presence or absence of superior athletic ability in specific races or ethnic groups. Much has been said, but little proven, about the Negro's superiority in athletics, but other than speculation, little or no definitive research has been undertaken to prove or disprove this view. Whether or not the Negro, or the Oriental, is physically or behaviorally superior to the Caucasian, and whether or not it is just a function of the social environments in which they live, are still burning issues when discussing individual differences in sport and physical activity. Cultural differences are even more difficult to determine because rarely is a *pure* culture available for evaluation and comparison. Historically speaking, some cultures such as Athens and Sparta have been noted for their athletic emphasis and prowess, but to ascribe the current successes in international athletics of the United States or Russia to individual differences arising from their cultures is quite tenuous. Whether or not certain unique factors operating in the American or Russian societies can be identified as the reasons for their superior athletic performances is particularly interesting from a strictly behavioral point of view.

Age differences and their influence on the performance and behavior of participants in physical activity are just as difficult to determine. Though most of the research on age differences has been done with younger children, more recently attention has been turned to changes in ability and behavior which accompany the aging process. Complex research designs are needed to separate out the effects of simply growing older biologically and the differential effects of a society which treats its older people differently because of their age. Of special interest in the question of individual differences as a function of age are the issues of: (1) at what ages does the potential for athletic performance appear and (2) at what ages does it start to disappear?

Finally, the study of individual differences in athletic ability and performance becomes intriguing when one considers the complex patterns of relationships between strictly behavioral variables such as the desire to excel in sport. Do all individuals participating in sport have such a desire, or do individual differences exist? And to what degree? And, if they do, why? Individual differences due to age, sex, race, and culture, as previously covered, are only a few of the causal variables that exist in such questions. Family structure, sibling order and rivalry, parental interests and attitudes, physical opportunities, physiological variables, body build, different needs at different ages, and many others all influence the existence of individual differences in any aspect of athletic behavior and performance. As soon as one starts to identify causal relationships between two or more variables in sport when attempting to answer questions of why people behave the way they do, one immediately discovers the thousands of combinations that exist in the behavioral area of sport.

The extent to which individual differences in sports behavior and performance exist in children of all ages necessitates providing different kinds of educational experiences from kindergarten through high school. A few children can perform superbly before entering school, others not until their teens. Our traditional curriculum practice in physical education and athletics has tended to treat these children all equally. This has resulted in some children meeting class standards, some exceeding them, and some not quite satisfying them. This lack of appreciation of the existence of individual differences in ability and behavior has forced a rigidity on the physical education system that virtually ignores above-par and below-par performers. On one hand, gifted children are forced into antiquated athletic systems while on the other, sub-par children are turned off and become drop-outs. With modern teaching methods based upon a recognition of the importance of assessing individual differences in both the ability and behavior of children, however, a drive for individualized instruction along the four continuums of physical, social, emotional, and intellectual development is now underway (Mosston 1966).

THE INDIVIDUAL IN A PHYSICAL MOVEMENT MILIEU

Scientists working in the fields of human behavior tend to attach considerable significance and importance to the nature and role of play and participation in sport in our childhood society. The significance and psychological meaning of participation in physical activity and sports in later life, however, has remained relatively unexamined. This is mystifying when one considers the emphasis and attention that the public has attached to sport and its place in society in recent years. People all over the world read and talk about sport possibly more than any other single subject. Sport everywhere claims large sections of our daily newspapers, and it is not uncommon for a sports attraction to draw the biggest television audience of the year. Added to this powerful attraction that competitive sport seems to have for millions of people throughout the world is the mass participation by millions of others in daily physical activity. Some recreative sports number their participants in the millions and in some countries, for example, Australia, it is said that the average person works only for the purpose of being able to enjoy his favorite sport during his leisure time. What, therefore, is there in physical activity and sport that attracts such widespread interest? Why do people watch and participate in sport? What is it that drives man to move in either a recreative or competitive milieu?

It is the thesis of this book that the answers to these questions, and questions like them, lie in the understanding of man's general and specific psychological behaviors. A basic premise from which to proceed is that as man evolves, psychological and sociological characteristics tend to replace physical and biological characteristics as the main determinants of human behavior. Such an assumption has two major implications. First is the realization that we no longer live in a physical world. Man lives and succeeds now on the basis of his mental qualities and his ability to integrate his life smoothly with that of his fellow man. No longer is man required to live by his muscles, no longer is he required to fight off wild animals to survive, and no longer is he required to outrun these animals if they are too big or too ferocious to fight. Modern man now lives in a mental world, in which the important skills for success are based in his psychological and sociological abilities. So to look for an explanation of his behavior with respect to *anything,* one must perforce look to the psychological and sociological dimensions of his life.

Thus, to explain man's fervent interest in sport we must examine the psychological and sociological dimensions of his behavior in a movement context. And, because of this strong, all-pervasive influence and dependence on man's mental abilities, each day coupled with lack of opportunity for physical movement, man has developed, even more sharply than before, a real and strong need for physical activity. This is reinforced by an instinctual need for movement that is rooted in his physical past. Groos (1901) suggests that play is the result of emerging instincts being fixated in actual, current behavior, and that the basic instincts rooted in man's primeval past lie latent in modern man, waiting for the relevant stimuli and opportunity to become manifest. Such an approach has intuitive attractiveness for explaining modern man's compulsion for both the excitement of competitive sport and the need for participation in physical activity. For thousands of years man had to compete and to move in order to stay alive, and such instincts probably remain as part of his evolutionary heritage.

Each person, however, who participates in sport, actively or passively, has his own distinctive interests, needs, pleasures, and motivations. Sport means different things to different people and no complete formula exists which can tell us everything we want to know about the individual participant. Rather, we must delve into a complex, nebulous, and often intangible structure of potentials, abilities, skills, and capacities, if we are to begin an understanding of man performing in sport and physical activity. We must realize perforce that the psychological needs, in particular those which participation satisfies, are many and quite varied. That sport may represent a man's response to the challenges of nature, that it may be a sublimation of survival activities, or that it may represent an acceptance means of dealing with aggressive impulses, are just a few that could be mentioned. Therefore, though it is evident that no single statement can be made to describe the individual performer in sport and physical activity, there is a need to operationally define or distinguish between the ordinary participant in sport and the "athlete."

A commonsense or intuitive approach to defining the term *athlete* could be:

Any person who engages in competitive athletics.

Conversely, the basis for the distinction between the ordinary participant and the athlete obviously lies in whether the activity is competitive or not. The ordinary participant in physical activity thus becomes a person engaging in physical activity for reasons other than could be construed as being solely competitive. In order to demonstrate whether or not this is a valid distinction, the scope and nature of man's movement milieu should be explored. In addition, the distinction must be explained in terms of what characteristics exist between the terms *athlete, participant,* and *movement* that are common to each and yet are different. The focus of this discussion now centers around:

The interaction of man and his movement in either a competitive or noncompetitive milieu.

Movement now becomes our frame of reference and, as such, must be examined in terms of its denotations.* Cratty (1964), in stating a case for the analysis of movement, feels that *"movement behavior"* refers to observable movements (or skilled performance movements), to movements which can be termed reflex in nature, or to movements which may seem randomless or purposeless. He further states, in an effort to narrow such a frame of reference, that "... acts which involve short-term execution and completion of an identifiable task may be considered as the motor performance aspect of movement behavior." Motor performance is thus considered as goal-oriented, purposeful, observable movement over a short period of time. *Skilled* motor performance implies that the movements have undergone a learning phase which has resulted in a smoothing out or coordination of the more observable aspects. As Singer (1972) observes, "... Skill is a relative quality, not to be defined in absolute terms." What may be skilled performance, for example, at the high school level is not necessarily regarded as skilled at the professional level.† However, the highly skilled performer is usually quite recognizable in that his performance seems to be very smooth, free of error, quite accurate, extremely forceful, very fast, and, most im-

---

*The *denotation* of a term is the collection of all those things to which the term refers.

†For an interesting discussion of "levels" in athletic skill the reader is referred to Levels of the Game, by John McPhee, New York, Bantam Books, 1970. This is an extensive analysis of the tennis styles of Arthur Ashe and Clark Graebner.

portant, highly successful. It is interesting to note here that one of the denotations of the term *movement* is *skill*, which has strong athletic connotations:* namely, that athletes tend to be highly skilled.

Competitive athletics, the remaining phrase in our definition, has three main connotations: first is that man struggles personally against another person or persons, second is that his struggle is impersonally against an objective, external standard, and third is that he struggles to better himself, i.e., he competes with himself. All three of these designations function within the context of games and sport. This is consistent with Starr's (1961) definition of competitive athletics as being "a wide range of games and sports which involve a rivalry or a match with one's self or with others." Competitive athletics, thus, become only a small part of the totality of man's movement. Physical movement is engaged in by man for many reasons other than competition and it is here that the main distinction can be made between the *athlete* and the *participant* in physical activity. If the performer is competing, in the above sense of the word, then he must perforce be regarded as participating in an athletic context; if he is simply engaging in physical movement for reasons that do not emanate from his competitive needs or desires, then he can be classified as a participant. Football players, mountain climbers, golfers, joggers, and even dancers, are all athletes, regardless of their ability levels, if their movements are primarily directed toward the pursuit of excellence or success. Little boys wrestling on the front lawn, people canoeing on mountain lakes or bicycling on their Exercycles in the basement, if the connotations of their movements are not directed toward competing, are participants. The pure joy of movement, accompanied by its myriad sensory incentives, thus can be distinguished, phenomenologically, from the competitive joy of movement. Thus, when one thinks in a competitive frame of reference one is usually thinking in terms of the athlete or of athletics. Though every athlete is a participant in physical activity, every participant is not necessarily an athlete.

Our operational definition of the *athlete* has now become:

> Any person who executes and completes an identifiable, short-term, skilled motor performance while competing against an objective, external standard, against another person or persons, or against oneself.

---

*The term *connotation* refers to the suggestion or significance of the term rather than its flat expression.

There are many other reasons besides the thrill of competition for participating in physical activity and sport. Weiss (1969), for example, feels the attraction that athletics and physical activity have for the young person lies in its potential for achieving excellence. It is his contention that the young person, realizing that excellence in most everyday pursuits is usually years in the future, recognizes that, in sport, excellence can be attained in a relatively short period of time. And this realization, coupled with the strong prestige and status implications that athletic excellence has for our younger generation, presents to the young person an opportunity for escaping anonymity in his particular society.

Closely related to this desire for excellence is the general human trait of needing to satisfy a basic desire for achievement. In an achievement-oriented society, the need for performing in a setting where public evaluation is explicit and immediate is very strong. Physical activity and sport provide perfect vehicles for satisfying this achievement need in a setting which is not only possible for the young person, but also extremely relevant.

Participating in physical movement situations also provides a person with the opportunity to satisfy his needs for aggression, power, independence, curiosity, and affiliation. That is to say, people use physical activity and sport to release aggressive tendencies within them which are either inherent to them as homo sapiens or which are learned tendencies in their culture but which have no socially acceptable outlets. Physical contact sports, in particular, appear to have profound potential for the release of such tendencies. Physical activity and sport also provide the person with the means for seeking and attaining close social bonds with other people. Belonging to a sports group or playing on a team satisfies such an affiliative need both in boys and girls and in men and women. Conversely, physical activity and sport also provide the opportunity for satisfying one's need for independence. The need a person has for being able to do things without the help of other people can be constantly observed as probably strongly operating in such activities as mountain climbing, surfing, and skiing, and in such sports as golf, tennis, and track and field.

Curiosity, as we shall see shortly, can be seen as a basic need operating in the play of young children, especially when it is considered in terms of mastering one's environment or pursuing some kind of competence. One is constantly curious about one's place in the meaning of things. One pursues this curiosity in many ways, one of which is through a movement dimension.

The need for power can also be seen to be operating in sport.

The desire for influencing or controlling other people around you is obviously central to many people's reasons for participating or being involved in sport. The so-called "ego trips" that athletes and coaches engage in are traceable to strong needs for power. Just by demonstrating athletic or motor excellence, however, one can influence other people, and it is the satisfaction one gains from such an accomplishment that may drive him to participate in physical activity and sport. For all these and other reasons people participate in physical activity and sport, and it is the purpose of this book to explore the more important of these.

ABILITY, CAPACITY AND SKILL

Three other important factors overlie the behavioral dimensions of physical activity and sport. These are the motor ability or athletic ability of the performer, his motor capacity, and his motor or athletic skill. These three factors place the individual participant into the movement context within which his behavior can best be viewed.

A commonsense definition of *athletic ability* would be the power or capacity to competently perform in any particular athletic activity. The evaluation of such ability is normally based on whether the performance is successful or not, so that when we see an athlete execute a superior performance, we tend to automatically think that he possesses *ability*. The concept of ability then becomes an operational one in terms of performance. For example, it is generally assumed that football players have, in varying degrees, athletic ability. But does a quarterback have the same ability as a lineman? Can it be assumed that there is some common ability cutting across all positions in football, or is it better considered that abilities are *specific* to specific positions? For example, if we consider speed of foot to be necessary in *all* football players, regardless of the position they play, are we saying that speed of foot is an undeniable component of athletic ability? If we do, then we have taken the first step to differentiating on a conceptual basis rather than on an operational one. Otherwise, in our example, all topnotch dash men would automatically be good football players. Such an assumption is a ridiculous one because we know that to be a good football player one must have, in addition to speed of foot, other important traits such as physical size, strength, aggressiveness, knowledge and insight into the intricacies of the game, and specific coordinations. By saying this we are tacitly assuming that football ability is the composite of a number of components and that the only thing remaining is the identification, description, and explanation of not only these relatively independent components and their relationships, but also their degree of contributory importance to the total structure of any particular kind of athletic ability.

Setting aside, for purposes of discussion at this time, the physiological components of athletic ability, let us examine the major pieces of information relating to athletic and motor ability. First, to be consistent with the previous distinction between athletes and participants, the distinction between motor ability and athletic ability can best be simply considered as regarding the term *motor* as being generally concerned with physical movement and the term athletic as being generally concerned with movement in an "athletic" context. Thus, ordinary motor ability becomes athletic ability when the ability or abilities involved become manifested in a competitive sport milieu.

The identification and definition of motor ability is not that easy, voluminous research ranging all the way back to Sargent (1887) through McCloy (1940) up to Fleishman (1964). *Motor ability* usually refers to the capacity or power of the person for action or movement in a physical sense; it is normally considered in terms of current status and with reference to the skeletal musculature. It is also thought to be an enduring trait that is affected both by heredity and learning. Implied in the usage of the term is an inherent consistency of competence in the execution of motor tasks and a general acceptance that ability is *latent* rather than active. This distinguishes it from *motor capacity* which is generally conceived as the ultimate development *potential* of the individual's ability. Thus, one may have a high degree of one but not of the other. For example, two boys could be considered to have the same ability (both can hit a baseball), but we might consider one of them to have a greater potential or capacity than the other (one will stay a .300 hitter while the other may become another Ted Williams and hit .400). (The same analogy can be made with respect to behavioral variables: two people might have the same current leadership ability but, because of certain other personality traits, one might have more capacity for becoming a better leader than the other.) In reverse terms we might even consider one person to be superior in capacity but inferior in his ability to put his already acquired skills into action. Such is the case with underachievers in sport; a boy who seems to have everything going for him just does not seem able to rise to his potential in performance.

Motor capacity also implies that some individuals will be able to acquire more ability than others. The ease with which such individuals acquire motor ability and the ease with which they learn new motor skills is referred to as *motor educability or motor aptitude*. Though these two terms have more or less fallen into disuse lately, they do have a conceptual usefulness for the student of physical activity. There is little doubt that some individuals have more of a readiness, facility, or quickness for acquiring new motor skills than others, and every teacher and coach is aware of this observation. Why some people learn easily and others do not is a question of particular interest in physical activity and sport. Are there certain factors that must be present in a person's makeup before he can start to learn a task or is his motor educability dependent upon his already established motor ability? McCloy (1940) felt the latter was the case and, consequently, went to a great deal of trouble to list factors which he considered prerequisites to the effective learning of motor skills. Factors such as strength, flexibility, agility, peripheral vision, and concentration, for example, were all felt to be requisites for educability or learning.

It is not inconsistent, then, to suggest that these concepts are also viable for behavioral factors as well as for performance variables. For example, the capacity a person has for *determination* in athletic performance may or may not be realized in an actual ability for determination; and this in turn is probably a function of the ease with which he acquires or learns how to be determined in specific performance situations. Behavioral capacity, ability, and educability, as we will see in the following sections of this book, are all combined into a complex network dependent upon one's personality characteristics, one's environment, and one's interaction with other people.

The concept of *skill* also has both performance and behavioral connotations. Skill generally refers to a specific task and the level of the person's proficiency in that task. A *motor skill*, then, is a highly developed capacity to perform a particular motor task or group of motor tasks. An *athletic skill* is therefore the level of motor proficiency a person has for performing an athletic task. A *behavioral skill* is the person's proficiency in a specific behavioral situation. In this context, an ability underlies or is general to the performance in question, while a skill is specific to the particular task. The most important distinction concerned with a skilled motor performance is that it involves a series or sequence of organized movements that are goal oriented. Thus a knee jerk movement is hardly a skill, whereas throwing a football obviously requires the smooth sequence of movements just noted. A behavioral skill has the same connotations: if a coach is highly skilled in communicating with his players, then he has acquired and developed a series or sequence of mannerisms and mechanisms which are successful in smoothly interacting with his athletes. Examples of such behavioral mechanisms are empathy, sympathy, and consistency of behavior.

NATURAL PHYSICAL AND ABILITY ENDOWMENT

Athletic talent is normally construed as being native to the individual and as being hereditary in nature. The question of whether or not a person is a *natural* athlete has twofold significance: first, is he considered a natural athlete because there is an inherent smoothness and ease in his performances or, secondly, is it because he is a superior performer at a large number of sports? The latter question will be explored shortly in a discussion revolving around the issue of task specificity. With reference to the first question, however, a simple explanation is not that simple.

The speed, force, and coordinated smoothness of a champion athlete's performance tend to be so effortless that people often make the mistake of thinking his success is due solely to his *natural* talent. Ignored in this assumption is the vast amount of time and effort which has been spent in learning, practicing, and perfecting the various skills required for any particular event. The question usually implied at this point is "... how much does heredity contribute to the making of an athlete, and how much is caused by the effects of his past environment?" That is, are outstanding athletes *born not made*? Are some people natural athletes or are they normally endowed people who have devoted hours and hours to diligent and dedicated practice under the careful guidance of a series of excellent coaches? Can anyone become a champion athlete if he is prepared and eager to sacrifice a large portion of his life to sport? Or does heredity *predetermine* those who will later become champions?

Even genetically speaking the questions are difficult to answer. From the actual moment of conception, rather than birth, environmental factors start to operate and interact with genetic inheritance received from each parent. Life in the mother's womb is influenced by the environment in which she lives during pregnancy. It is soon evident, however, that in the early stages of life, one factor, namely physical appearance, is predominantly hereditary in nature. Children do tend to inherit their physical endowment or appearance from their parents. Studies on identical twins whose physical characteristics are little affected by their environments support this observation.

Whether or not other physical considerations such as reaction time, agility and flexibility are also the result of the genes inherited from each parent remains to be seen. Other physical characteristics, however, such as speed, would appear from subjective observation to be largely natural to the individual and relatively unaffected by practicing or being coached. A boy tends to be either fast or slow in running or skating and though running or skating can certainly be improved through coaching and practice, there is little doubt in the coaching ranks that some boys are natural runners or skaters. It is, incidentally, of no help to examine the physical and athletic ability of a boy's or girl's parents. There is almost no objective basis for thinking that a child will be naturally athletic if his parents are both champion athletes. The reason for this is that genetics is very clear and succinct on the point that each offspring is an *individual entity* and not so many parts of this and that. Though each offspring inherits 23 chromosomes from each parent, the pairing up of the chromosomes in prophase of meiosis is done in a haphazard manner with respect to the relative position of the pairs in relation to each other. That is, all the chromosomes inherited from the father do not line up on one side and all those from the mother on the other. Rather, the offspring may inherit a chromosome from the first pair from his mother, the next from his father, and so on in any combination of dual arrangement from 23 pairs. Added to this is the fact that the arrangement of the 23 pairs varies in every germ cell during meiotic division and that there may be crossing-over occurring in the genes.

What this means is that with the 50,000 or so genes that exist in the 46 chromosomes, the odds are about 1 in 200,000 trillion that parents will ever present the same package of genes to more than one child. So even though the rough physical characteristics seem to be transmitted from parent to child, it is highly doubtful that athletic ability is inherited. What happens is that parents with athletic interests and attitudes have a significant effect on the environment in which their children grow and develop and, in this way, either consciously or subconsciously, orient them toward a life in athletics.

The question of *innate* ability (ability that exists from the time of birth) is just as complicated. This is the question that is concerned with how a particular trait, present from birth, is modified by environment. Though it is virtually impossible to distinguish the influence one's external environment might have on a particular trait from that which internal maturation might have, there are ways of describing *how much* of the total change might be due to environmental conditions. All that is in the genes, or *innate,* is not necessarily inherited because there is always the chance of mutations occurring between parent and child. Also, what is *congenital,* or present at birth, need not be innate since post-genetic effects may occur in the womb. And, finally, the individual is influenced by broad *constitutional,* or general physiological, contributions which modify the trait following birth.

When a trait such as athletic ability, either in a performance or behavior context, varies in a graded way, presumably because of the cumulative effect of many genes, we generally find that some part of the observed variance is due to changes in environmental factors. Cattell (1966) describes a method by which we can estimate the differential effects environment has on the traits of identical twins growing up in the same or different environments. This can be subjectively observed in the correlational situation that exists between hereditary and environmental influences. For example, it is quite possible that a boy (or girl) who is outgoing, vigorous, and active in temperament will receive additional encouragement and opportunity from the people around him to participate in athletics, thus magnifying the effects of his inherited characteristics.

The task, then, of being able to attribute athletic ability or even behavioral traits that are highly loaded on successful athletic performance to *innate* or *natural* causes is very difficult. Even though some individuals do seem to possess a greater potential than others for superb athletic performance, the answer probably lies in their constitutional and environmental histories. The question of the *all-around* athlete is much simpler to answer. The boy who can perform well in a number of sports or activities has long been thought to possess a thing called *general athletic ability.* Such ability is seen as transferring from sport to sport and enabling the individual to be immediately good at anything he takes up. This concept has fallen into considerable disrepute lately due to the work done on the specificity of performance in various tasks which are similar if not virtually identical to each other.

The theory of task specificity states that the ability of a person in one particular task provides little information as to his ability in another task. This has been found in experiments in which low correlations are consistently found between the performances of subjects on highly similar tasks. Though task to task performance does correlate slightly, the relationship is not high enough to warrant being able to predict performance from task to task. This is a strong indication toward task specificity: namely, that skills required to successfully perform a particular task are specific to that task rather than general to a large number of tasks.

The person who performs successfully in a large number of skills, or the all-around athlete who is good at a number of sports, then, is a person who has successfully developed the specific skills required for each of the tasks or each of the sports. They are individuals who have a high command of a number of specifics. For example, research tells us, and this can be confirmed from the reader's own experience most likely, that the relationship between being able to throw a basketball as compared to a football, extremely similar skills in appearance, is very low. In order to throw a football, one must learn the appropriate skills for throwing a football, which, in the main, are subtly different enough from throwing a basketball that they could be termed specific. You wouldn't send a boy out to practice throwing a basketball if you wanted him to learn how to throw a football. Considerable research on task specificity underlies such a commonsense assumption.

Overview

An attempt has been made in this chapter to show how broad behavioral dimensions underlie performance in physical activity and competitive sport. The intention was to show how the final performance of an individual is a function of not only natural physical endowment, physical fitness, motor ability and capacity, and the acquired skills specific to the sport, but also is very much dependent on the general psychological makeup of the person. Emphasis on the latter was absent in this chapter simply because that is what the rest of this book is about. In the remaining chapters the attempt will be made to show *why* people behave the way they do and how this affects their performances in various physical activities and sports. It is also important to look at physical activity and sport from a behavioral standpoint for the simple reason that one must have some understanding of why some people participate and some people do not, why some people are better than others, why some people are more competitive than others, and why people must be taught and coached on the basis of their own individual needs, desires, interests, and attitudes. The key to this book will be to provide you with the necessary insight for treating people as *individuals* and not just as members of a class or a team.

THE PSYCHOLOGY OF PLAY

Preface

Research workers and educators have long been interested in the phenomena of play as a means for gaining further insight into the group and individual behavior of both adults and children. The study of play as a prelude or precursor to the complex games, sports, and athletics in an individual's later life gives one the opportunity to trace a consistent phenomenon over a long period of time. Its immediate value to the child has been described as being essential to his physical, emotional, and intellectual development, as well as being necessary for the natural expression of his inherent impulses. If, then, the study of play can provide us with information concerning an explanation of why people play games, it should provide a foundation for explaining the later behavioral aspects of athletic participation and performance. Authorities in sociology, social history, and anthropology indicate that play, as a basic mode of behavior, has served to both direct and reflect the patterns of development in various cultures throughout the history of man. Psychological thought, on the other hand, has been directed more to describing what *meaning* or significance play has for the individual with the ultimate objective of answering the question of *why* people play.

INTRODUCTION

For thousands of years, and in all societies, man has subconsciously developed his basic instinct for play into the organization of complex games and sports having definitive rules and specific boundaries. Such organization has been undoubtedly reinforced by wide social acceptance, with participation being enhanced by the popularity of sport to such an extent that it has now become an integral part of our modern society. The organizing of play into a complex structure has developed to such a super-technological level in some sports that there are many people concerned that the play element may disappear entirely from sport. Although this is mainly a viewpoint concerned with "values," it is of obvious importance for people involved in sport to understand exactly what meaning the term *play* has for them, and to determine what role it possesses in the larger context of sport. This chapter is an attempt to describe and explain some of the more important psychological and sociological positions on play and to direct a focus toward the role of play in sport during childhood.

The term *play* is derived from the Anglo-Saxon word *plega* meaning to guarantee, stand up for, or take a risk for something, and to risk danger or devote oneself to a single purpose (Ulrich 1968). Though this derivation is somewhat obscure in terms of the current consideration of the term, when one is studying the interaction of man and his movement, play, and its various connotations, becomes an important central concept. Movement for man is a dominant characteristic throughout his life and, because of this dominance, has been continually interpreted in biological terms.

Theories such as the surplus energy theory of Von Schiller and Spencer have taken this biological point of view, but generally, movement is now interpreted more in terms of its psychological and sociological implications. As *man moves to live so he lives to move.* Because his movement has purpose, and because it reflects his needs, his interests, and his attitudes, it becomes a fundamental part of his nature. Movement, in this respect, as reflecting the total fabric of life must be mainly considered in terms of its play aspects. Though movement involved in work is necessary, it is during man's leisure and recreational pursuits that movement becomes both an end and a means toward an end. Except possibly for the professional athlete, who must move to earn a living, man moves predominantly because he wants to, not because he has to. Thus, in play, most of our analysis of movement occurs.

As compared to work, play is natural and spontaneous. It is only later, when play submerges into the more organized and complex games in sport, that man begins to seek satisfaction of needs other than mere free enjoyment of movement. Play in children, as a means and an end in itself, must be considered separately, and it is in the description of what constitutes play that its fundamental characteristics emerge. Knowledge of the most representative positions in play theory thus provides the reader with some knowledge of these characteristics. This theoretical framework of play has been the exclusive domain of psychologists and psychiatrists for many years and has resulted mainly from information concerning the place of play in personality formation. Though the implications of this research have had an indirect influence on more specific conceptualizations in athletics and physical education, the fact still remains that an analysis of the converse side of these results should provide meaningful insight into the psychological aspects of motor and athletic ability. Thus, while the child psychologist concentrates on determining how useful a tool like free play can be for both diagnosis and treatment in child psychiatric problems, the sports psychologist will be concerning himself with the same literature but from the point of view of what use this information has in terms of analyzing the psychological aspects of athletic and motor ability.

Not only does the study of a child's play provide us with insights into his personality but it also provides us with a framework with which to view the cause and effect relationship between personality and physical activity as they both develop as a function of an increase in age. In addition, it should be possible, within these terms of reference, to trace a pattern of change in the psychological significance of play in exercise and sport as the transition is made from childhood through adolescence to adulthood. The objective, therefore, is not only the analysis of psychological characteristics as evidenced by the development of games and sports, but also the analysis of the developing psychological makeup of the future participant in physical activity and sport.

It is already well accepted that the various stages of maturation and aging contain their own specific problems of adaptation and adjustment, and it is thus quite obvious to expect motivational patterns in play to vary at different age levels. And though no one universal, all-inclusive theory exists which can explain the various motivational aspects of play and sport at each stage of life, it should be possible to trace a pattern of change in the psychological significance of play and sport during a person's life. This must necessarily be done in general terms owing to the changes caused in each life stage by changes in the culture.

It must not be taken for granted by the reader that "people play because it's fun," that the phenomenon of "fun" in play is a settled issue. It is not the least bit satisfying to say that "people play because it is in their nature to do so." Any position that holds that pleasure in play lies in doing something for its own sake simply skirts the edges of a very complicated problem. As Reider (1967) notes, "We can accept a child's statement that he plays because it's fun or because he likes it, but we cannot be content that this *explains* play or even certain kinds of play." Buhler's (1935) concept of functional pleasure (*i.e.*, that play gives pleasure in its very indulgence, in and of itself) and Huizinga's (1955) theory that fun in play defies logic or analysis are also of no help in explaining the significance of play. At the other extreme, the explanation of play as a means of reducing tension is just as empty and dissatisfying. Whatever theoretical explanations are offered, all have a strong tendency to categorize play as belonging to late infancy and childhood and to evaluate it in either strong negative or positive terms. However, none of these generalizations really explain play. So the reader is, as always he should be, left to formulate his own position.

TRADITIONAL THEORIES OF PLAY

Traditionally, play theory at the turn of the century centered around play as a biological phenomenon, instinctive in nature and physiological in function. Such an "instinct" approach considered play as a device to either conserve or expend surplus energy. The four theories covered in this section represent this position rather thoroughly and, though their beginnings can probably be traced to the social and philosophical literature of the Nineteenth Century, they can be seen as precursors to the later psychological positions on play (Diagram 2). These writers did not consider the theoretical overlapping of their positions to be a problem — thus indicating a rather sophisticated dialectic view of play. And, in fact, Groos (1898, 1901) went to considerable effort to describe the separate, though connected, mainstreams of thought on play. He categorized play theory into biological, physiological, sociological, pedagogical, and aesthetic divisions, a sophisticated position for that era.

Play as Result of Surplus Energy. Succinctly, this position holds that play is the *result* of a surplus of energy which exists because the child has been freed from the necessity of self-preservation through the actions of his parents and the society in which he lives (von Schiller 1875, Spencer 1873). This energy surplus finds its release in the aimless but exuberant pursuit of pleasure. The theory postulates that a certain amount of surplus energy will always exist in the individual and that there is a tendency to expend this energy in *goalless* activity (*i.e.*, play). For adults the theory implies that man will never be able to expend all his energy in work and that the surplus is automatically directed toward wholesome activity that makes him feel good. Play, in this sense, provides an opportunity for the discharge of this surplus and, it would seem, in an age of decreasing work commitments and increasing leisure, man would be likely to have increasing surpluses of energy, and thus be involved in more playful pursuits.

This position has the strong connotation of viewing play as "blowing off steam," a seemingly reasonable point of view when one considers the hyperactivity of some children. The justifica-

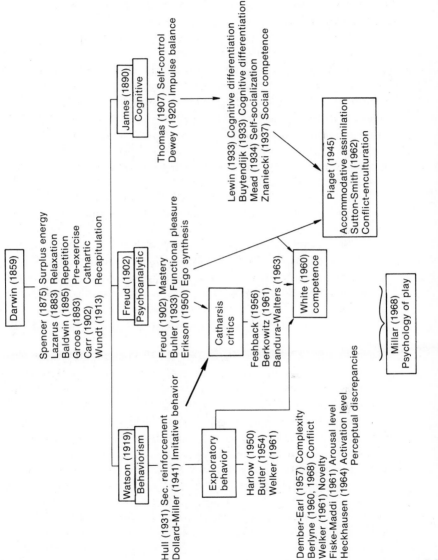

DIAGRAM 2. A MODERN PSYCHOLOGICAL PERSPECTIVE OF PLAY.

tion of extra athletic and physical activity facilities has always, in part, been based on this viewpoint of play. The building up of surplus energy in the child can eventually reach a bursting point and, if activity facilities and programs are available, it is hypothesized that the so-called energy can be directed along constructive lines, such as athletic programs. This *tension-reduction* explanation of the value of play, though popular in the psychological theory of the day, is inadequate when explaining why some children continue to play even when utterly exhausted, or why some adults, who never seem to play at all, do not appear to be overly burdened with surplus energy. Play, of any kind, can naturally act as an incentive to the person. The pure fun of playing is a *raison d'être* in and of itself, and may have no connection whatsoever with the level of so-called surplus energy in the individual. For the overly fatigued child, his or her response to play is simply a reaction to specific stimulation, *i.e.,* the child has been so conditioned to playing when the opportunity occurs that he will play regardless of his fatigue. The businessman's work is probably his play, and as such, absorbs his energy potential quite easily.

The explanation of play as the result of an over-abundance of energy is obviously inadequate for answering most of the puzzling questions we might have about play. It does, however, show us a link between the biological and psychological factors of exuberantly releasing one's tensions in the form of physical activity. Schoolchildren, who burst out of the doors at recess to run and jump, climb and tussle, probably exhibit a combination of release from physical inactivity during classes and a psychological realization of the situational stimulus, *i.e.,* one does these things when one comes out of school during recess. Their activity is both a biological and psychological explosion of energy.

Play as Pre-Exercise.   Groos (1898, 1901) hypothesized play as the product of emerging instincts in the individual, something that brings instincts to the surface, fixes them, and then exercises them in preparation for the time when the individual matures. Groos emphasized the idea of *playful experimentation* in terms of the child's sensory apparatus, *i.e.,* touch, vision, hearing, etc. This emphasis focused on the relative helplessness of the infant as a precursor to motor activity. In a sense, Groos felt that the repetitive perception of pleasant sensory stimulation, *e.g.,* music, bright colors, would give a familiarity and a sense of pleasurable differentiation between the child's *self* and the external world, and that it is in this repetition of pleasure that play begins. This focus was further reinforced by Groos' belief that muscular exercise is experienced as pleasurable (a forerunner of Buhler's

(1935) later psychological theory of play as "functional pleasure," *i.e.*, that pleasure experienced in performance is without regard to the success of the task).

Groos was strongly influenced by Charles Darwin's theory of natural selection in animals. Darwin's premise was that those animals survive who are best fitted to handle their existing environment and whose progeny are most capable of adapting to the new and changing conditions of their surroundings. Darwin felt that if animals can be said to play, they do so only because it contributes to their struggle for survival, that play is the practice and perfection of skills necessary in later adult life. Such a "pre-exercise" interpretation views play as a generalized impulse to practice what comes instinctively to the individual.

Those of us who endorse aggressiveness, fighting, and competitiveness in some of our sports today would suscribe quite heavily to Groos' position. People who support this kind of behavior in play and sport justify their actions by saying, that if a child is going to be successful in later life, he must learn to be aggressive and competitive. They then *use* play and sport to improve and reinforce an incomplete hereditary instinct, such as aggression, by encouraging their young athletes to practice aggressive skills. This is a straight pre-exercise justification of play. Interestingly, Groos felt that "play-fighting" was more of a lead-up to courtship than to survival, in that the victorious competitor claims the female prize after subduing his opponent. This also has connotations in our modern sport, where considerable status and prestige resulting from successful performance does in fact help in the achievement of female prizes.

One weakness of Groos' position is its inability to explain the frivolous play of already mature adults. Though practice benefits probably do occur in adult play, they are no longer the fundamental *raison d'être* for their play. Adult play, strange as it may seem, probably is justified on the basis of fun even more than is children's play. Nevertheless, a large number of professional people involved in sports still feel that, in this sense, play, as a conditioning instrument important in molding relevant personality traits, makes its most significant contribution to society. Overendorsement of such values in play carries with it the danger of eventually negating the fun element in play.

Play as Recreation. This theory states that one plays in order to recuperate from the fatigue and tensions which result from the trials of daily life (Lazarus 1883). It is felt that play has the power to act as a restorative for powers nearing exhaustion, that fatigue accumulated from working could be eliminated by indulging in active recreation. This is an "energy" theory in reverse — rather than looking at play as the *result* of a surplus of energy, play is seen as the means to *revive* one's energy stores. Playing tennis or golf after a hard day in the office is seen as "relaxation" for the person, which not only alleviates boredom and psychological tension but also seems to replenish one's physical energy stores. This explanation is rooted in the premise that, at our present stage of evolution, man is required to use his mental powers more than ever before. This results in greater mental fatigue which can be alleviated by resorting to phylogenetically older, more deeply rooted racial habits, which involve the relaxing use of muscles, such habits usually manifesting themselves in the form of play. Play avoids such mental fatigue and thus has the effect of acting as a restorative.

Though this theory does not explain play unpreceded by mental fatigue, it does have implications for a large segment of adult play in modern society. In a highly technological milieu, where man is constantly required to survive by his wits rather than his muscles, his intense use of leisure time in active recreation must have some basis in recuperation or restoration.

Play as Recapitulation. In this theory, it is assumed that play, rather than being an activity devoted to the development of future skills (as in Groos' pre-exercise theory), is an activity which recapitulates the cultural stages in the evolution of man (Hall 1906). Recapitulation rests on the notion that *ontogeny repeats phylogeny, i.e.,* that the development of the individual repeats the development of his race or species. Some of the stages through which the human fetus passes are similar to the stages through which man has passed from fish to homo sapiens. Such a view states that the child is an evolutionary link between animal and man, and states that play is a reliving or recapitulation of the history of his remote ancestors, both animal and man. Play activities such as swimming, climbing trees, canoeing, hunting, archery, and hiking all show interesting relationships to the struggle for life in our past history.

G. Stanley Hall felt that play exists in children today as a vestige or spirit of man's animal, savage, nomadic, agricultural, and tribal pasts. Play is a link to these remote origins on an instinctual level. Though such a Lamarckian view of evolution (*i.e.,* that acquired characteristics are inherited from one generation to another) has been in disrepute for many years, one must speculate on the animal ferocity, aggressiveness, and violence that continually crop up in sport and play today as having some connection to acquired traits which were necessary for survival in man's past. Not even animals play as brutally as man — probably because of some regulatory survival instinct which animals seem to possess but man doesn't (*i.e.*, play-fighting is good practice for later achievement but has no rationale for destroying one's own species). The physical aggression we see constantly in sport these days may, in a sense, be the instinctual recapitulation of one's violent evolutionary struggle.

Summary

It is obvious that these traditional theories of play tend to be quite consistent with modern thought, in many cases as we will see, actually predating a great deal of current thinking. Though lacking in the orderly study of details and the important recognition that a large part of the meaning of play lies in a person's subconsciousness, these turn-of-the-century views provided a solid, pragmatic base for later theorizing. Certain speculations, relevant to modern athletics and physical activity, are of interest.

Intuitively, we can agree that the explosive, unstructured play of young children at school recess, or after school, is probably the release of surplus energy. Though hard to define, there probably is a *need* * for physical activity in the human being that becomes pent up or frustrated by even short periods of physical inactivity. Sensory isolation experiments, in which people forced into complete inactivity resort to all kinds of mental games, confirm such a speculation. The important implication here is that when dealing with young people in an athletic or physical activity setting, one must provide as many outlets for actual movement as one can — otherwise a tense, frustrated psychological and physical atmosphere is created. Forcing young people to stand around listening to long involved skill or strategy instruction will defeat its own purpose, simply through the boredom it causes. Kids come to athletic settings to *move*, not to stand around. Instruction and coaching, then, must constantly be delivered or presented in a movement context.

Groos' pre-exercise explanation of play is also interesting in that it supports the view held by many physical educators that play, games, and sport can be used to prepare a child for the harshness of real life. That sport can be used as a "training ground" for the youth of the nation is a concept that has been popular for centuries in different societies. Whether or not play can be explained precisely in pre-exercise terms remains to be seen, but there probably is, within the individual, a tendency to

---

* For a fuller explanation of the term *need*, the reader is referred to the Introduction in Chapter 8.

regard play situations as variations of real life and to react to them in a realistic manner. There is no doubt that play can become quite serious, and when it does, Groos' views assume more validity.

The relaxation and recuperative properties of play have also long been accepted. And if one wishes to accept the therapy derived from play as being its basic purpose, then Lazarus' views would seem to be quite pertinent. It is a particularly appealing position when attempting to explain adult play, especially when dealing with highly active, but mentally fatigued, businessmen. It is less adequate for understanding the play of children.

Recapitulation, as an explanation for play, is more difficult to understand or justify. There is the realization, however, that a great deal of play activity does have strong instinctual overtones. That a child may be recapitulating or reliving an activity inherent in his genetic or evolutionary background is quite possible. Any of the play activities which involve a struggle against one's natural environment may have as their fundamental explanation a recapitulation justification.

TWENTIETH CENTURY THEORIES OF PLAY

Although they took different forms, the 19th century theories of play generally reflected the all-pervasive influence of Darwin's theory of evolution. It wasn't until the turn of the Twentieth Century that new currents of thought began to appear as to how behavior could best be explained. Since then "psychological" theory in play has been mainly influenced by three major methodological positions within the total field of psychology, namely: *psychoanalysis, behaviorism,* and *cognition.* Until the decade from 1910 to 1920, instincts and other biological mechanisms were the basic foundations upon which play theorizing rested, and this was exemplified by McDougall's (1917) famous list of 14 instincts. However, Ross (1908) and others began to emphasize the importance of *environment* and *learning* as influences on human development, and in 1919, John Watson, the "father" of behaviorism, delivered his famous denouncement of the term "instinct" by saying it had become useless and should be removed from all psychological literature. From this approximate point in time the biological position on play theory split into the three already mentioned streams of thought: the psychoanalytic with emphasis on instinctual energy and the unconsciousness of motivation, the behaviorist with emphasis on learning, and the cognitive with emphases on cognition, symbolic learning, and interpersonal interaction. Although the three streams of thought can be identified, they are not completely independent of each other. There is considerable overlapping in various psychological views of play, as we will see.

The Psychoanalytic Position on Play

Of the three emerging branches of psychological theory mentioned above, the psychoanalytic school was probably the most in accord with traditional thought on play. Although psychoanalytic play theory was introduced by Freud (1908, 1920), it can be seen to have much in common with earlier cathartic theories of play, *i.e.*, the release of tension or energy through play. Already mentioned in this vein are the surplus energy theory of Spencer and von Schiller, Groos' views of play as a repetition of pleasurable experiences, and Baldwin's (1895) and Appleton's (1910) emphasis on play as repetition for mastery. Gilmore (1966) states that the roots of cathartic play theory can be traced back to the writings of Aristotle, though it wasn't really articulated until 1902 by Carr (1902). According to this theory, play is the attempt by the child to master situations which at first are too much for him. Freud drew heavily upon these ideas and placed them within the context of his psychoanalytic ideas, thus popularizing them.

Play as an Outlet for the Release of Tension. Fundamental to Freud's theory was a basic sexual instinct as the source of all motivation (1908, 1920). This instinct was given several names, of which the most popular were "libido" and "eros." "Sexuality" was used in a very broad sense by Freud to include all the manifestations of striving for pleasure. He outlined five developmental psychosexual stages (oral, anal, phallic, latent, and genital) that the libido goes through prior to maturity. Such libidinal development was viewed as a stream which constantly required outlets for its healthy existence. If the libidinal energy was dammed up or restricted in any way, it would be emitted in disguised forms (*i.e.*, sublimated) or erupt in socially unacceptable forms. Early childhood experiences in these various developmental stages were felt to be crucial in determining the success of one's adjustment in later life. Overindulgence or frustration (*i.e.*, repression) of the libido at any one of these stages would result in "fixating" the libido at that stage, and the infantile expressions of that stage would appear later in adult behavior. Everyone was said to experience such frustrations and conflicts during life from instinct-dominated infancy to socially adjusted adulthood.

Play was viewed as one important outlet for the anxiety developed from such frustrations. It was felt that play in the child reflected his wishes and conflicts at each of these developmental stages. Play was seen as being a response to either of two unconscious wishes: (1) in accordance with the "pleasure principle," play was felt to reflect a child's wishes to be big and grownup, or to be someone more fortunate who always seems to be having more fun or (2), consistent with cathartic theory, play was seen as a manifestation of an inherited tendency to repeat, over and over again, any experience that had previously been too much for the child. This seeking of a "sense of mastery," which was restricted by Freud to play, is supposedly used to reverse a previously painful experience. This view is given broader interpretation in the later writings of Erikson and White.

Play, then, for the child is the seeking of pleasurable experiences and the avoiding of painful ones. Play is determined by the wishes of the individual, not by the hard facts of reality, even though objects and situations are borrowed from reality in order to create a play world which is familiar to the child. The child distinguishes play from reality by creating a world of his own, in which he can order and alter events in such a way as to derive only pleasure. The child wishes to be grownup and do what adults do. In play he can structure his activity so as to accomplish this. The little girl who is bossy to her dolls is wielding an authority denied her in real life, while the little boy who plays Little League baseball can achieve a status and recognition that would normally be years in the future for him.

Freud also felt that people are constantly attempting to reduce their levels of nervous tension, that high activation levels are distressing and uncomfortable to the average person.* He hypothesized that play enables the child to master distressing events by actively bringing them about rather than being a passive and helpless spectator (Millar 1968). Such an action, especially in the form of active play, is a direct attempt to reduce the effects of unpleasant situations. The frustrations and conflicts of daily life, can thus be solved by the child in competitive sport, where he is allowed to endlessly repeat or re-create the frustrating circumstances bothering him in real life. So the Little League baseball player who is frustrated over being ordered around constantly by his parents in real life can redirect his frustrations into the ordering around of his teammates, or indirectly can relieve such tension by playing hard or running hard.

---

*A completely opposite view to this position can be seen in the Fiske and Maddi theory on Level of Activation in Chapter 5.

Generally speaking, then, Freud's view of play is as the projection of wishes and the reenactment of conflicts and unpleasant events in order to master their disturbing effects. He felt that play can reveal the inner life and the motivational structure of the individual.

Play as Ego Mastery. Much of the effort of the Neo-Freudians (*i.e.*, those modern psychologists who basically believe in Freud's approach, but interpret his material slightly differently) has been to elucidate the *ego-functioning* within an individual in meeting the realities of everyday life. Erikson (1950) is a key figure in this extension of ego-psychology but still retains the basic elements of a Freudian position. He recognizes eight stages of ego development and acknowledges the systematic relationship between the individual and his social environment.

Following Freud, Erikson (1950) calls play the "royal road to the understanding of the infantile ego's efforts at synthesis." He says further:

> Play, then, is a function of the ego, an attempt to synchronize the bodily and the social processes within the self . . . the emphasis, I think, should be on the ego's need to master the various areas of life, and especially those in which the individual finds his self and his social role wanting. To hallucinate ego mastery and yet also to practice it, an intermediate reality between phantasy and actuality is the purpose of play. . . .

Thus play allows the child to gradually master his environment while keeping his anxiety at a manageable level.

Erikson recognizes three distinct developmental stages which the infantile ego goes through to maturity: the autocosmic (the world centering on his own body), the microsphere (the small world he shares with others), and the macrosphere (the large world shared with adults). Each sphere is endowed with its own sense of reality and mastery, and the child progresses from stage to stage. Although possessing the shortcomings of the libido model of human behavior, Erikson's theorizing recognizes the uniqueness of adult play (recreation) and the function of symbolic play for children.

Probably Erikson's most useful contribution is the distinction he makes between adult and child play. He states that the playing adult *sidesteps* into another reality; while the playing child constantly approaches mastery of his existence. Adult play is a "vacation" from reality, from seriousness, from consequences, and, in a sense, must be uninvolved and light. Play must *not* be work. For the child this is simply not possible because he never has to work. Children's play, then, cannot be explained as a flight from work. Because of this deficiency, Erikson felt that most adults try to explain children's play as either being work itself or as pure nonsense (since the child is really *nobody* yet). This feeling, that child's play has mastery as its objective, is consistent with the view that play *must* have some *use*, and supports most of the contemporary thought today that play can be used to teach children various important values.

The Behavioristic Position on Play

Behaviorist theory may be described as that school of thought which focuses upon the objective observation of overt behavior in experimental situations, and is in marked contrast to the introspective methods of the mentalists like James and Freud. Although behaviorism was first popularized by Watson (1919), the most representative position on play is the work of Clarke L. Hull (1943).

Play Through Secondary Reinforcement. Hull's theory of learning, with its emphasis on primary and secondary drives within the context of learned associations between stimuli and responses (*i.e.*, S-R psychology), has been of central importance in Western psychology. In Hullian terms, playful behavior is explained in terms of secondary reinforcement. This reinforcement may be in the form of either learned cues indicating rewards or conditioned stimuli produced by the individual's own responses.

Hull, like other behaviorists, assumed that reward was essential for learning—that learning occurs when drive states are reduced by satisfying the needs that create them. Primary rewards (*e.g.*, food and water) for primary drives (*e.g.*, hunger and thirst) obviously are essential for the individual if he is to learn how to reduce hunger and thirst needs. The same is true for secondary drives. Praise, recognition, status, prestige, money, or toys, as secondary rewards, are recognized as having an immediate effect on learning as well. It is in the satisfaction of secondary drives, such as the drives for achievement, affiliation, and independence, that the importance of play as a variable in learning has been identified. It is during childhood that many of these secondary needs are satisfied by one's mother and become secondary motives in a child's psychological structure. Behavior, such as play, which is engaged in without any apparent primary reinforcement, actually is reinforced by a number of secondary cues in the form of rewards. Young participants in age-group sport, for example, quickly learn that good performance produces (*i.e.*, is rewarded by) recognition, status, and prestige, not only from their peers but from adults as well.

Play as Imitative Learning. As an extension of Hull's view that playful behavior can be explained in terms of secondary reinforcement, Miller and Dollard (1941) felt that *imitative learning* could also be applied to an explanation of play. They contended that selective reinforcement of matched responses leads to a generalized habit of imitation, or an *acquired imitative drive.** A child's "make-believe" play, for example, can be interpreted in terms of a learned imitative drive. Imitation, as a generalized habit, is not necessarily learned on the basis of rewards; it can also be described by assuming that children learn to attend to relevant cues in their environment. "Role-playing" occurs in the free play of children constantly as a type of imitation, and is, to a large extent, dependent on the cues a child perceives. For example, the boy who does most of the scoring in a hockey game will become aware of cues indicating leadership to him, and he will thus start to imitate those leadership prototypes with which he is familiar, *i.e.*, his father, his coach, his teacher, and others.

The meaning of imitative play, then, is mainly in terms of role-playing and the reenacting of memorable events. The repetition of something that was previously pleasurable to the child can constantly be observed in the overt play behavior of some children. What is repeated and rehearsed in imitative play are the actions of significant others *whom* the child has observed, or those events which were significant or important to him. So when a child sees a Bobby Orr score a goal or a Hank Aaron hit a home run, he goes out to the rink or the diamond to attempt the same thing. Such an explanation lies in the realm of imitative learning.

Play as Exploration and Investigation. One other general view of play, which is also a modification of Hullian drive-reduction theory, is of importance at this point. This is the view that play is involved in the *investigative* and *explorative* needs of the individual. Here the premise is that if too much emphasis is placed upon drive-reduction as the basis of reinforcement, behavior involving exploration, investigation, and manipulation, is ignored. Evidence from sensory deprivation and self-stimulation research has shown conclusively that exporatory play behavior can be reinforced without drive-reduction occurring.

Exploratory play behavior is seen by Berlyne as an attempt to reduce conflict within the individual by acquiring more information about his environment. Conflict is viewed as the result of competing response tendencies (*e.g.*, a child wants to play foot-

---

*The concept of drive is examined more extensively in Chapter 8.

ball, but he is afraid to because he's fearful of injury, or he doesn't know anything about the game, or he's been told not to, etc.). Berlyne feels that explorative play is thus caused by the attraction of novelty, change, complexity, or uncertainty, in his environment. These arouse his tendency to investigate or explore. A situation, for example, which is relatively novel to a child (*e.g.*, learning to ride a bicycle or first learning to throw and catch a football), will possess a strong stimulation for him. The complexity of an organized sport such as football, hockey, or baseball, will also strongly stimulate him. When he willingly enters these kinds of situations, Berlyne feels that he is doing so in order to reduce the stimulation. The high stimulation that a child experiences in riding a bicycle, or playing football, becomes pleasurable, because it is invariably followed by a reduction in excitation, and is therefore associated with reward. The suspense, or even moderate fear, engendered by this kind of explorative play, may even be viewed as enjoyment by the participant. This is a view which emphasizes conflict reduction as the essence of exploratory play behavior.

Dember and Earl (1957), on the other hand, account for exploratory play behavior by postulating that it is an effort to *optimize* stimulus complexity rather than reduce it. Such a motive is viewed in much the same terms as the primary drives in traditional play theory. The level of stimulus complexity, which is generally altered by temporal and/or spatial variation in stimulation, is said to be optimal when it is just above the individual's present complexity level. Play is thus viewed as an attempt on the part of the individual to maintain the complexity of the stimuli impinging upon his body at his particularly ideal level. So, high active children (as contrasted to low active children) who need higher levels of activation in their lives, will tend to optimize whatever stimulation is available to them by plunging into situations which provide high stimulus complexity. For example, some boys are just not content to stand on the sidelines and watch football—they have to play it.

Play as a Need for Competence. White (1959), though drawing heavily on Freudian theory, and postulating a central nervous system motive for competence, states that play behavior is motivated by an urge within the child to develop an effective familiarity with his environment. This motivation he has termed *effectance motivation*—a motivation that is not a simple drive-like process, but a *self* or intrinsic motivation. He feels that, through competent interaction with one's physical and social environments, the person receives positive feedback from his actions, and experiences a feeling of *efficacy or self-competence*.

In this very important sense, play is a serious business, although to the child it is merely interesting and fun. Competence motivation thus is an intrinsic need within the individual, distinct from primary drives, which is partially satisfied by a person's gains or successes in certain activities.

Competence, as an objective in play, is a value close to our hearts in Western culture. With our intense societal drive toward success and "getting ahead," all of our institutions are seized upon as agents in promoting such a cultural orientation. Play is no exception. The values of our society which we consider important are reflected in the play activities of our children. Competence, of course, is a highly desirable value. The massive reinforcement that a child receives for becoming competent will undoubtedly cause what White calls an *intrinsic need,* but which is probably more a motive to achieve. This is particularly evident in the way in which many adults perceive "play" in organized sports for children. Here the drive for excellence becomes an end rather than a means in play, and White's formulations assume a specific significance.

Play as the Seeking for Novelty, Complexity, and Uncertainty. Many of the aforementioned "activation" theories of play are placed in an interesting framework by Heckhausen (1964). He states that play and other "useless" activities are governed by an *activation cycle* which consists of alternating drops and rises in the daily tensions of people. He attributes these drops and rises in activation to *perceived discrepancies.* These discrepancies are divided into four categories:

1. *Novelty or Change*: the discrepancy between the current perceptions of the child and earlier perceptions or experiences.
2. *Surprise Content*: the discrepancy between current perceptions and what were one's expectations based on earlier experiences.
3. *Complexity*: the discrepancy between parts of the perceptual field which the child views.
4. *Uncertainty or Conflict*: the discrepancy between different expectations.

Heckhausen feels that there is a motivation intrinsic in the individual which compels him to keep his level of activation or stimulation at an optimal level. Movements of short duration toward and away from this optimum are experienced as pleasurable. Generally, play increases a child's arousal potential and, in doing so, compensates for the lack of unpredictability, risk, surprise, and danger in his everyday life. Maybe it is better described as a need for variability in one's life. This is an interpretation of play as a seeking for novelty, complexity, surprise, and uncertainty in life, and, if true, considers play as a contributor to a child's level of activation. Heckhausen is saying that the *seeking* of tension, rather than its *reduction,* is the chief purpose of play and that there is an alternating between these two needs depending on the circumstances. A need for variability in a child, for example, might manifest itself in his choice of basketball over baseball, the former more filled with variable situations than the latter. The alternating play activities of children could be explained in Heckhausen's terms. Children could be playing either to relieve tensions or increase them.

The Cognitive Position on Play

Neither the excessive behaviorism of Watson nor the reliance of the Freudians on the physiological-libido explanations of human behavior satisfied a number of scholars. These workers considered the study of human cognitive functioning and experience as the prime subject matter. This was in direct contrast to the behaviorists, who were willing to consider only observable behavior as worthy of scientific study. A second feature of the cognitive point of view was the recognition of the importance of both biological and environmental factors influencing behavior. Most cognitive theorists considered the proper method of study to be the examination of the human species itself, as opposed to the species-comparative approach of the behaviorists. Thus, the detailed study of the role of symbols, language, and thought in human play moved to the fore.

Included in this general grouping of cognitive positions are the gestalt traditions of Kohler (1921) and Lewin (1933), the genetic and phenomenological positions of Buhler (1935) and Buytendijk (1933), and the social behaviorism of Thomas (1907) and G. H. Mead (1934). Of most interest and direct relevance for explaining play behavior are Mead and Jean Piaget (1932, 1945).

Play as Role-Playing. George Herbert Mead (1934) and the "Chicago School" of sociology, which included such scholars as Dewey, Thomas, and Znaniski, saw man as an essentially *social* creature. They considered society to be a complex network of symbolically interacting members, all of whom have *selves.* The "self" is built up in interaction with other social members, so that the way one thinks he is, is a function of the way he thinks other people see him. The "mind," or thinking, was thought to be socially constituted and was involved with the use of symbols and language built up in the child's play activities. Each individual was seen as an active novelty-seeking and novelty-producing organism, with his perceptual and cognitive processes being built up through interaction with others during play.

The major process involved in becoming a social being was that of developing a *self-concept*,* *i.e.*, by becoming able to attach meanings to oneself by taking the roles of other people and generalizing back to oneself. Infant play and game play was seen by Mead as being central to this process, a process which occurs in two stages. In the first stage, called the *play* stage, the child is able to take on individual, discrete roles, without which he would be unable to view himself, and thus have no unified conception of himself. Playing by himself and with other young children his own age, he gradually builds up this conception of himself as a real person. In the second, or *game*, stage the child completes the image of his "self" by learning to handle various situations in which he must take a number of roles simultaneously. By doing so, the child in a sense manages to get different views of himself, which he gradually integrates into a total picture of himself.

Mead uses the game of baseball to demonstrate this development of multiple and simultaneous role-taking. The young boy learns to be a baseball player, a hitter, a fielder, a runner, a catcher, all at the same time. He also learns that he is viewed differently by his teammates, his parents, his friends, his coach, and others — all are viewing him in different terms — and, upon realizing that he is enacting several different roles, he is better able to arrive at a total conception of himself. He is thus able to complete his self-conception and to learn how to empathize with his fellow players. Play has thus become a socializing agent in the child's life.

This concept of the role of play in life represents life as a "game" or a "drama." It is a "symbolic interaction" of play with life which is seen as a series of games, each requiring preparation and socialization. Stone (1962), for example, stresses that life must be viewed as a continuous socialization for the child and the adult, that life is a series of careers with each critical turning point marked by a definite change, the new upcoming "game" being rehearsed immediately prior to entry upon the appropriate field of play.

Again, such a view of the role of play is consistent with our modern attitudes. Most of the people involved in age-group sport for children *do* feel that sport "is" life, or, at least, a preparation

---

*Self-concept is covered in Chapter 6.

for life. The symbolism attached to sport constantly rises to the surface—the smaller boy struggling against the bigger boys and winning, the lone defender girding himself against the onrushing hordes, the fierce aggressiveness of the athlete in a tough spot— all symbolize and recapitulate the way people instinctively feel real life is. This general attitude is subconsciously passed on to the children, who already are playing "real life" games in their play, in such a manner as to make play an *actual* symbolic inter-action with real life.

Play as Assimilation and Accommodation. Jean Piaget (1932, 1945), the famous Swiss developmental and educational psychol-ogist, represents what could be considered a current "endpoint" of the cognitive position. His theory of the cognitive and intellec-tual development of the child emphasizes the "inevitability" of play as but a part of all infantile dynamics. Though Piaget's basic concern was with the intellectual development of children, or how children actually come to think logically, he soon found that the play of children was closely bound up with the growth of in-telligence. This biological-adaptive growth process was felt by him to consist of two polar sub-processes: *assimilation,* the bend-ing of external reality to fit the individual's currently existing cognitive categories, and *accommodation,* the adjustment of these cognitive categories to fit external reality. Assimilation, in this sense, refers to the process whereby the individual changes the information he receives by making it a part of his own knowl-edge (*i.e.,* he integrates external objects and events into his own cognitive view of the world). Piaget felt that when such a process predominates the child is probably indulging in play. The child plays because of the "functional" pleasure he experiences, (*i.e.,* play is fun because the child feels he is becoming a grown up, functioning part of the adult society). Piaget recognized three types of games which seemed to appear in succession and which were an integral part of what he viewed as the two major periods of intellectual development in the child. That is, practice games, symbolic games, and games with rules were seen as occurring successively during what he called the child's sensory-motor period and his representational stages of development.

Piaget felt that play begins in the child's *sensory-motor* period of development, a period spanning approximately from birth to two years of age, and which is a major aspect of the sub-process of assimilation. Play becomes a repetition of achieve-ment in order to integrate and consolidate this mastery into one's cognitive self. Play gradually, during this period, becomes more than just the successful repetition of pleasurable associations—it also becomes repetition with variations. It now assumes an emphasis in systematic experimentation and exploration. The various possibilities of what can be done with objects is recognized, explored, and coordinated, and the child starts to achieve mastery over simple objects, events, and other people. He can now throw his rattle out of the crib and know that someone will retrieve it; he is starting to walk; and he is learning that balls bounce back off walls when he throws them. He is, in Piaget's view, achieving during this period, a motor coordination necessary to perceive and manipulate objects both in space and time.

In the *representational* stage of development, from two years to about eight years of age, the above accomplishments are repeated on symbolic and verbal levels. The child starts to perceive and manipulate objects and events by symbolizing and generalizing their relationships to each other. A stick becomes a baseball bat or a golf club, a tin can becomes a soccer ball, or a piece of lawn becomes a battlefield or a football field. Though this point of view is still confined to himself only and he views things only in relation to himself (*i.e.*, pure egocentrism), this type of representational play is very much assimilation to Piaget. The repetition and organization of thinking and performing in terms of images and symbols is slowly being mastered. Anything important that has happened to the child is repeated in his play, even though it may be distorted because of his egocentrism. No attempt at adaptation of this representation to reality is made, so that make-believe play, though highly elaborate and organized, will bear only a slight relationship to what it is representing. Little boys playing baseball or hockey, for example, appear to be reproducing the actions and behaviors of adult athletes whom they have seen on TV, when actually they may be only assimilating and consolidating particular emotional experiences for themselves, *i.e.*, the excitement of the game, its dangers and thrills. With growing experience, their play starts to become a closer representation of reality and their social adaptation to each other, as integral and important parts of their play, gradually is substituted for the more symbolic and unreal aspects of their previous play.

Play now becomes less egocentric or self-oriented, and is strongly modified by rules and codes of conduct, especially in terms of cooperation with others. Games with rules now replace the individual symbolic, make-believe games and last into adulthood. They have the prime function of both individual and social assimilation and are the integration of new experiences. Though Piaget represents play and games as a microcosmic moral-social system in the development of his intellect and social behavior, he does provide us with certain interesting speculations.

First, is the fact that, generally, Piaget's representational stage of development closely corresponds to that time period when many children are first introduced to organized and competitive sport. Immediately, two questions are of interest: (1) Can children in this age period cope with the intricacies and complexities of the games? (2) Is the introduction of competitive sport at this time a *good* thing for them? Both questions, of course, are difficult to answer in any terms. However, in terms of Piaget's views on moral and social development, one could speculate that up to approximately the age of seven, most children are far too egocentric for organized sport. They are in a stage where they may know the rules, but still adjust them, ignore them, or invent them for their own particular gratification. Children, at this period of their development, are still playing symbolic games with themselves, games in which they may be player, parent, opponent, and referee, all rolled into one. Games, at this time, are only representational to them, not real, and to put them too soon into a reality context may retard their social development or negate the functional fun that games have for them.

From ages seven and eight through ten the child does in fact, learn the rules and codes of conduct and how to operate within them. Though he may simplify some of these rules, or invent slight modifications to rules he dislikes, he generally is probably at a stage of cognitive development which can cope with games bound by rules and limits. Too much emphasis on the rules at this time by adults, however, may have the result of "turning the child off." He will think that the game is more important than he is, and though his egocentricity is starting to diminish at this time, there is still enough present for him to fight any encroachments upon it.

From ages 10 and 11 up, organized sports are usually perfect modalities for children. This is because most children are starting to make rules a part of their personality structures and are internalizing all kinds of morality patterns and codes of conduct. It is very important during this stage of development for adults to follow rules to the letter of the law, especially in sport. The child is at a stage in his life when he *wants* rules and limits, so that he can better learn how to handle himself in the adult world.

In answer to the second question—whether or not competitive sport is good for children around the ages of seven or eight— one must examine his own particular philosophy of sport. If one thinks that sport should be *used* to socialize the child, to make him better prepared to handle his role in real life later, then one would probably think that sport participation at this age is a good thing. Piaget, for example, would probably support this view. If, on the other hand, one thinks that the most important thing for the child at this age is to have *fun,* then the introduction of competitive sport at this time may simply serve the purpose of turning him off. This would be due simply to the overemphasis on playing according to the rules (both real and imagined) by adults in organized sport. If the child is not yet ready to negate part of himself for the sake of some rule at this stage, then he will feel that the situation is unfair to him. This either spoils the sport for him and makes him quit, or serves the purpose of making sport overly restrictive for him. The egocentricity which Piaget talks about during this stage of development is still very strong in most children, and must be realized and handled very carefully by adults involved in age-group competitive sport.

Overview

Intuitively, any discussion of play theory is predicated on the question of *why* man plays. This implies a context of motivation, and it is in this motivational framework that most of the psychological theories are presented. Though the issue as to what *meaning* play has for the individual is far from settled, the role of play in early life, and its gradual submergence into complex games and sports, would seem to be of fundamental importance for the student of physical activity and athletics. The question of why children play should be answered, at least partially, in order to shed some light on the more important question of why people participate in sport.

The development of psychological theorizing on play was seen to parallel very closely the general development of psychological-sociological thought prevalent at any one time. And the evolution of these streams of thought were naturally part and parcel of the chronological periods in which they took place. Therefore, most psychological theories of play must be viewed in their proper historical contexts. With the current strong emphasis on social-psychological analysis, for example, play theory has already assumed strong sociological overtones, and the student must take this into account when coming to some decision of his own about why people play. Historical precedents must not be ignored just because they are old, but only if they don't appear to add to one's understanding of the phenomenon under question. If some formulations appear to have a bearing on the question, or seem to have some meaning for you the reader, then it is phenomenologically proper for you to include it in your formulation. Understanding the phenomenon is the important thing regardless of the sources of understanding.

The traditional theorists, working under the strong influence of Charles Darwin, obviously reflected a biological model of man and so explained play in these terms. Instinct, the recapitulation of phylogenetic stages, surplus energy, and cathartic positions represented this kind of thought. The energy-reduction view, in fact, was extended into the more refined and sophisticated thought of the behaviorists and the psychoanalysts. It was interesting, at this point, to see the psychoanalytic people further refine the idea of play as tension-reduction, while the behaviorists assumed a position emphasizing learned behavior and environmental influences in interpreting play. The cognitive branch emerged as an attempt to explain uniquely such human phenomena as thought and language, and again play was gathered under a theoretical blanket oriented in specific directions. Piaget and Mead are excellent examples.

Now emerging on the current psychological scene are the activation, relativistic models of behavioral man, and, as we will see in other chapters in this book on motivation and personality, play explanations will again be subtly determined by the major trends in psychological thought. Man is generally presented in these views as a "tension-seeking" organism, and play and sports participation lend themselves quite nicely to such models. In addition, certain topical themes are now starting to influence play theorizing. Recently, for example, aggression in play has received considerable attention (*e.g.*, Berkowitz [1962] and Bandura and Walters [1963]).

Some prominent psychologists such as Schlosberg (1947) and Berlyne (1968) have even expressed the view that play is a totally vague and useless concept, and should be eliminated from the psychological literature. Berlyne, for example, feels that most of the various explanations of play simply mean that people are under the "sway" of intrinsic motivation, a motivation that dominates other kinds of behavior as well. He feels the concept of play should be given up for either wider or narrower categories of behavior.

Such criticisms, though valid for disciplines such as psychology, have little validity for people interested in physical activity and athletics where play, as a concept, has a strong implicational meaning. However, one implication of such criticism is important in that we must be careful not to treat *all* manifestations of play behavior as being the same or attribute global causes to it. Susanna Millar (1968), in her excellent book, The Psychology of Play, has expounded this idea. She feels that we should reject any idea of a special motive for play, and emphasize the varied conditions under which playful behavior is reinforced. She points out that play may involve aspects of aggression, exploration, and sexual behavior; that it may be solitary or social; that it may be violent and widely dispersed or quiet and concentrated. In fact, according to Millar, the one common characteristic of play is its paradoxical nature, *i.e.*, there always seems to be a paradox between the major behavior from which some play behaviors take their name and the play behaviors themselves; for example, aggressive play is a lot different from real aggression.

Millar also does not accept the "uselessness" of play as a concept. Rather, she explains these apparent useless actions by suggesting that it is only the interpretation of the observer that makes play behavior appear purposeless; the play behavior may, in fact, serve useful biological and social functions completely different from the interpretations given them. Among the unobservable biological functions which she suggests that play might serve are learning through exploratory play, excitement reduction through familiarization with one's environment, and the achieving of an ability to interact with others through social play.

Thus, as students of physical activity and athletics, it is important for us to realize that play, as a concept, requires a complete dialectical approach — that no one explanation is comprehensive enough to cover all forms of play behavior. Rather, we must require ourselves to attempt a broad understanding of the underlying psychological structure of the individual when attempting to understand his behavior in physical activity and athletics, especially in terms of how he "plays" in these contexts.

THE SOCIO-PSYCHOLOGICAL NATURE OF GAMES, SPORT AND PHYSICAL ACTIVITY

Preface

In order to study the psychology of sport,* we must first have a reference framework within which the concepts of sport and physical activity can be discussed. Several basically sociological frameworks are available in the literature, and it is out of these that we can extract a psychological concept of sport and physical activity. As will be emphasized again and again in this book, the content material is presented as logically and fairly as possible, with the main intention to provide the reader with a basis upon which he can formulate *his own view* of the particular concept. Limitation in space will, of course, restrict complete and comprehensive treatment of each concept; nevertheless, an attempt will be made to present the main representative positions.

INTRODUCTION

Four basic terms, *play, games, sport,* and *physical activity,* lie at the root of this area. Definition of each one, independently, or as a mutually exclusive cluster, is at best elusive; however, with the common intuitive understanding that most people have of these terms, certain fundamental elements begin to appear upon examination. It is the intention of this chapter to discuss those common elements which are of a psychological nature.

Play, which was fully discussed in Chapter 2, is best consid-

---

*Generally speaking, the term *psychology of sport* as used hereafter in this book will refer to *the behavior of the individual* in a sport or physical activity milieu. Only indirectly will *performance* and *group behavior* be covered.

ered as a type of behavior engaged in for purposes of fun and enjoyment, with no utilitarian or abstract goals in mind. As Avedon and Sutton-Smith (1971) observe, the main problem with this term has been that though a biological interpretation of play has deemed it as unfunctional (*i.e.*, function as defined in terms of servicing particular psychological or sociological needs), upon closer examination it does, on the contrary, seem to have fundamental implications for explaining why man behaves the way he does in both real life and in sport. This is especially true from a *species* point of view—man acts quite differently in his play than do most animals. It is here that a connection can be made between play and the later complex games of adolescence and adult life. That is, that play is preadaptive—that it *prepares* each individual player in a general sort of way for the complexities to come.

As was stated in the last chapter, many varieties of phenomena are hypothesized as being *preadaptive* in the concept of play, but it is important at this point to realize that preadaptation implies the increasing of a person's range of responses so that under pressure he is better able to tap a larger number of resources. Sutton-Smith (1968) modifies this view by noting that such a concept of adaptation is restrictive in that it gives insufficient emphasis to the development of voluntary controls in man. He feels that play can be regarded as an "exercise in voluntary control systems," with voluntary control implying such things as mastery, anticipation of certain outcomes, choice of instrumental behaviors, persistence or single mindedness, sequential control, and freedom from innate sensory capacities. This means, in essence, that when a child is playing he is gradually developing a capacity for controlling or mastering his environment. He does this by achieving a sense of mastery *from* his play, by learning how to anticipate certain outcomes caused or emanating from his play behavior, by freeing himself from the control of his basic sensory controls (*e.g.*, emotion), and by learning how to sustain the direction of his behavior so as to have more alternative responses to choose from. It is in this view that the easiest connection to *game* participation can be made. When participating in the more complex play structure of games and sports, the person is now better able to function because of the preadaptive experiences achieved in previous play. Pure play behavior thus becomes a precursor to play in games and sport.

When does play become a game? In terms of criteria, probably when it becomes repeatable, systematic, and predictable. In a cultural context, play is a uniquely individual piece of behavior, whereas a game can be repeated by others because it has a systematic pattern with outcomes that are, to a greater or lesser degree, quite predictable. Play is open-ended in terms of outcomes, *i.e.,* one does not necessarily know what will happen in any particular play situation. Also, in a game, one becomes involved with goals, or the anticipation or expectation of goals. Play in a game situation assumes a "goal-directedness" and becomes more instrumental rather than consummatory behavior. Thus, play relinquishes a certain amount of its voluntary control in a game situation simply because it is restricted or subordinated to the pursuit of real goals. In addition, games usually imply some opposition between a player and some standard, or between the players themselves, so that even in simple games, stylized repeatable patterns caused by rules regulating the opposition further restrict and subordinate the pureness of free or independent play. In order to better understand the distinction between *pure play* and *playing within a game structure,* it would seem appropriate to analyze what constitutes a game.

THE NATURE OF GAMES

Though several attempts have been made to classify games according to some organizational pattern, probably the most influential of these is that by Roger Callois in 1955. Following up on the general views of Huizinga (1955), characterizing play as being free, separate, and regulated, Callois has suggested that games should be considered along two dimensions: 1) the *descriptive behavior* which predominates in various games, and 2) the *spirit* with which this behavior is characterized. Callois then goes on to classify games into four categories, on the basis of the behavior that predominates: competition (agon), chance (alea), pretense (mimicry), and vertigo (ilinx). The spirit dimension is seen as being on a continuum from extreme, *paida,* which denotes spontaneity, noise, laughter, and agitation, to extreme, *ludus,* which denotes patience, acceptance, perseverance, and discipline (Diagram 3). Each game is thus characterized on the basis of the principal kind of behavior that is dominating and to what extent this behavior tends to be spontaneous or planned.

Some understanding of analysis of what constitutes individual behavior in games is important simply because games have evolved, or been created, for a number of reasons in our Western culture. Most of the play behavior in our society occurs in games — pure, *non-game* play can be seen to decrease suddenly at around the age of 8 years, or once children start school. Why does this happen? Why does the pure play of little children gradually, or suddenly, become structured play? What do games provide

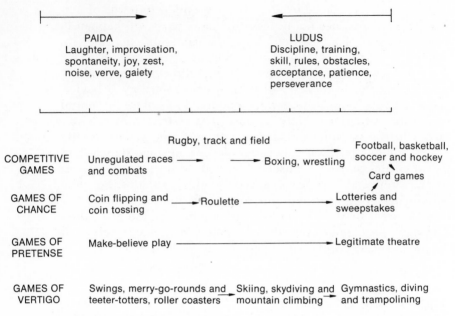

DIAGRAM 3. THE BI-DIMENSIONALITY OF GAMES (CALLOIS 1955).

that free, unstructured play does not? And why does interest in game participation continue on into later adulthood? Finally, do games always involve play? Though no real, specific answers exist for these questions, one can make the following general speculations. First, games are simply structured play; *i.e.*, they are structured in that rules, temporal and spatial limits, and agreements on acceptable behavior now exist where they didn't before. What, then, are the advantages or the attractions that this structuring has over no structure? Well, first, it would seem that structure provides a better opportunity to the player to prove his superiority over other people or over his environment. Games provide more *objectivity* to the play situation. Next, games can be seen as the structuring of play situations in order to achieve certain definable goals such as excellence, participation, health, fun, enjoyment, and relaxation. Structure also provides the opportunity for a repetition of play situations that are attractive or enjoyable to the player.

Structure provides an opportunity to compare one's abilities and capacities with those of other people in a fair and acceptable way. Structuring play may also provide the player with more meaning to his behavior, especially in cultural terms. And, finally, games seem to provide opportunity for the affiliative tendencies of people that independent, unstructured play cannot. Callois' classification of games more accurately describes this structuring of play and, therefore, is as follows.

Competitive Games (Agon).* Games in which agon is predominant are struggles in which a superficial equality is created in order to ensure an ideal confrontation between the players. When such a confrontation is achieved, triumph or victory is considered worthwhile, and it is hypothesized that the outcome of the contest depends ultimately on a single ability or combination of abilities — fitness, skill, speed, strength, endurance, or other — which the player possesses and which is unaffected by external forces. Most of our modern sports and athletic contests fit nicely into the *agon* category. The victor or winner triumphs because he is *better* than his opponent. The key to understanding agon is that the competitors start equal and strive under equal conditions. Such a principle is even obtained by assigning handicaps in games like golf and shooting when it is thought an inequality exists. Sport, in its usual sense, is predominantly agon in makeup, particularly sport which is competitive in nature. Callois makes an interesting observation when he notes that such a system exists for wrestling (a muscular type of agon) just as much as it does for chess (a cerebral type of agon). Such an observation very clearly classifies chess as a competitive sport (thus clarifying a recent controversy).

The core of games in which agon predominates is the pursuit of excellence and recognition. Such pursuits naturally imply dedication, sacrifice, training, practice, concentration, and the like on the part of the participant. Such a *raison d'être* for participation, we will see, is innate to the person and is part of the culture in which he functions. Sports of this kind provide man with the opportunity to rely on his own abilities and capacities in an arena where he can prove to himself and others that he is worthy or capable. A great deal of the psychological content of our modern sport is rooted in the agon principle of *equal struggle.*

Games of Chance. Games in which *alea* predominates are virtually the converse of agon games, *i.e.*, alea games are based on an inequality caused by external forces over which the players have no control. Here it is more a question of triumphing over one's destiny rather than over an opponent. Fate and luck determine the outcome, and when rivalry exists, victory simply means the winner was luckier than the loser. Dice, roulette, flipping a

---

*The terms agon, alea, mimicry, and ilinx are an attempt on Callois' part to choose the most significant and comprehensive term for each category of games that would keep them distinct from each other. He utilizes this nomenclature in order to avoid using terms which refer too directly to concrete experience.

coin, and lotteries are examples of games in this category. In these games the player is passive, waiting for fate to tell him whether he is a winner or a loser. He has no opportunity to display any abilities, skills, or resources which he may possess—he has, in essence, become a pawn. Games of alea virtually negate all the qualities of games of agon. No training, practice, concentration, or dedication are required, nor is any ability important—all that is necessary is a resignation or surrender to the caprices of luck. This can be seen or interpreted as a deliberate shirking of responsibility on the part of the player—he does not have to struggle, work, or compete; all he must do is gamble and wait for the result. The fundamental attraction of alea games is, of course, that in one great stroke of luck a player can win more than a lifetime of work and patience could ever provide him.

The inherent implication of alea is that superior skill or ability, dedication and sacrifice toward a goal, and concentration during participation, are all abolished. This makes *all* players completely equal—even more than in games of agon. Under the capricious eye of Lady Luck all are equal. For people of inferior ability, for people who are lazy, and for people who lack purpose, games of alea are most attractive. Card games, however, are not pure alea—rather they are an interesting combination of alea and agon. In the dealing of hands to each player alea is predominant, the subsequent playing of the hands is more *agon* in nature, although even here luck or chance operate. Agon can be quite strong in card games such as poker and bridge, in that one can mount a concentrated effort to overcome or exploit what luck has dealt him.

In the psychological context, both agon and alea present the player with conditions of absolute equality, something which is denied him in real life. Playing games thus becomes a *clear* situation; one is good and he wins, or one is lucky and he wins. Real life is far too confused or complicated for this to happen with any consistency.

Games of Pretense. In all games there exists the temporary acceptance of an illusion which is closed off from real life. There is an acceptance that the milieu is fictitious or imaginary, and that one is no more than an illusory character behaving in a manner appropriate to the setting. The player is pretending he is someone or something which he isn't. Such manifestations are termed *mimicry* by Callois, and they emphasize the primitive, elemental, and semi-instinctive nature of play. Mimicry is manifested in the little girl playing mother and in the little boy pretending he's Hank Aaron hitting a baseball. Mimicry also includes any person who wears a mask or disguising costume to a party. The enjoyment of mimicry resides in being someone else temporarily or in trying to convince other people you are someone else. Mimicry is probably quite evident in children's sport (it certainly is in their presport play activities), if one is prepared to accept the possibility that they are enacting certain roles which they deem important. For the little boy who is apprehensive about contact sports, mimicry is operating when he pretends he is the big, brave hockey or football player who is just as tough as anyone. Such a manifestation becomes important when understanding the behavior of young children participating in competitive sport.

Games of Vertigo. Callois' last, and most modern, category deals with that species of games in which the *pursuit of vertigo* seems to be predominant. There is little doubt that great numbers of people seek out activities and sports which provide them with feelings of dizziness, giddiness, seeming loss of control, and a strong element of danger. Undoubtedly these activities provide fun and enjoyment to the participants — no other reason seems applicable. Merry-go-rounds, Ferris wheels, swings, and teeter-totters, still the principal playground items, provide us with the initial manifestations of this type of pleasure, with these activities gradually giving way to the more sophisticated and dangerous sports such as skydiving, ski jumping, surfing, scuba-diving, car racing and mountain climbing. The attraction of this category is strange and difficult to explain, but it nevertheless does hold some place in the schemata of games — otherwise why do people, just off a roller coaster ride, shaken, pale, and trembling, immediately rush over and buy another ticket? This category is described further as a subdomain of physical activity by Kenyon (1968a), in another section of this chapter.

So what does Callois tell us about the psychology of sport with his classification of games? What further insights can we gain from a study of games and their seemingly principal behaviors? Some of the more obvious implications are as follows:

1. Most of our competitive sports are obviously agon in nature. They are activities deliberately structured to create an equality of chance within which two individuals or groups can struggle for the prize. For many people, the joy of competition, on an equal footing, is the main attraction of sport. The pure enjoyment of succeeding is a strong motive impelling people to participate — this is apart from the many external or artificial incentives that normally accompany victory or triumph. As Callois notes, agon is "the purest form of personal merit ... it presupposes concentration, effort, and the will to win ... [and] it implies perseverance and discipline." What better characterization of modern competitive sport?

2. *Alea,* in Latin, is the word for the game of dice and its milieu is pure chance, over which the player has no control. To enjoy activities centered in this category the individual must enjoy gambling and risk taking. Though the psychology of gambling invariably revolves around the issue of "compulsive losing," the alea category is possibly useful in understanding part of the attraction sport has for the modern multitudes of spectators. For the spectator, unable to compete because of inferior skill, size, or courage, who vicariously enjoys sporting contests through identification or sublimation, the element of pure chance as to who wins or loses adds a certain amount of spice to the game. This can be observed in their "calling to the gods" to favor their team or blaming a loss on "bad luck." If their identification with a player or team is strong enough, losses are invariably explained as bad luck. Some players even tend to rationalize their poor play in this manner. Such indications would appear to underline the subtle existence of alea in those activities which are more agon in nature.

3. *Mimicry* has its most obvious implications in children's play and games. Here the child can and does enter a fantasy world when participating in games. It is a chance to step out of real life and temporarily become someone else. For children (and a lot of adults), this can be strong attraction and can partially explain the reason sport and games have such a hold on them. Callois observes that, even though mimicry is not inconsistent with agon (*i.e.,* even when pretending one wishes to be the best or to excel), the child engaging in *mimicry* while playing a game will *not* wish to submit or adhere to the rigid forms of behavior, rules, or regulations that agon presupposes. Rather, the child defines his own structure of the game as he goes along. For him, it is the pretense that is important, not the outcome of the game. Rules of the game are only relevant as they help to structure the pretense itself, and are ignored otherwise.

It is here that Callois makes the jump from pure play to games. He feels that "rules are inseparable from play as soon as it acquires . . . an institutional existence (Loy and Kenyon, 1969)." Rules transform play into a cultural instrument to teach, condition, and socialize children, and they become initially prevalent in the game structure of our society. Play, in games form, with rules, is no longer truly free, relaxing, or diversive, although these elements reside at its source. As games become more complex, the structure becomes more rigid. Society has now achieved a control over play by making it an instrument for civilizing the player and impressing upon him the importance of obeying rules and regulations.

4. The pursuit of *vertigo* has instant implications for explaining sports such as skydiving. Man has always been attracted to activities in which he is unable to maintain complete control of his body or his immediate environment. Kenyon's (1968a) development of this category follows along these lines, whereas, Callois is more concerned with the vertiginous, or whirling out of control, aspects of the category. Little children simply spinning around and around are pursuing vertigo and the giddiness that it produces. Proceeding gradually through all the playground apparatus and amusement park rides, the pursuit of vertigo, for some people, eventuates in vertiginous sports such as springboard and tower diving, trampolining and gymnastics.

THE NATURE OF SPORT

The term *sport* means many things to many people and, even though it has ambiguous connotations, an analysis of this term is very important. Again, many authoritative statements have been made regarding the term, but in successfully distinguishing it from the terms play and games, the treatment of sport as a term has probably been most successfully made by John Loy (1968) in his article The Nature of Sport: A Definitional Effort. Loy contends that sport is best discussed as a *game occurrence,* as an *institutionalized game,* as a *social institution,* or as a *social system* (Diagram 4). He feels that if discourse on sport is to be fruitful, then a frame of reference must be established in order to achieve understanding.

It is probably in his interpretations of the social institutionalization of sport that Loy makes his most interesting points. The importance of viewing sport in a social context is obvious — man does not exist alone or unrelated to other people. Man lives and functions as part of a group, and in that group his individual behavior becomes a function of his interaction with other people. A child may play by himself in his earliest years but by the time he is participating in sport, he is by necessity involved with other people. Social groups form because certain needs can only be satisfied through membership in a larger unit; the needs for affiliation and social comparison are prime examples.* Thus, in order to gain insight into individual behavior, one must shape his understanding in terms of the social context within which that behavior occurs. Participation in sport thus becomes an interac-

---

*Affiliation and social comparison are thoroughly discussed in a later chapter.

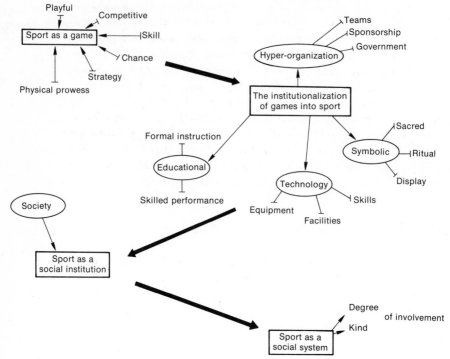

DIAGRAM 4. A DIMENSIONAL SCHEMA OF THE NATURE OF SPORT (LOY).

tion between man as both a biological-cognitive and social organism, and it is with this in mind that we can now look at Loy's treatment of the nature of sport.

Sport as a Game Occurrence. Most people think of sport in this context. That sport, as an all-encompassing or general term, consists of a large number of independent *sports*. Thus, sport is made up of games, such as baseball, and sports events, such as a track meet. When we turn to the sports page in the newspaper, buy a sports magazine, or watch sport on television, we are expecting to read about or see some game or event. The nature of sport, in this context, is regarded then as a game (or event) occurrence. A game (or event) in this sense is defined by Loy "as any form of playful competition whose outcome is determined by physical skill, strategy, or chance employed singly or in combination." Under this definition is subsumed all sport as we know it, except professional sport, which is, of course, pursued for reasons other than fun, enjoyment, or personal satisfaction.

If sport is considered as a game occurrence then the *play elements* as described by Huizinga (1955) and Callois (1961) must be taken into account. That is, any given contest has one or more elements of play inherent or explicit within it. Briefly, these play elements are as follows. Play has *freedom*—no one is required or forced to participate in playful activities. Play is *separate*—separated from our cognizance of life by being spatially and temporarily limited, *i.e.*, most forms of sport take place in a particular circumscribed environment, such as a football field, and within a certain, set duration of time. Play is *uncertain*—the outcome is unpredictable or cannot be determined beforehand. Play is *unproductive*—playing a game does not result in the creation of new goods or materials, *i.e.*, play is nonutilitarian in nature. It is here, probably, that professional sport ceases to become sport and becomes something else, such as work, business, or entertainment. Play is *governed by rules*—all games and events have formal or informal agreed upon rules and regulations that govern the conduct of the sport. Here, mere games generate into "sports" because of the larger and more complex structure of rules that accompany sports. Play is *make-believe*—it stands outside ordinary or "real" life and is characterized by an "only pretending" quality. In the ultimate analysis, playing a game must be considered unreal, if only for the reason that it *really doesn't* make any difference what happens. Its effect on real life is only temporary at most.

A game possesses not only the elements of play but also the variable of *competition.*[*] The competitive element in games connotes a struggle or contest for some prize that is awarded on a disproportionate basis. Competition can be between two individuals (*e.g.*, wrestling), between two or more groups of individuals (*e.g.*, baseball), between one person and a standard (*e.g.*, trying to set a record), or between one or more individuals and some element of nature (*e.g.*, mountain climbing).

Roberts and Sutton-Smith (1962) feel that most games can be classified according to their *outcome attributes*: games in which the outcome is dependent on the players' *physical skill*; games in which the outcome is largely determined by rational choices in *strategy*; or games in which the outcome is determined by *chance*. Most game occurrences are, of course, a mixture of these three elements.

It is these elements of play, competition, physical skill, strategy, and chance that most games tend to share in common. There is, however, one additional characteristic which sport possesses that many games do not and which does distinguish between the two. This is the element of *physical prowess*. Loy

---

[*]Chapter 4, The Psychology of Competition, deals thoroughly with this aspect of sport and physical activity.

suggests that the demonstration or exhibition of physical prowess, by which he means the employment of highly developed coordinated motor and physical skills in order to achieve a particular goal, easily separates what is commonly thought of as sport from other games. Most games require minimum skill whereas most sports require maximum skill levels. Maximum skill level implies considerable training, practice, and execution and thus suggests high levels of proficiency. It is here that the distinction between games and sport is most evident. A pick-up game of football or hockey on the street is a *game*; a highly organized football or hockey game in a stadium or arena, involving higher and more complex levels of proficiency, is a *sport*. Also, the more organized a game becomes, as in the above examples, the more quickly it becomes a sport. Such increases in organization are best described as an increasing *institutionalization* of the game.

The Institutionalization of Games into Sports. Loy conceives of sport as an institutionalized game as a "distinctive, enduring pattern of culture and social structure combined into a single complex." This complex is seen to include those values, norms, knowledge, proficiencies, and social roles and statuses which are particularly peculiar to that sport. Sport thus becomes a broad institutionalized *blueprint*, which guides and forms the organization and behavior within game occurrences and sporting events.

The establishment of rules and regulations for a game, or the mere presence of related organizations to a game, does not necessarily imply institutionalization. Rather a game, as conceptualized by Loy, becomes institutionalized when it has a past history of specific organization and conduct and a format for its future intentions. The more organized a game becomes in consistent and realistic environments, the more institutionalized it becomes. Sandlot baseball or street hockey are definitely related to major league baseball and hockey in terms of similar institutional patterns, but the latter are more institutionalized. Thus, the degree of organization which a game possesses is a direct measure of the extent of its institutionalization.

The institutionalization of sport proceeds through what Loy describes as the "spheres" of sport. He terms these the *organizational, technological, symbolic*, and *educational* spheres. The *organizational* aspects of sport are discussed in terms of *teams, sponsorship*, and *government*. In teams, the point is made that competing sides are more carefully selected and have a more stable social organization with increasing institutionalization. In relation to sponsorship, it is shown that both direct and indirect social groups which act as sponsoring bodies become more and more involved in sport. With respect to government, Loy feels that games become more institutionalized when, instead of rules and norms of conduct being merely passed on by word-of-mouth from year to year, such aspects become quite numerous, are formally codified, and are enforced by regulating bodies. The *technological* sphere of institutionalized sport refers to the involvement of superior material equipment and the high levels of skill that are required. If improvement in equipment and skill is to have some potential for the future, a complex technology evolves in order to translate this potential into fact. Increasingly complex skills, strategy, tactics, and analysis of skill, accompanied by highly improved stadia, playing surfaces, player equipment, and opportunities for spectator involvement, all serve directly to facilitate institutionalization. The *symbolic* sphere of sport includes the dimensions related to *secrecy,* display, and ritual. Secrecy is stressed in sport in order to explicitly separate it from the real world. Closed dressing rooms, secret tactics, exclusion of the fans from player-coach confabs, all serve to exploit this factor, and the more involved it becomes the more institutionalized the game becomes. The "dressing-up" or "display" attached to big-time sport causes a mere game to become an entertainment spectacle. Several writers (Stone 1955, Goffman 1961, Leach 1964) feel that this need for spectacular display in sport comes about because of the discomfort in the individual spectator over the unpredictability of the outcome of the game. They imply that the display attached to sport provides spectators with predictable, certain expectations—they are comforted by knowing what's going to occur and happen. The band, the cheerleaders, the pennants, the hot dogs, all contribute to this feeling of stability. The rigid ritualization of games is also an indication of increasing institutionalization in that attempts are made to make the game more dramatic and meaningful to both the competitors and the spectators. The *educational* sphere is concerned with the increasing formality of skill instruction and acquisition that accompanies institutionalization. In a game, skill acquisition is non-directed, relatively informal, and only indirectly related to achievement. People interested in playing a game are more casual regarding the level of skill or the amount of knowledge required of them to participate. The transmission of this knowledge and these skills to other people is also very informal and casual. In sport, however, skill and knowledge are acquired in a stylized, formal way. Increased emphasis is directed toward formal instruction, and the ability or capacity for skilled performance becomes very important. Thus the educational implications inherent in sport become highly institutionalized, whereas in mere games they do not. In sport, many irrelevant people become relevant, *e.g.*, teachers, instructors, coaches, trainers, managers. In games, only the player is necessary.

Sport as a Social Institution. The notion of sport as an institutional pattern is broadened if one is prepared to consider it as a *social institution*. The institutions of our society (*e.g.*, business, education, religion, art) define various aspects of our social order, particularly the value systems, interests and attitudes that revolve around the major concerns of daily life. These institutions have the function of educating the individual in how he should act, feel, behave, and believe. They have the function of organizing, facilitating, and regulating human behavior along those directions which the society-at-large deems desirable.

The magnitude of sport, and its broad permeation into all aspects of society, force one to consider it as a bonafide social institution. This is particularly true now, when sport influences such disparate things as business, television, the mass media, clothing fashions, social prestige, hero worship, advertising, and the like. Sport has been used, for centuries, as a vehicle for socializing people into the mores and value systems of society (learn to be competitive in sport and you'll be competitive later in the real world). If sport reflects, or mirrors, the society in which it operates, and if it successfully transmits the important aspects of that social order, then it can be considered an institution of that society. Loy feels that the facilitation and regulation of human behavior requires sophisticated social machinery. This is reflected in sport by the extensive organizational, managerial, and bureaucratic aspects that now are accepted as necessary in running a sports program. Even in age-group sport, such as Little League baseball and minor hockey, the hyperorganized atmosphere supposes institutionalization, and the values which people attempt to transmit to the children engaged in these sports is primary evidence of sport being regarded as a social institution.

Sport as a Social System. Loy covers one other social dimension which is important in the understanding of individual behavior in sport. This is the view that a person's behavior is governed, to a large extent, by the structures and processes inherent within the social group in which he is functioning, and that sports situations can be identified by considering what social systems are operating in a particular context. That is, a social system exists when a group of people possess certain identifiable characteristics primarily caused by the type of relationships developed through their interactions with each other (Caplow 1964). Thus, two teams playing against each other in a basketball game are just as much a social system as are four people playing bridge. Each situation has identifying characteristics which shape one's evaluation of exactly what is occurring. This is a valuable, but ignored, approach for interpreting behavior. Too often we do not take into account the peculiar social characteristics of groups participating in sport. We tend to be too inclusive in our judgments and evaluations. For example, we are likely to think that individual behavior will have the same implications in hockey as it does in basketball or football. This is quite erroneous. The social system operating within a football team has certain specific characteristics which are totally independent from that of a basketball team. In terms of Loy's thesis, the differences between these two situations are rooted in the particular kind of social interactions that occur between the players of each team. If why people get involved in sport is of concern, then the analysis of a person's interactions with other people has identifying characteristics which shape one's evaluation of exactly what is occurring.

Loy suggests that we interpret sports involvement in terms of the *degree* and *kind* of involvement that occurs in sports situations. He feels that a person's commitment to a specific sports situation can be assessed by its frequency, duration, and intensity. An evaluation of the *degree* of involvement by a person sets a baseline from which we begin to evaluate why he participates, or why he does not. For example, the degree of involvement in sport by children can be compared with that of adults by examining how many times children and adults participate over a set period of time, how long they participate in each period, and how energetic is their participation. With objective comparisons such as these we can begin to examine both the individual and social motives underlying sports involvement.

In examining the *kind* of involvement that occurs in sports situations, Loy suggests that we consider the people in a specific situation in terms of their relationship to the *means of production* of a game. This again is a useful categorization of the roles people play in particular situations, and is important for distinguishing the various interactions and relationships people have with each other. He feels that people who have direct or indirect access to the actual production of sport are "producers" and those who are only vicariously involved are "consumers." Producers are the players, coaches, trainers, cheerleaders, officials, and other sundry game personnel. Consumers are spectators, television viewers, radio listeners, media readers, and people who just converse with each other about sport.

Sports involvement thus becomes a highly complex network of roles, interactions, and relationships. This is but a surface treatment of the social context of sport, but it does serve to lucidly present the distinction between what is a game and what is sport. In the following chapters of this book we will be constantly referring to analyzing individual behavior in *sport* and the reader is cautioned to be aware that these descriptions and explanations must always be considered in the social context in which they occur. Though no clear lines separate the psychology, sociology, and social psychology of sport, each discipline supports and supplements the other in the analysis of sports behavior.

THE NATURE OF PHYSICAL ACTIVITY

Though the characteristics which distinguish *physical* activity from other types of activity would seem to be self-evident, one soon realizes that human movement is, indeed, a highly complex phenomenon. Paddick (1967), in his analysis of the field of knowledge in physical education, feels that, because of the complexities and interactions that occur between such disparate phenomena as sports, games, exercise, training, play, and dance, the study of physical activity can best be described as the *study of the interaction of man and his movements*. It is within such a context that the nature of physical activity can be examined. Paddick feels that physical activity (*i.e.*, physical or motor performance), which is the basic underlying commonality of the above phenomena, can be analyzed in terms of five basic processes: namely, the mechanical, energy, organizational, growth, and learning processes that denote human movement. Though these processes are in constant interaction with each other, so that no ultimate distinctions can be made between them, the continuity of each with each serves only to emphasize the integration that is necessary to establish what is meant by physical activity. Later, a discussion of physical activity as a sociopsychological phenomenon will be made; however, at this time, some comments on these processes is appropriate.

Change in motion is the result of forces, so it is necessary to determine how man produces the forces upon which his motion depends. The regularities in the manner of production of these forces constitute the *mechanical process*. The process is circular: forces which are produced cause alteration in subsequent responses. Man produces these forces by the tension he develops in the muscles acting through his skeleton, with these forces dependent on the relative length of limb segments and body proportions. Changes take place in man as a result of the forces he produces, and these changes further affect the forces that can be produced. Regularities such as the increases in muscle size and strength associated with certain kinds of movements, and the loss of strength associated with disuse are universally accepted.

In producing these forces, *energy* is used. This energy for motion must be supplied over and above that required for basic metabolic processes. The identifiable regularities in the production, supply, and utilization of energy underlie this process. Study of the energy process involves the relative importance of such factors as oxygen consumption, supply, and distribution and calorie supply, utilization, and storage. Two major kinds of energy processes operate (aerobic and anaerobic) in such a way as to make available movement of great intensity over a short period of time regardless of the immediately available oxygen. Through interaction with the other processes, the various energy processes are modified to make different movements available.

The presence of an *organizational process* is obvious when one realizes the complexity of man's movement. Organization, or the coordination and regulation of organized responses, that occurs is automatic, *e.g.*, the relaxing of antagonists or the increase in circulation. However, man can also consciously direct his activity—he not only can form some concept of his movement but also can develop some feeling or attitude toward it. If he decides the movement is of value he continues it, if he doesn't, then he terminates it. Thus, the fact that man can pay attention to his movements means that a kind of filter-amplifier is applied to all movement at the organismic level. In this sense, then, perception becomes all important. It is through perceptual organization that external stimuli are organized with internal factors such as the hormonal processes associated with emotion, motivation, maturation, and inhibition.

That movement is learned is without doubt—however, how *learning* occurs is a matter of considerable controversy. Metheny (1965), for example, has stressed that motor learning, though traditionally considered separate from other learning processes, is, in fact, the same process. Also traditionally, the learning process underlying physical activity has been confined to movement considered as skills. Now, however, learning in the ability to exert forces has been indicated (Morehouse 1965). This has been an area generally regarded as training and has been usually distinguished from the study of learning.

As children *grow*, their ability to perform movement and their physical activity change. Equally, it is clear that the aging process is accompanied by changes in man's capacity for physical activity. The mechanisms that relate growth and aging to movement, however, are less clearly understood. Though a distinction between *incremental growth* (*i.e.*, the balance of retention over loss in the continuous interaction man has with his environment) and replacement growth (*i.e.*, the replacement of discarded cells) can be made, the processes involved are undoubtedly complex

(Frank 1963). There is little doubt, however, that growth processes have importance for understanding training effects such as increases in the cross sections of muscles and for the understanding of the role of movement in rehabilitation.

The preceding conceptual development of the nature of physical activity represents only *one* way of satisfactorily describing one aspect of reality. Many other characterizations could be made. However, the very complexity of physical activity necessitates avoiding a sole emphasis on the isolation or fragmentation of certain processes without a continued attention to their synthesis and integration. Conceptualizing the complexity of physical activity, however, permits us to do three things. First, it permits us to organize and integrate an already considerable amount of information dealing with the understanding of human performance. Secondly, it provides an orientation for future investigation within the area of physical activity, so that all kinds of research growing out of that orientation will contribute to further organization. And thirdly, it will help in accounting for all relevant variables, thus avoiding artificiality and fragmentation in describing the concept. This is particularly true when one considers those characteristics of physical activity which are socio-psychological in nature. The following section explores this aspect of physical activity.

In an attempt to answer the question "what is meant by the term physical activity?" Kenyon (1968) has developed a conceptual model in which the major domain of physical activity has been subdivided into six subdomains. These subdomains, characterized by what distinct meaning each has, in terms of physical activity, for the individual, are labeled *social experience, health and fitness, pursuit of vertigo, aesthetic experience, catharsis,* and *ascetic experience* (Diagram 5). These quasi-independent

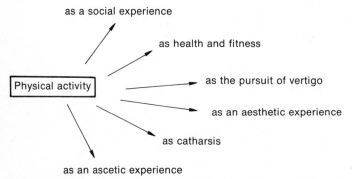

DIAGRAM 5. THE KENYON CONCEPTUAL MODEL OF PHYSICAL ACTIVITY.

subdomains are hypothesized as representing the major manifest and latent instrumental values that physical activity has for the individual participant. It is this "perceived instrumentality" of physical activity which Kenyon feels offers the best basis for classifying physical activity into subcomponents. There is little doubt that various aspects of physical activity offer differential satisfaction to different individuals. Because of this, physical activity can be characterized as a *sociopsychological* phenomenon and reduced to more specific, meaningful components. Such a treatment interprets physical activity as a "psychological object" toward which people develop interests, attitudes and values. Though interpreting the term physical activity in a programmic sense (*e.g.*, as team vs. individual activities, dance, combatatives, racquet sports, aquatics) has operational value for neatly organizing programs and curricula, it has no use whatsoever when attempting to conceptualize physical activity. For example, the categorization of tower diving and synchronized swimming under the rubric *aquatics* implies that these physical activities have large commonality and naturally group together; this is ridiculous, the *only* thing they have in common is that water is involved in both. Such heuristic categorization, Kenyon feels, based solely on pedagogical grounds, has held back thought in physical education in terms of accurately denoting physical activity. To avoid this approach he has denoted physical activity as "organized, non-utilitarian, gross human movement...(as it is)...manifested in active games, sports, calisthenics, and dance" and has constructed a model which he feels better represents the phenomenon.

The Subdomains of Physical Activity. Initially Kenyon's attempt to construct a model of physical activity consisted of subdomains termed *physical health, mind-body dichotomy, cooperation-competition, mental health, social intercourse,* and *patriotism.* These came together as a result of traditional and intuitive observations of what constituted physical activity. Subsequent research, however, failed to indicate the validity of these concepts. In a second attempt, physical activity was examined as a *recreational experience,* for *health and fitness,* as the *pursuit of vertigo,* as an *aesthetic experience,* and as a *competitive experience.* The integrity of this structure proved to be much stronger than in the first attempt, except for the two subdomains of physical activity as recreational and competitive experiences. These two were subsequently reformulated as *social experience* and *ascetic experience,* to complete the model as it now stands. The rationales underlying the perceived instrumentality of each of these dimensions of physical activity are as follows:

1. Physical activity as a *social experience* is characterized as those physical activities whose *primary* value lies in providing the participant with the opportunity for making new friends, for maintaining close social bonds with other people, and for general social intercourse. Almost all physical activity provides such opportunity and, even though specific activities such as bowling, golf, and curling immediately come to mind, this dimension must be considered as an all-embracing subdomain of physical activity. For thousands of people, participating in physical activity has its strongest meaning in terms of the social experiences it provides and the social needs it satisfies. Playing football or table tennis thus may be rooted in this dimension; it depends not so much on the type of activity but rather on why the person participates in an activity that provides the real meaning of physical activity. Conversely, all who play football or table tennis are not doing so for the same reasons, *i.e.,* football and table tennis *mean* different things to different people. Any information as to why people participate in different or the same physical activities is immediately of value. As we will see later, a strong need or motive for affiliation operates in sports participation and, to a major extent, determines what activity a person chooses. Thus physical activity, in a social context, must be viewed as a means toward satisfying an individual's affiliative needs.

2. Physical activity as *health and fitness* is characterized by those activities whose main or immediate contribution is to the improvement of individual health and fitness. For great numbers of people in the Western world this is the *only* context in which physical activity is viewed, and, whether they participate themselves or not, it is in terms of physical fitness that physical activity has meaning for them. The President's Council on Physical Fitness in the United States and the Fitness and Amateur Sport Directorate of the Federal Government in Canada are only two examples of the official emphasis placed upon the importance of physical fitness in Western society. Coupled with the constant stream of warnings from both the medical and physical education professions, health and fitness through physical activity has become almost a household phrase. Some activities such as circuit training, weight training, calisthenics, and training exercises for various sports are quite obviously directed toward this dimension. Many other activities, however, although they contribute directly toward fitness, may not have that particular meaning for people. Track and field events, swimming, jogging, and various Y.M.C.A. programs would also seem to be oriented solely toward this dimension, but one must be careful. Implicit in these activities is the possibility that they do not necessarily have this mean-

ing for the people who participate in them. Activities which appear to be oriented toward health and fitness may be taken up for completely different reasons. Again, it is important to realize that people who participate in physical activity for reasons grounded in health and physical fitness will exhibit distinctly different patterns of behavior than people participating in these activities for other reasons.

3. Physical activity as the *pursuit of vertigo* is characterized by "physical experiences providing, at some risk to the participant, an element of thrill through ... speed, acceleration, sudden change of direction, or exposure to dangerous situations..." (Kenyon, 1968). This characterization is a modification of Callois' (1961) views on the basic attraction vertigo has for people. Callois felt that people who pursue vertigo deliberately attempt to destroy their bodily and perceptual equilibrium in order to generate a giddiness or convulsive shock that is pleasantly intoxicating to them. Riding the roller coaster at the fairgrounds or simply playing on the teeter-totter in a playground produce such sensations and the basic attraction of these activities is hypothesized as being the pursuit of vertigo. Kenyon has taken this characterization and added the dimensions of danger, thrill, and risk. By broadening the scope in this manner, he has made available an intuitively attractive rationale for explaining why some people mountain climb, ski jump, surf, or sky dive.

Kenyon, however, does make the important reservation that, though people may *pursue* vertigo in these activities, they do not necessarily achieve it. He also emphasizes that the instrumental value of such activities is probably latent within people, *i.e.*, they know they like such an activity but are unable to articulate their reasons. There is no reason to believe that ordinary physical activities such as gymnastics, football, hockey, and basketball also do not possess strong elements of vertigo. So again the dimension underlies many diverse activities that in the past have been neatly placed in different categories. Attempting to explain what it is about an activity that attracts or repels a person is significantly more valuable to us than just knowing what activities he participates in.

4. Physical activity as an *aesthetic experience* characterizes those activities which have aesthetic value for the person in terms of grace, beauty, or other artistic qualities. This is a much stronger dimension of the attraction of physical activity than one might expect. Aesthetics deals more with those things which are beautiful than with those which are right or practical. It is here that the emotional feeling one has for sport is manifested, and because of this, physical activity is dealt with in a much more

subjective manner. Many athletes view and appreciate physical activity as a medium for artistic creation and, in doing so, put themselves outside of reality. When physical activity is considered by the person to be a creative art form, the activity exists only for itself, or enclosed within itself, and thus becomes an experience. Physical activity thus is pursued for its own sake and no other. Lovers of sport and physical activity who hold that all physical activity is beautiful can easily achieve an aesthetic experience in viewing the way a player skillfully moves or performs in a contestant's use of his imagination, in the poise of a champion, or even in just a beautiful girl in leotards. So again, though certain activities such as gymnastics, figure skating and ballet may connote aesthetics, there is the realization that beauty and grace can manifest in *any* physical activity. Because of this, aesthetic experience becomes an underlying dimension of physical activity.

5. Physical activity as *catharsis* is a conception denoting the release of tension generated usually from frustrations caused in the vicissitudes of daily life. That is, one characteristic of physical activity is that it provides an outlet for "blowing off steam." The *catharsis hypothesis*, a favorite of writers on aggression, has been a useful one for physical educators for a century. It develops from the premise that within everyone there exists a need for physical activity—when this need is unsatisfied, tension arises and can only be dissipated through violent physical activity. Many school physical education programs have been justified on this basis and allowed to continue because the children need to blow off steam if they are to learn their other school subjects properly. In addition, physical activity has been used as a vehicle for releasing pent-up aggression in socially acceptable ways and, for many, this has been one of the basic justifications for competitive sports programs. Again, however, it is probably a legitimate dimension of physical activity simply because of its perceived instrumentality: that is, if people think physical activity has a *cathartic function* then it probably will—for them. It is highly doubtful (as we will see in Chapter 10, Aggression in Sport), however, that physical activity does actually have the cathartic effect it is said to have.

6. Physical activity as an *ascetic experience* is characterized by those activities involving long and strenuous training, conditioning, and practicing, where "deferred gratification" is demanded of the participant. This dimension arose from previous attempts to characterize physical activity as a competitive experience which provides the contestant with a means for expressing his excellence or superiority. It was thought that the charac-

terization of physical activities which required high dedication and long sacrifice must of necessity be related to a basic desire within people to aspire to high levels of achievement. People who are prepared to "pay such a price" are envisioned as being prepared to undergo a kind of ascetic experience. This is very much a dimension of physical activity when it connotes high excellence or success to the participant. Championships come out of, or are the result of, long hours of drudgery, sacrifice, and boredom.

Kenyon's model characterizes physical activity in terms of sociopsychological phenomena and attempts to describe, in conceptual terms, the *multidimensionality* of physical activity. The meaningfulness of each subdomain is interpreted as the perceived instrumentality it has for the individual, *i.e.*, what value each concept has in defining physical activity for the individual. Considerable subsequent research has validated this model of physical activity and has shown the subdomains to be relatively univocal and independent.

Overview

A perspective of sport and physical activity has been presented in this chapter in order to provide the reader with a reference point from which to view psychological behavior in an athletic context. The content of this chapter is naturally far from complete; the concepts of games, sport, and physical activity are vast and would require whole textbooks themselves for complete treatment. However, an orientation, especially in terms of *context,* has been provided in order to outline what constitutes sport and physical activity, to show the sociopsychological variables which influence behavior in sport, and to set the stage for further understanding and insight. Further clarification of these concepts will develop gradually as the book progresses through the basic underlying psychological dimensions of sport and physical activity, because, if nothing else, sport is an individual thing. The reality of sport exists in each individual's mind and it is through his overt behavior that his interpretation of this reality can be seen and, hopefully, interpreted by others. Life is a complex of physical, intellectual, emotional, and social developmental patterns, and for a large number of people, especially children, sport and physical activity are integral parts of these patterns. Thus an understanding of behavior in sport and physical activity will aid us in helping people to better fulfill their lives.

THE PSYCHOLOGY OF COMPETITION*

Preface

In contemporary Western society it is normal and important to be competitive. In everyday life, business, and certainly athletics, individuals and groups of people are constantly engaging in competitive behavior for success, prestige, status, and social approval. Margaret Mead (1961), for example, has noted that three basic components of behavior operate in any society to give an overall indicator of that society's general tendencies: cooperative, competitive, and individualistic behaviors. Although all three of these components very definitely operate within Western society today, it is competitive behavior that seems to be of primary importance for success in physical activity and athletics. What is this competitiveness which everyone talks about, where does it come from, and how does it develop? This chapter is an attempt to provide the reader with a behavioristic frame of reference within which one can better understand the construct of competition.

INTRODUCTION

Though many definitions of competition exist, the operational interpretations by most people center around some reference to a *struggle between individuals or groups of individuals, for some common goal or object.* Church (1968), however, provides the most precise definition in his distinction between cooperative and competitive situations. He feels that certain social phenomena such as aggression, power, and imitation should be defined in terms of behavior, while other social phenomena such as cooperation and competition are better defined in terms of social situations. The distinction he makes between cooperation and competition has an immediate implication for

---

*The author wishes to acknowledge the contributions made by Dr. Leonard M. Wankel of the University of Waterloo who, as a graduate student during the writing of this chapter, thoroughly examined the nature of competition and its interaction with motor performance, Specific references to Dr. Wankel's work are made to Wankel (1971).

situational behavior in athletics and physical activity, namely, that *a cooperative situation* exists when the "payoff" (*i.e.*, reinforcement) for each individual in the situation depends upon the *joint behavior* of two or more of these individuals. For example, success in a particular cooperative endeavor occurs when either of two persons achieves a specific goal, when both people achieve a specific goal, or when their joint efforts result in a shared goal. The parallel to team sports is obvious. That is, a cooperative situation exists in football when any one particular person on the team achieves his particular objective (*e.g.*, scoring a touchdown, kicking a field goal, making 90% of his blocks during a game) when two or more of the players on the team together achieve success (*e.g.*, the offense scores, the defense prevents a score) or when the combined effort of everyone on the team meets a specified criterion (*e.g.*, winning the game). A *competitive situation* exists, on the other hand, when the payoff or reinforcement depends on an individual's performance *relative* to the performances of one or more other people. That is, a competitive situation is one in which the payoff is allocated among two or more individuals as a result of their performances. Thus, differential reinforcement exists in all competitive situations in that one person either wins everything or wins a higher degree of the goal than the loser or losers. In this general framework, then, an acceptable or workable definition of *competition* is *any situation in which two or more individuals struggle for the complete or larger share of a particular goal, and in which the success of their performances is relative to each other.*

Ross and Van den Haag (1957) define the two major types of competition in our society by the outcomes which result. They suggest classifying competition as either being *indirect* or *direct*. In *indirect* competition the person struggles for achievement against a non-personal, relatively objective standard, against his own previous achievements, or against "records" which represent the best performances at his ability level. This designation incorporates such diverse competitive activities as struggling against par on the golf course, climbing a mountain, canoeing or cross-country skiing, performing against one's previous marks (*e.g.*, doing 32 push-ups instead of 31), or just going out and running against time on the local track. Just about all physical activity and sport can be considered in terms of indirect competition, especially the so-called individual sports. Such a view ranges all the way from describing the competitive element involved in the middle-aged jogger trying to reduce his best time right through to the professional athlete constantly attempting to achieve perfection in his own specific skills. This designation is also impressive in that it clearly emphasizes physical activity and sport as being primarily competitive. In *direct* competition people struggle against each other in a clearly personal context. In direct situations each performer attempts to maximize his success while at the same time minimizing that of his opponents. Tennis, handball, wrestling, fencing, boxing, and practically all the team sports exemplify direct competition.

Malpass (1962) feels that too much emphasis is placed on considering competition only as "direct": that is, people reinforce only the subduing and degradation of one's opponent rather than motivating the participants to achieve excellence. In fact, excellence is usually reinforced only as a means toward the end of winning. Winning thus replaces excellence as the main value of competition in sport. A psychological explanation of this preference of people for winning can be found in Alfred Adler's (1930) theorizing on the fictional finalisms of superiority and perfection. Adler feels that the core tendency in a person's life is to strive toward superiority and perfection, and that the basis for this tendency lies in the person's physical weaknesses and incapacities, in his feelings of inferiority regardless of his physical condition, and in his compensatory attempts to overcome real or imagined inferiorities. The direction of these compensations is toward what he terms *fictional finalisms*, or the ideals of perfect living. Superiority over other people thus becomes an ideal or goal in one's life, and any blocking or thwarting of these goals causes frustration in the person and consequently feelings of inferiority. The use of direct competition in sport caters to such a view of life. Sport is used to demonstrate superiority, not excellence. This is an emphasis which should be unattractive to professionals in the field.

It is also interesting to note in this context Luschen's (1970) view of sport as *zero-sum* type competition, *i.e.*, competition wherein one competitor wins and the other loses. The outcome of any competition thus results in a zero value. *Non-zero-sum* type competition, on the other hand, allows for varying degrees of partially winning or partially losing. The distinction between these two types of competition rests upon how one defines "success." If success is evaluated only in terms of winning then all sports competition is of an all-or-none variety, *i.e.*, a zero-sum outcome. However, if success can be evaluated in other terms such as enjoyment, satisfaction, getting better, or increasing one's self-confidence, then performance relevant to a referent standard becomes involved in non-zero-sum type competition.

Several important questions emanate from the above definitions and distinctions regarding competition in sport, and it is toward understanding these questions that the remainder of this chapter is devoted. For example, what is competition? Is it a psychological, biological or social phenomenon? In what kinds of terms can we explain competition? Can we explain what occurs during competitive situations? What is competitiveness? Is it behavior that is innate to animals or is it socially induced and propagated? Do individual differences in competitiveness exist, and, if so, are these differences based in one's personality or in his environment? What are the various sources of influence on competitiveness? What are the various dimensions of competition? Does socioeconomic background determine how competitive a child will be? Can competitiveness be objectively assessed? How does competition affect learning and performance in physical activity and sport situations? And lastly, what is the difference between cooperative and competitive behavior? And which is most effective for success in group performance?

Various paradigms in the literature exist for analyzing the theoretical structure of competition and the manner in which people behave in competitive situations. Generally speaking, this is social behavior theory simply because most competitive situations involve more than one person in one way or another. Individuals competing in isolation from other people are better observed in terms of motivational indices, while people competing with each other can be looked at in both motivational and associative behavior terms. Thus, theory on competition can explain human behavior on the basis of associative connections between individuals and situations without any reference being made to separate motivational or intervening drive-arousal systems, or it can explain behavior simply in motivational terms which replace most cognitive constructs with mechanisms such as drive and arousal (motivational theory). Both general types of theories have been utilized in analyzing competitive behavior.

DIFFERENTIAL REINFORCEMENT IN COMPETITION

Church (1968) attempts to explain the effects of competition in terms of *differential reinforcement, i.e.,* the winner of a competition always receives more reinforcement for his behavior than do the other contestants. He suggests that in order to understand competitive behavior one need know only the basis upon which the distribution of reward is made. No reference to the cognitive or connative states of the individuals is necessary. He further states that social facilitation* from competition is at its optimum when the probability of success is slightly less than 50 per cent—that success is more likely if your opponent's ability is just slightly higher than your own. This is straightforward behavior theory, in which the effects of social facilitation that accrue from competition are explained in terms of the reinforcement of desired responses. Such a Skinnerian approach to behavior phenomena implies that it is the *situation* which must be analyzed in order to explain the effects which occur. In this context then, it is of primary importance to determine under which conditions a competitive situation optimizes an individual's or team's performance. Consider a wrestling match—the winner is reinforced, the loser is not. Such allocation of reward thus depends on (or is a function of) some characteristic of each person's behavior (in this case, his wrestling skill).

Does such a competitive allocation of rewards cause the person to wrestle better? Does it raise his motivational level? It certainly does if skill is chosen as the basis for the competition. The competitive allocation of rewards leads clearly to differential reinforcement, and this in turn leads to an increase in skill (or whichever response characteristic is being rewarded).

Thus, Church (1968) defines a competitive situation *as "one in which the available reinforcements (e.g., prizes, money, status, etc.) are allocated among two or more individuals as a function of some characteristic of their behavior relative to one another."*

Competition, in this sense, implies a struggle between two people for the same object, without implying that it is necessary for one's opponent to be either physically or mentally present. For example, many aspects of athletic competition do not require the presence of competitors. One can "compete" with athletes around the world simply by trying to be better than they in some particular event such as throwing the javelin. Also, no reference need be made to any subjective cognitive or connative states of the person when explaining competition—one need only determine to what extent differential reinforcement contributes to the manner in which people behave in competitive situations. In solitary individual competition, performance is ranked on the basis of behavior of a single subject, without any reference to other people (*i.e.,* indirect competition). In other competitive situations such as football, hockey, and baseball it is almost impossible to rank subjects on the basis of individual performance,

---

*Social facilitation is a term which refers to the enhancing of an individual's actions or behavior by the presence of others doing the same thing.

simply because too much "interaction" between individuals occurs.

Church feels that motivational interpretations do not adequately analyze or explain the effects of competition. Such interpretations revolve essentially around the position that a competitive situation increases motivation which, in turn, results in response facilitation (improvement) or response decrement, depending upon the level of motivation and the complexity of the particular task. In terms of the Yerkes-Dodson Law (1908), performance on any task is a function of the level of motivation and task complexity—that there is an optimal level of motivation for any task and that this optimal level decreases as task complexity increases (see Diagram 6). Church feels that without independ-

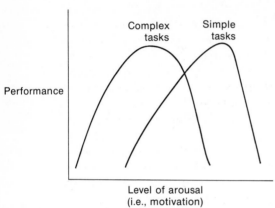

DIAGRAM 6. PERFORMANCE, MOTIVATION AND TASK COMPLEXITY.

ent measures of motivation and task complexity, and with only a "hazy" notion as to what the relationship of these two variables is to performance, any motivational interpretation of the effects of competition on performance tends to be weak. He feels that it is more plausible to describe the effects of competitive situations in terms of the differential reinforcement of some previously present response characteristic rather than to some motivational factor which may or may not be present.

SOCIAL FACILITATION AND COMPETITION

Festinger (1954) views competitive behavior as a response to the interaction of two basic drives within the individual: namely, the drive upward to constantly improve one's abilities and the drive that exists within people to constantly evaluate their abilities, opinions, and emotions. In the absence of objective criteria by which to evaluate one's ability, individuals seek out social situations for the purpose of comparing themselves with others. This process of social comparison is engaged in with appropriate referent persons — people of similar abilities — and covers not only an evaluation of one's abilities but also of one's opinions, attitudes and emotions. Competition, as viewed by Festinger, is seen as resulting from an interaction of these two drives. A child's competitive behavior in sport, therefore, is interpreted as resulting from both a desire within him to become better in his athletic ability *and* a desire to discover how good he is by comparing himself with both his teammates and his opponents. If both these motivational drives are strong within an individual, he will be highly competitive. Also, in most sports situations there exists a high potential for expressing these two drives, thus automatically causing situations which are essentially competitive.

It is generally accepted in our western culture that doing well, or doing better than someone else, is highly desirable, so that the better one performs, the more desirable is the performance. This is what Festinger is referring to when he talks about a *unidirectional drive upward.* Individuals are constantly oriented toward some point on the ability continuum that is slightly higher than their present level of ability or the current level of ability of the group within which he is functioning. As long as the person desires continual improvement, he is competitive. There always exists a pressure to be slightly better than the people one is using for comparison purposes. For some athletes whose ability levels are considerably higher than that of their referent group (*i.e.,* their teammates' ability levels), a dilemma immediately exists. Should they continue on upward, increase the discrepancy between their ability and their teammates' ability and risk a certain amount of negative feedback (*i.e.,* jealousy, etc.), or is it better to stop improving, and try to bring their teammates' ability levels up closer to their own. This latter alternative rests on the idea that individuals prefer reasonably similar bases for comparison simply because of the competitive behavior that is involved in comparison. If the individual chooses the latter alternative, he probably becomes *less* competitive, and there is a plateau in his skill improvement. Somehow, the coach-teacher and the athlete must recognize such an occurrence and re-orient the athlete back on to a competitive basis.

One more explanation is of interest. Some children participating in competitive sport lose a high degree of their competitiveness once they have made the team. The reason for this is partially explained when one realizes that the child has probably reached the same level as the average ability level of his referent group (the team) or has successfully fulfilled his level of aspiration (*i.e.*, he has reached that "slightly better" point on the ability continuum). When this happens, the situation becomes *less* competitive for him. Coaches and teachers usually correct such a situation by having the child reset his level of aspiration higher.

In a further attempt to clarify the phenomenon of competition in terms of social comparison, Jones and Gerard (1964) have differentiated between what they call *comparative* and *reflected* appraisal. Comparative appraisal refers to the evaluation of one's own relative standing with respect to a particular ability or opinion by comparing one's ability level with the ability levels of other people. Reflected appraisal is an evaluation of one's own ability level that is inferred from the behavior of other people during one's interaction with them. The person indulging in the evaluation judges his own worth from the cues emanating from the other person's behavior. So an individual can engage in social comparison not only through a straightforward comparison but also through inferring from other people's behavior toward him approximately what they think of his ability. Thus, the competitive behavior of an individual participating in sport depends on his judgment of the way teammates, coaches, opponents and spectators regard him. For some children in sport, strong positive reinforcement is needed in order for them to become competitive; they must be given a positive image of themselves. If a coach's behavior toward a particular athlete indicates that he thinks the boy is not worthwhile, then the boy will detect this attitude, incorporate it into his own self-picture and actually start thinking he really is not worthwhile. This might occur directly in the face of positive approval flowing in from various comparative appraisals he is making at the same time. Comparative and reflected appraisal processes arise out of the broad socialization that is constantly occurring during a child's daily life. Jones and Gerard feel that a child is dependent upon others, especially adults, for the direct satisfaction of his primary needs (*i.e.*, food, clothing, shelter, nurturance, etc.), and for information pertinent to his environment and the meaning of his environment. The former is termed *effect dependence,* the latter *information dependence.* It is through these two forms of dependency that the child is socialized into recognizing and incorporating the relevant values, mores, beliefs and customs of the culture in which he lives. And one important aspect of this socialization is the social comparison he engages in through comparative and reflected appraisal. If competition holds an important value in his culture (and this is certainly true in Western culture), then the child is "socialized" into being competitive.

Competition, in a social behavior context, was also treated by Allport (1924), one of the important pioneer workers in the field of social psychology. Allport identified two separate social factors operating in competitive situations. First was *social facilitation,* which he described as the enhancing of an individual's actions or behavior by the mere presence of other people doing the same thing. The second factor, *rivalry,* was concerned with the emotional reinforcement of actions and behavior when accompanied by a desire to win (*i.e.,* rivalry is seen as a motivational component in competitive situations where there exists a cognitive desire to win). The implication here is that, in the absence of an implicit or explicit desire to win (rivalry), a strong competitive element exists in most social situations simply from the sight and sounds of other people engaged in the same activity. Thus, in physical education classes, children will sense a competitive situation existing simply because of the presence of other children doing the same thing.

Allport referred to a group of people engaged in the same activity as a *coacting* group. Social facilitation is comprised of the effects of coaction which are generally beneficial. Zajonc (1965) used this term when he theorized that social facilitation should be further subdivided into *audience* effects and *coaction* effects. He felt that a real distinction exists between the effects that the mere presence of spectators have on performance and the effects due to other individuals performing the same task. Competitive behavior, it is felt, will be higher or stronger in a coaction situation than in a mere audience situation. Cottrell (1968), in a criticism of Zajonc, has taken this paradigm even further. He feels that Zajonc's description of "audience" as the *mere* presence of others is inadequate to explain audience effects on competitive behavior. He prefers a learned or secondary drive explanation for the audience effect, and a relationship can be seen with Jones and Gerard's views on comparative and reflected appraisal. Cottrell feels that a distinction must be made between whether or not the audience is important, relevant, or referent for the individual. That is, an individual's actions and behavior will be more significantly facilitated if the person is *directly concerned* about how the audience is evaluating him. It will be affected by his *past experience* in audience situations, his general *attitude toward the task* he is performing, his *attitude toward the audience,* and the *general response of the audience* to his performance. All these specific audience factors are hypothesized as raising the drive or arousal level in the person and thus facilitating his behavior. In particular cases, of course, performance will be negatively affected rather than enhanced. Such arousal or drive is considered to be learned (*i.e.,* a secondary drive), as the result of continuous exposure to performance situations in front of spectators over a period of time.

In practical terms, then, the point being made by the above social psychologists and sociologists is that, apart from his inherent personality makeup, specific variables operate in a social situation to influence a person's behavior and performance. They say that competition situations consist not only of a cognitive desire to win (rivalry) but also of a general effect called social facilitation. This social facilitation (or raising of arousal level) is a function of both coaction and audience effects. Thus, the intensity and direction of competitive behavior in sports and physical activity situations can be shown to be a function of the interaction between an individual and his teammates or between an individual and spectators. Regardless of whether performance is positively or negatively affected, an individual's behavior is facilitated (*i.e.,* his level of arousal is raised) in the presence of both passive and coacting others. Practicing in isolation when one is to compete in front of people thus may result in poor performance. Children, especially, must be conditioned into performing in front of people.

REINFORCEMENT IN THE ACQUISITION OF COMPETITIVENESS

Critical to any discussion of competition in physical activity and sport is the question of whether competitiveness is an inherent or acquired characteristic.* Though it is beyond the scope of this section to delve thoroughly into the biological nature of man, a definite attempt will be made to outline one specific aspect of basic psychological theory underlying the *acquisition* of particular behaviors. Such theory, it is hoped, will provide some understanding of how individuals become competitive and how they remain competitive. Also, some implications will be covered as to how one can maximize competitive behavior in the individual athlete. The theoretical area covered in this section is generally

---

*For thorough discussions on whether man is inherently competitive or basically altruistic, the reader is referred to Ardrey (1966) and Montagu (1964).

subsumed under the rubric *learning theory* or, more specifically, *stimulus-response (S-R) theory.*

Ivan Pavlov (1927), the distinguished and famous Russian physiologist, is usually considered the father of S-R theory, and it was his formulation of a new kind of learning called *classical conditioning* which laid the foundations for later theorizing on behavior acquisition. Pavlov demonstrated that through the continuous and simultaneous presentation of an unconditioned stimulus (*e.g.,* food) and a conditioned stimulus (*e.g.,* a bell), the conditioned stimulus would eventually elicit a response (*e.g.,* salivation) that originally was elicited only by the conditioned stimulus. This act of salivating to the sound of the bell was referred to as a *conditioned response* (Diagram 7).

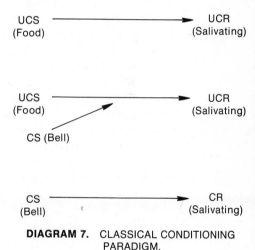

DIAGRAM 7. CLASSICAL CONDITIONING PARADIGM.

This process of conditioning was accepted and embraced by a number of American psychologists, and quickly adapted for explaining behavior other than just learning. Watson (1925), who at the time was rejecting the prevailing introspective approach to behavior, proposed that behavior should be studied using the same kinds of objective techniques that other natural sciences were using. He felt that it was important to build a psychology dealing only with observables, and seized upon classical conditioning as a particularly useful means for observing behavior. At the same time, Thorndike (1932) was constructing his Law of Effect, designed to demonstrate the all-encompassing importance of reward and punishment in the learning process. This fundamental theorizing laid the basis for numerous formulations over the next thirty years in American psychology, with such famous names as Hull, Tolman, Guthrie, Miller, Dollard, Spence, and Hilgard all assuming a dominant interest in this general approach to learning. No real justice can be done to the development of S-R theory over this period of time, especially in this particular section. Rather, it is sufficient to say that the phenomenon which is of interest here has emanated out of Clarke L. Hull's (1943)[*] theory of behavior and has been elaborated by Dollard, Miller and Spence. This section is concerned with the writings of these particular people.

A great deal of Dollard and Miller's (1950) work rests on an interpretation of Hull's famous learning theory in terms of its personality implications. As with Hull, the concept of habit is centrally crucial to the formulations of these authors, and the core of their position on the structure of personality is a description of the learning process. They feel that behavior acquisition is the study of the circumstances under which a response and a cue-stimulus become connected. Competitive behavior thus can be viewed as a habit connection between certain cue stimuli and various responses. That is, one *learns* competitive responses. They feel that learning, in its simplest form, is a function of the particular circumstances under which *habits* are formed, and that the strength of habit increases only under certain conditions and is not just a matter of continuous practice. Thus, the individual must be forced, in certain situations, to make the desired responses in the presence of certain cues for which he is then rewarded (or reinforced). The fundamental factors in a learning situation thus become *drive, cue, response* and *reward* (Miller and Dollard 1941). A paradigm of the learning principles which these authors have applied to emotional behavior in everyday life can be seen below in Diagram 8.

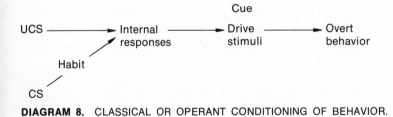

DIAGRAM 8.   CLASSICAL OR OPERANT CONDITIONING OF BEHAVIOR.

What can be seen in this diagram is that, as in the traditional classical conditioning sense, an initially neutral stimulus (CS) is paired with an unconditioned stimulus (UCS) which regularly

---

[*]The Hullian model of learning receives a more thorough technical treatment in Chapter 8.

elicits a characteristic behavior pattern (the conditioned response in the Pavlovian paradigm). Miller (1941), however, hypothesizes that a series of internal events occur between the observable stimulus (UCS) and the overt behavior it produces. As can be seen in the diagram, the unconditioned stimulus elicits a number of internal responses usually associated with some kind of emotion. These responses, in turn, elicit or give rise to an *"internal pattern of stimuli"* which have drive properties and are thus known as *drive stimuli* (SD). These drive stimuli have the same capacity as external sources of stimulation and set off or *"cue"* still further responses characterized in the diagram as *overt behavior*. Drive, in Hullian terms, is a motivational concept which is thought to impel or activate behavior. Such drives are usually primary in nature, but Miller feels that any stimulus, external or internal, if strong enough, will evoke a drive and cause behavior. Thus, after repeated presentations with the UCS, the neutral CS will eventually become paired with it and elicit similar, if not the same, internal responses. When this connection between the CS and the internal responses is made it is represented by the concept of *habit*. Thus, the learning that has taken place is characterized by the building of this connection, that is, the formation of a habit. For a habit to be established, the stimulus and the response must occur close together, both spatially and temporally, and the response must be accompanied by reinforcement or reward. Eventually, over a period of time, the originally neutral CS not only elicits the internal responses (originally only elicited by the UCS) but also sets into operation the whole sequence of internal events previously elicited by the UCS. Now the drive stimuli (SD) and the CS act as cues to elicit overt behavior. This behavior, in addition, is energized or aroused by the drive stimuli. As this drive is *now* elicited by a learned response (*i.e.,* the result of a habit being formed), it is best described as being a *secondary drive*. For example, if the UCS in a situation is a pain-provoker then a neutral CS can be paired with it to cause the usual responses to pain, *i.e.,* fear or anxiety. Through the above explained sequence of events, then, fear or anxiety becomes a learned response *and* a learned or secondary drive. In a drive- or tension-reduction sense, situations that reduce or decrease the drive stimuli will increase the strength of a particular response in terms of overt behavior. Such situations or events become *reinforcers* of this behavior. Conversely, behavior unaccompanied by events which eliminate drive stimuli is weakened or not repeated. Behavior thus becomes a function of reinforcement. The occurrence of the reinforcing event depends on the response being actually made; that is, the response or overt behavior that occurs is *instrumental* in producing the reinforcing event. This is what B. F. Skinner (1935) called instrumental or *operant* conditioning.

We can now trace the development of competitiveness, or aggressiveness, etc., in physical activity and sport as a learned or acquired drive in the individual through Miller and Dollard's learning paradigm. *Habit* is the key concept of their theory. And habit is the connection between a stimulus (or cue) and a response. External and internal stimuli are both important in acting as cues to the desired behavior. Miller and Dollard feel that a person's personality consists primarily of habits which in turn are developed from the unique events to which the individual is exposed. So for a child to become competitive he must be presented with clearcut stimuli which will elicit competitive responses. This happens constantly in our culture, in which competitive responses are invariably rewarded or reinforced. When a stimulus such as a sports situation is presented to a child, he will make a competitive response, or the situation will elicit competitive behavior if in the past his competitive behavior has been reinforced or rewarded. It must also be realized that habits involve internal responses that further elicit internal stimuli which possess drive characteristics. So a habit of competitiveness may involve such internal responses as enjoyment and satisfaction or tension and arousal, which in turn act as drive stimuli to elicit competitive behavior. These are secondary or learned drives and they also constitute (along with primary drives) part of a person's personality. In our society a large number of these derived or acquired drives tend to replace the original functions of various primary drives. In this connection, certain rewards or reinforcements which are also of a secondary or learned nature come into existence. Secondary rewards, in fact, often serve by themselves to reinforce behavior. Competitive behavior thus can be seen as an acquired characteristic, originally elicited by primary drives, but now part of the habit structure of a person, which receives reinforcement of a secondary nature.

Thus, if an athlete exhibits competitive behavior, he is reinforced in terms of prestige, money, recognition, and praise. The drive stimuli, *or cues* in this learning sequence are what the person notices, and to which he attaches importance. For example, though a competitive response to a competitive situation is quite natural, we must also recognize that this competitive response will generate or elicit cues such as cheering or praise or exhilaration in the person and thus these will generate overt competitive behavior. Competitors very easily discriminate between stimuli elicited by their responses to certain events and are reinforced or negatively affected by them. The development of competitiveness, or the maximization of competitive behavior, thus evolves through the cues (drive stimuli) that an individual notices.

Malpass (1962), in an article on the values of competition, agrees with this general view of behavior theory and takes it one step further by stating that "instrumental or operant conditioning stresses not only what *precedes* behavior but also what *follows* behavior." This, of course, is a massive simplication of the whole area of Skinnerian psychology, but it does have several implications of importance for athletics and physical activity. Malpass states, in operant conditioning terms, that the simple S-R formula in real behavior situations now becomes as shown in Diagram 9.

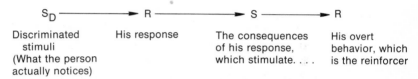

S_D	R	S	R
Discriminated stimuli (What the person actually notices)	His response	The consequences of his response, which stimulate. . . .	His overt behavior, which is the reinforcer

DIAGRAM 9. THE CONDITIONING OF BEHAVIOR

Malpass's views are directly consistent with Skinner's on how certain behaviors are learned in the everyday world. That is, operantly conditioned behavior is behavior that acts upon one's environment to produce certain desired effects. A person's behavior is shaped and maintained by the success of its consequences; if a person engages in a certain type of behavior which is successful in terms of influencing his own way of life, his environment, or people around him, then the consequences of his behavior act as reinforcers and cause him to repeat that particular behavior. So, in terms of the above diagram, boys and girls in physical activity and sports situations acquire certain behaviors because the conditions of the situations are arranged to cause these children to notice relevant stimuli (SD), respond to these stimuli, and, then, on the basis of the consequences of these responses, act in certain ways. When the behavior of these children results in an *altering* of their immediate environment, these responses are called *reinforcement contingencies,* and it is the behavior that acts as the reinforcing agency; *i.e.,* a positive reinforcer strengthens the acquisition of a particular behavior when it is made contingent upon that behavior.

So, in terms of competitive physical activity and sport, this behavior indicates the following implications:

1. A person's competitiveness* is a function of three factors: his genetic endowment (his biological make-up as a member of the species homo sapien), his past environmental history as an individual, and the specific situational aspects of his current environment. Some children bring more competitiveness to sports situations than others simply because they have been exposed to reward structures in their family and social environments that were oriented toward being competitive. This *preconditioning* then has an effect on what stimuli or cues in their present environment they attend to. Thus, such children are usually no problem in terms of their levels of competitiveness. However, children who come from family and social environments which have tended to minimize (*i.e.*, not reinforce) competitive behavior require explicit stimuli to which they can *learn* to respond to competitively. Previously neutral stimuli, such as praise, recognition, and small social rewards, must now be presented in such a way as to elicit competitive behavior. This causes the child to learn that certain kinds of behavior, especially competitive, will be effective in terms of altering his situation such that he will receive reinforcement (*i.e.*, be rewarded) by acting in a certain way. In essence, the child's environment is structured in such a way that his competitive behavior reinforces his competitiveness and his non-competitive behavior goes unrewarded. It is not so much that we reward his competitiveness, but rather that his own behavior reinforces his behavior. If the child learns that he can *alter* his own environment (*i.e.*, become a successful participant, make people notice him, etc.) by being competitive then this becomes the reinforcing agent in and of itself. All types of stimuli (discriminated stimuli) can be presented to the child to elicit the desired competitive responses. Verbal stimuli such as encouragement, criticism, praise, and exhortation are obvious, but it is generally felt that personal demonstration is more effective. The way the coach or teacher acts and behaves is more powerful in terms of stimulating appropriate behavior. Actions speak louder than words. The example a coach conveys to his players comes more from what he does than what he says.

2. The consequences of a child's behavior are more important in establishing a particular behavior than what precedes his behavior. Antecedents such as specific stimuli are only important if the consequences of the child's responses to these stimuli act as positive reinforcers in such a way that he will repeat the desired behavior in future situations. One can put a child con-

---

*Competitiveness, as a term, can be defined as a strong urge or desire to succeed in competitive situations.

stantly into competitive sports situations but he will not necessarily become competitive *unless* his competitive actions act as positive reinforcement to his desire to alter his environment. Success, for example, is more important for younger than older children in most sports situations, *i.e.*, there is a risk of turning small children off if they are constantly put into situations that have high failure potential. If the child can succeed in a particular sport by engaging in competitive behavior, then his competitiveness will become more consolidated in his personality structure.

3. Teachers and coaches must determine their own particular system of reinforcing stimuli, while remembering that it is the general environment of each situation that determines a child's response. Each system, naturally, will be a function of the individual's own personality and past environmental history, with one coach or teacher doing it his way, while another does it differently. However, certain fundamental factors operate in all situations. For example, *continuous reinforcement* enhances the *learning* of a particular skill or behavior, but once the skill or behavior is learned, people work with greater intensity and for longer periods of time when reinforcement is introduced intermittently than when it is continuous. Secondly, behavior is shaped and maintained by the consequences the behavior produces. Competitive behavior, or competitive situations, must produce satisfaction or enjoyment in the child, otherwise it will not serve to reinforce itself. Too much competition at an early age, before the child can expect certain positive feedback, may serve to discourage him rather than motivate him to continue. Competitive athletic situations for young children (who are still *learning* competitive behavior) must be structured very carefully to provide the right kind of reinforcement. If a child experiences constant failure in sports situations (or never gets to participate), his behavior will act so as to weaken his resolve to continue or it will actually cause him to remove himself from that particular environment.

4. There is no way of predicting what will be reinforcing for different individuals. This introduces the necessity of avoiding rigid or stereotyped structuring of competitive sports situations for children. Somehow, the coach or teacher must analyze what environmental conditions are right for each child and, then, utilize them to allow them to provide the positive effect necessary for the reinforcement of behavior. Some children, for example, are reinforced through achievement-oriented stimuli (just achieving excellence is rewarding in itself), whereas others seek affiliation in sports (they merely want to be accepted as a part of

the group). Generally speaking, ridicule, criticism, and contempt invariably operate to negate the behavior one wants to produce or consolidate in children participating in competitive sports situations. One must carefully analyze and then manipulate those environmental (*i.e.*, situational) conditions which will act as reinforcement contingencies for each child's behavior.

5. It is virtually mandatory that coaches and teachers analyze what discriminative stimuli they have been making available to their players and students when their behavior is inconsistent with what was originally sought. When a child performs or behaves badly it is usually because the wrong reinforcement contingencies are operating. If a boy behaves badly during a game or other physical activity situation, then, before blaming the child for his bad behavior, one should examine the specific and general environmental conditions influencing, or maybe even causing, such behavior. An examination of the factors in sports situations where winning is overemphasized, for example, would probably produce a considerable number of behavioral instances that are way out of proportion. Also, pressure on the young athlete caused by overemphasis on winning (rather than on excellence, for example) will sooner or later negatively affect his performance.

LEVEL OF TASK DIFFICULTY AND COMPETITION

When evaluating the effects of competition on learning and performance, it is imperative that the level of task difficulty be taken into account. That is, competitive situations will cause either positive or negative effects on the learning and performance of various motor tasks depending upon how hard the task is for the individual. Several important psychological viewpoints are relevant in this discussion and are interpreted in the following section.

Competing Responses: Spence (1956). This position is centered around the concept of *drive* embodied in Hullian-Spence behavior theory. Anxiety is the drive which is of main concern here, and it is generally postulated that an increase in drive causes an increase in the strength of all responses in any situation. If one can assume that competitive situations in sport generate higher levels of anxiety (drive), then the responses (performance and behavior) a person makes will be of a stronger intensity than in similar situations without competitive influences. The effects of increased drive, caused by competition, on the learning of a task depends on how complex the situation is, and particularly on how dominant the *correct* response is over other competing responses that are present. According to this theory, if the dominant responses in a situation are the correct ones, then increased drive improves performance; if the dominant responses are incorrect, then performance deteriorates in high drive situations. Considerable evidence corroborates this postulation when tasks are simple, but its application to complex tasks is less than clear.

Spence and Spence (1966) state that one must be careful in simply equating complex tasks of high difficulty with tasks having dominant incorrect response tendencies, and simple tasks with those having only dominant correct response tendencies. Although this is generally the case, it is not always so. For the coach and teacher, however, it is important to be aware of the effects of competition on performance where competing response tendencies are operating. If, in performance or behavior, the task is of a level of difficulty high enough that the person has a medium or high probability of making the wrong response, then an intense competitive situation will probably cause the incorrect response tendency to dominate. Children who play poorly in some competitive situations may simply do so because their ability does not meet the level of difficulty of the task. Many coaches and teachers intuitively try to avoid this by breaking complex skills down into simple parts that are easy to learn and perform. This instills correct response tendencies into the task and makes it possible for the child to perform better in competing response situations. A quarterback in football is constantly required to integrate highly variable situations, and one attempts to condition him into making the correct response more or less automatically. This is why experience is so important for good quarterbacking in football and good goaltending in hockey. Over the years these athletes gradually build an extensive repertoire of motor skill programs which are dominated by correct response tendencies and which they can instantly elicit when the situation arises. The longer the period of time one plays and the more experience he receives, the more motor programs he has integrated into his general ability structure. Also, some authors have found that subjects with high levels of anxiety tend to perform more poorly than low anxious subjects on complex tasks. It has been reasoned by Mandler and Sarason (1952), for example, that complex tasks usually present an explicit threat of failure to high anxious people which may produce interfering responses during their performance and cause it to fall off.

Arousal Theory and Competition. As has already been noted, the Yerkes-Dodson Law (1908) dealt with the relationship between stimulus intensity and performance in such a manner as to give a picture of what happens to performance under stress (see Diagram 6, p. 78). Generally, it was thought that every task has an optimal stress level for best performance and that if this optimum is not reached, or is exceeded, top performance will not occur. Furthermore, it was hypothesized that such an optimal level of stress is higher for simple tasks than it is for complex ones. Slightly more current views on this phenomenon of arousal are held by Duffy (1962) and Hebb (1955).

Advocates of this position feel that not only stress but also stimulus conditions and the individual's personality contribute to the level of arousal which is related to performance as it appears in an inverted U-shaped manner. Duffy (1962) hypothesizes that human behavior is basically a function of two variants: direction and intensity. A person either approaches or avoids situations, and does so with varying degrees of intensity. Duffy also argues that approach or avoidance behavior can always be described in relation to some condition of the environment. In a typical sports setting, the main condition is comprised of the effects of competition. The intensity of an individual's response is thought to be measurable both in terms of the force of his overt behavior and in changes in his internal processes associated with a release of energy. This internal release of energy is referred to as an individual's level of *activation,* the degree of *arousal,* or as the degree of *energy mobilization.* This so-called arousal varies on a continuum from low (in deep sleep) to high (in extreme effort or intense excitement). At the crux of this viewpoint is the fact that variations in a person's level of arousal are usually accompanied by concomitant variations in overt behavior and performance. It is this relationship that is relevant when discussing the effects of competition. A person's level of arousal would seem to affect the speed of his responses, their intensity and, certainly, their coordination. In general, the optimal degree of activation appears to be a moderate one: namely, too little or too much arousal is usually acquainted with less than optimal performance. Several factors, however, tend to influence this general relationship.

Ryan (1962), for example, feels that a person's ability to inhibit and coordinate his responses under high degrees of arousal will have an effect on what is optimal arousal for effective performance. This is probably a function of the individual's personality, as we will see in Eysenck's (1964) extraversion-neuroticism scale. Also, it appears that if an increase in arousal level is produced by factors extraneous to the specific task, the resultant increase in tension is accompanied by a decrease in performance; if the increased arousal, however, is a function of the concentration on the task at hand, the tension level may correlate positively with performance. Of course, if a person is already operating at his maximal level of skill (as in the case in many athletic situations), then increases in tension can only cause deterioration in performance.

Duffy (1949, 1951, 1962) describes the intensity of one's internal processes in terms of *energy mobilization, i.e.,* it is the internal processes which supply the energy for overt behavior. A person's energy mobilization varies with: 1) fatigue; 2) stimulants or sedatives; 3) general changes in fitness; 4) changes in the activity in which he is engaged; and 5) variations in his interpretation of the demands of the situation. Thus, competitive conditions inherent in most sports situations will cause a general rise in the individual's level of arousal or activation. In terms of Duffy's observations, the influence of competition will affect a person's behavior both in its direction and its intensity. In some people this arousal increase will cause them to avoid rather than embrace competitive situations. If a person engages in avoidance behavior his competitive performance will naturally deteriorate. Other people, however, as we know, enthusiastically approach competitive situations, and this is directly a function of a rise in their level of arousal. Such an interpretation depends upon what significance the competitive situation has for the individual. People will come into competitive situations exhibiting approach behavior (keen endorsement or acceptance of the situation) if they can interpret the situation as a means of reaching particular goals. They will ignore the situation if it has no significance for them. Also, some people, depending upon whether arousal affects them positively or negatively, will, respectively, attack or avoid specific obstacles. If a person's interpretation of competitive situations, as it relates to him, is incorrect, then an increase in level of arousal will negatively affect his performance. Thus, a certain high degree of responsibility falls to the coach and teacher to adequately direct the behavior of their athletes and students in order to take advantage of increases in arousal level.

Hebb (1955), on the other hand, takes Duffy's viewpoint one step further. He relates arousal level and performance by introducing what he calls *cue function,* which guides behavior, and *arousal function,* which is similar to Duffy's directional and activational aspects of behavior. Hebb assumes that activity in the brain cortex is facilitated by "bombardment" from the ascending reticular activating system in the brain stem, and it is this system that he feels is the *arousal* system. When arousal level is low (bombardment is minimal), a response that increases stimulation will cause greater arousal and facilitation of performance and will thus tend to be repeated; that is, the response has a *cue* function for facilitating level of arousal. When arousal is already high, as in competitive sport situations, greater bombardment from the reticular system may interfere with cue function effectiveness, perhaps by facilitating irrelevant responses, with the consequence of poorer performance. He agrees, then, with Duffy that an optimal level of arousal will exist for effective behavior and performance. Easterbrook (1959), in agreement with Hebb, contends that whether or not a course of action is enhanced or interfered with depends on the complexity of the task and upon the range of cue utilization inherent in the task. He feels that increased arousal interferes with incidental cues but tends to facilitate central, relevant cues, which sharpens and concentrates a course of action. Coaches, teachers, and athletes, then, are advised that increased arousal caused by competitive circumstances will facilitate performance *if* one can manage to eliminate irrelevant cues and stimuli and emphasize only those cues which are directly related to performance. Golf is a particularly good example of this. The outstanding golfer is normally one who can shut out all that is not relevant to hitting the ball. Easterbrook (1959) describes such a situation by stating that the simultaneous use of both task-relevant *and* task-irrelevant cues reduces the effectiveness of performance; and that as a performance becomes more skilled, it is the task-irrelevant cues that are excluded first. Thus, reduction of the range of all utilization reduces the proportion of irrelevant cues employed and improves performance. Easterbrook, however, feels that such cue reduction can be taken too far, to the point where relevant cues are excluded, thus causing performance to deteriorate. Hence, the inverted U phenomenon between level of activation and performance.

One other dimension of the interrelationship between arousal and performance deserves mention at this point. This is the question as to whether different personality types are differentially affected by an increase in arousal caused by competitive situations in terms of performance on tasks of differing difficulty. Though many personality theories provide information on this aspect, probably the most relevant is that proposed by Hans Eysenck (1960). On the basis of previous work by Pavlov (1927), and Hull (1943), Eysenck suggests that individuals differ in their personalities because of the nature and extent of their nervous activity. He has developed two broad personality dimensions; the E scale, which is a continuum between extraversion and introversion, and the N scale, which is a continuum between neuroticism and stability (Diagram 10). Though this is essentially

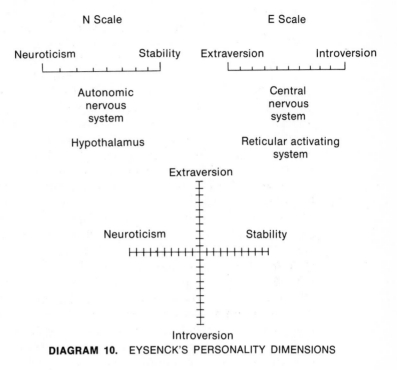

DIAGRAM 10. EYSENCK'S PERSONALITY DIMENSIONS

a behavior description of personality, he does attempt to *link* overt personality characteristics with their causal biological sources. He believes that behavioral characteristics can be explained at the neural level, with the E scale reflecting the strength of both the excitatory and inhibitory functions of the central nervous system (*i.e.*, the cortex), and the N scale reflecting the excitation of the autonomic nervous system.*

Recently, Eysenck (1967) has proposed that the extraversion-

---

*The *central nervous system,* or C.N.S., consists of the brain and spinal cord. The spinal cord integrates incoming and outgoing impulses involved in reflex activities and also provides channels for ascending and descending nerve impulses. Various parts of the brain provide the neural basis for higher psychological functions such as remembering and thinking. The autonomic nervous system or A.N.S. consists of the sympathetic and para-sympathetic systems, and basically serves the internal organs such as the heart, lungs, and viscera. The A.N.S. is, by definition, a motor system which comprises two basically antagonistic subsystems. Emotion, for example, is to a large extent dependent on the control of behavior by the sympathetic nervous system.

introversion dimension involves the reticular activating system, while the neuroticism stability dimension is more associated with the hypothalamus. This proposal is founded in the belief that cortical excitation in response to external stimulation (such as the effects of competition) is higher in introverts than in extraverts. This is postulated because introverts are seen as having weaker nervous systems than extraverts. Conversely, it is postulated that extraverts possess stronger inhibitory mechanisms. This view can be interpreted as indicating that extraverts are low on excitation and high on inhibition, with introverts being the opposite. Athletes, then, would react quite differently to a rise in arousal level from competitive circumstances depending on whether or not they are mainly extraverts or introverts. For example, an athlete high on extraversion would have more trouble "getting-up" for a game than one high on introversion, but would be better able to handle and channel arousal later in the game because of strong inhibitory mechanisms. This interpretation is consistent with Gray's (1964) summarizing of weak and strong nervous systems when he states that, though a weak nervous system (introverts) is more sensitive than a strong nervous system, it *begins* to respond at stimulus intensities which are ineffective for the strong nervous system, and throughout the stimulus intensity continuum its responses are closer to the maximum level of responding than the responses of a strong nervous system. Eysenck's extraversion-introversion continuum parallels this strong-weak continuum of nervous systems. Eysenck believes that the cortical supremacy of introverts puts constraints on their behavior in accordance with particular conditioned and learned patterns of response which characterize these people as introverts. The relative absence of this cortical supremacy, leading to the *absence* of constraints on behavior, conversely characterizes extraverts. This neural causal level is seen as being manifested in surface personality traits.

With respect to the causal basis and neural structure underlying the neuroticism-stability dimension, Eysenck's explanation revolves centrally around the hypothesized instability of the autonomic nervous system. He maintains that autonomic nervous system reactions are rooted in the person's constitutional structure, which mediates the reaction of the sympathetic nervous system to incoming stimuli. Though people react differently to sympathetic stimulation and to the way the parasympathetic system is controlled, Eysenck, nevertheless, feels that it is the autonomic nervous system that does, in fact, control *emotionality.* In this context, introverts are seen to be more chronically aroused than extraverts, and unstable (*i.e.,* neurotic) people tend to become aroused more easily than stable people. Welford (1968), for example, expects extraverts to perform less well than introverts, and stable introverts less well than unstable introverts. Evidence, however, on this prediction is contradictory. There is also some reason to expect unstable introverts to do well under easy conditions (or on simple tasks) but to break down under difficult conditions (or on more complex tasks). On the basis of considerable research, Eysenck makes several interesting predictions, two of which have immediate relevance:

1. Introverts tend to perform better on vigilance tasks, have a greater tolerance for sensory deprivations (isolation, etc.), and have less tolerance for physical pain.

2. Extraverts have superior memory or recall over short periods of time, have higher thresholds of arousal, and show greater physical persistence.

In terms of the interaction between arousal level, difficulty of task, and performance as a function of Eysenck's two personality dimensions, the following observations can be made:

1. People who score high on introversion and neuroticism will tend to perform better on easy or simple tasks than people high on extraversion and stability.

2. On difficult tasks the reverse tends to be true, i.e. stable extraverts perform better than neurotic introverts.

3. No predictions have been made on the intermediate personality types.

These predictions are based on the theory that higher arousal levels (partially caused by external conditions as in competitive situations) will not cause as much disruption in the performance of people possessing strong nervous systems (extraverts) simply because extraverts possess strong inhibitory potentials; that is, they can shut out the negative or deleterious effects of high drive situations. Introverts, on the other hand, are more sensitive and respond more quickly to situations of low intensity, as appears to be the case in low arousal situations or with easy tasks.

INDIVIDUAL DIFFERENCES IN COMPETITIVENESS

Some people are more competitive than others — or seem to be. And though we have already examined the effects of various competitive situations on behavior and performance, in terms of the arousal or activation that is generated, we still must be aware of the degree of competitiveness which people carry with them into any situation. Several factors constitute sources of influence on whether or not a person can be said to be competitive, and it is these factors which cause individual differences in competitiveness. Generally, *individual differences* can be said to exist in any trait when, after measuring or observing a large number of individuals on repeated occasions, some individuals score consistently high and some individuals score consistently low on the trait being measured.

Age. First it must be understood that competitive behavior is not manifested by *every* child in any particular age group. This variation is probably caused by a number of factors such as the child's physical development at that particular age, his temperament, his training, his family milieu, etc. *Generally speaking however,* corroborative evidence (Greenburg, 1932, Buhler, 1937, Graves, 1937, McClintock, 1969) indicates that the degree of competitiveness increases with increasing age, but that competition between children is not present in more than 50 per cent of the children in a particular age group, until between 4 and 5 years of age. Greenburg's (1932) evidence, for example, is diagrammed below (Diagram 11). McClintock and Nuttin (1969)

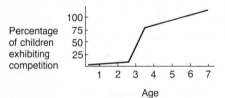

Percentage of children exhibiting competition

Age

DIAGRAM 11. COMPETITIVE BEHAVIOR IN YOUNG CHILDREN

take this evidence further by concluding in their study that competitiveness continues to increase during games up until grade six (ages 11 to 12). This general increase with age in competitive behavior seems to be a function of several specific factors. First, the particular tasks involved in a situation. Children experience no sense of competition toward tasks with which they are unfamiliar or which they have not yet mastered. This is probably linked with evidence indicating that until a child works on a particular task there is no desire to excel in it, and until a desire to excel appears, along with the desire for mastery, no competitiveness is generated. Secondly, competitiveness appears to be a function of the realization that other people are present. As soon as a child becomes interested in the fact that other people exist, and are involved with what he is doing, his competitive behavior again starts to increase. This has a direct relevance to considering competitiveness as a social phenomenon. Thirdly, with young children there is considerable evidence indicating that though competitiveness is a human inclination, it is largely nurtured and directed by education. Thus, the real upsurge in competitiveness at the beginning of school attendance — the mere presence (audience) of other children doing the same thing (coaction) — causes a competitive situation to which most children respond. From school age up into the late twenties and thirties of a person's life the urge for competitive sport endures. Though this is mainly because we live in a competitive culture, individual differences continue to exist in competitiveness throughout this age range. Competitiveness in sport seems to be at its extreme during adolescence, but again this would appear to be heavily influenced by social rather than individual psychological factors.

Sex. It would appear that boys derive more social facilitation from competition than do girls. Incentives such as praise, recognition, status and prestige seem to be much more available for boys than for girls in sport. Evidence accruing from the effects of competition on physical fitness test performance indicates more facilitation of boys than of girls (Strong, 1963). There is, however, no *real* evidence to indicate that competition in sport has a differential effect on girls as compared to boys. Also, there is no *real* evidence to indicate that boys are more *biologically* competitive than girls. Rather, individual differences in competitiveness as a function of the person's sex are quite obviously culturally determined. The taboos, mores, and value systems of traditional Western society have tended to suppress what natural competitive drives women might possess for sports and physical activity. Values such as getting married and raising a family have been substituted for participation in daily and athletic competitive pursuits. Men and boys have always received massive reinforcement from society to be competitive whereas women and girls have not. This has resulted in a conflict between what a large number of girls would like to do and what they are pressured to do by their culture.

This general view of sports competition for girls and women is quickly changing. The success of women athletes in other countries of the world in international competition has forced North American authorities to reexamine traditional views of the value of sports competition for women. The gradual changeover to this modern view has already shown that women are equal in competitiveness to men, and it can now be seen on our sport scene that formerly negative incentives, such as derision, reproof, and criticism, are being replaced by positive incentives, such as prestige, status, and recognition, for successful and competitive women athletes.

Competition, it would appear, has much the same effects on girls as it does on boys. Several studies quoted by Neal (1969) indicate that high school girls who participate in competitive sports generally are better adjusted both personally and socially than girls who do not. Considerable nonpublished research in the form of theses and dissertations indicates the same findings. As has already been thoroughly discussed in the preceding sections of this chapter, competitiveness and competitive behavior is mainly a function of the attitudes each person brings to the situation and the specific reinforcement contingencies that are operating with respect to each individual. There is absolutely no reason to believe that women are not as competitive as men if subjected to the same cultural conditioning relevant to competitiveness in sport.

Culture. Though individual differences in competitiveness as a function of one's cultural environment are mainly a sociological issue, there are various psychological implications. As Margaret Mead (1961) has outlined, three basic types of behavior occur in all cultures: competitive, cooperative and individualistic. The predominant behavior of the individual reflects the perspective held by that society and is reinforced by it. In Western society competition is the dominant form, and thus our major values reflect achievement, excellence, success, and struggling for identifiable goals. In other societies, such as Eskimo, Indian, or Guinean, the cultural emphasis is probably more on cooperation and individualism. In spite of the major cultural influences, however, individual differences in a particular behavior, such as competition, still exist. These differences exist mainly on the basis of the kinds of reinforcement contingencies that are available for the child when he is young. If, in a particular family environment, a child continually receives positive reinforcement for competitive behavior, he will become basically competitive in his general behavior. This will occur in spite of, or partially because of, the particular culture within which he is functioning. In addition to the reinforcements provided by significant other people, there will exist certain environmental conditions which will serve to reinforce particular kinds of behavior. In Western society, for example, there is a massive set of influences operating in practically all sports situations that connote competition. To win the prize, make the team, become more skilled, win recognition, etc., are all specific cultural conditions that influence individual behavior. It virtually becomes natural to behave competitively.

At this point, it is interesting to note the recent findings of Nelson and Kagan (1972). These authors have conducted a series of investigations examining cross-cultural differences in competitiveness and cooperativeness in young Mexican and American children. They state that though the competitive spirit in American children is "alive and well," it has generated a "culture whose children are systematically irrational." The investigations revolved around tasks that required either competition, cooperation, or a combination of the two, to acquire or achieve the reward. Their findings indicated that Anglo-American children repeatedly failed to achieve rewards because they competed in tasks that required cooperation. Some of these children even worked hard in some tasks (and sacrificed their own rewards) just to prevent or reduce the rewards of their peers. And it has been found that such irrational behavior increases with age; the drive to compete even overrides self-interest in many cases. The Nelson-Kagan studies also found that the situation was different with rural Mexican children. These children were observed to: 1) cooperate in situations for rewards that eluded the American children; 2) avoid relatively simple conflicts in order to attain rewards, and 3) refuse the opportunity to prevent rivals from receiving rewards they had already earned. They also managed to avoid competition in some situations which, by being competitive, would have resulted in achieving the reward. Such findings strongly supported the authors' contention that competitiveness is *not* universal, that it is, in fact, very much a function of one's culture. The reasons responsible for these types of irrational behavior were hypothesized to be related to how American and Mexican mothers reinforce their children's behavior. Nelson and Kagan state that rural Mexican mothers tend to reward their children regardless of whether they succeed or not (non-contingency reinforcement), whereas urban American mothers reward strictly on the basis of success (contingency reinforcement). That is, rural Mexican children very quickly learn that what they get is not necessarily related to what they do, whereas urban American children quickly realize that it is. This research very clearly demonstrates cultural differences in competitive behavior and indicates that value systems which emphasize *only* competition or cooperation can lead directly to frustration and irrational behavior.

Personality Traits.   Sooner or later, most discussions about competitiveness revolve around whether or not it is a function of one's personality. This is easily answered because competitive people all have personalities. The problem lies in identifying clearly *which* personality traits are most related to competitiveness, and whether or not such traits consistently appear to be very strong in people who are said to be highly competitive. A considerable amount of research has attempted to isolate those traits which characterize the outstanding competitor. Booth (1958), for example, using the Minnesota Multiphasic Personality Inventory, selected 22 items which he felt identified individuals who would react positively to competitive situations. Subsequent research, using these items, failed to substantiate Booth's scale. Though Mogar (1962) found good female competitors in a mental block test to score higher on the dominance and succorance traits of the Edwards Personal Preference Schedule, there were no differences in the personality profiles of males facilitated by competition and those who were not.

Several studies have attempted to identify anxiety level as a personality trait related to good performance under competitive conditions. Ganzer (1968) and Cox (1966, 1968), for example, found low anxiety subjects performed better under audience conditions than did high anxiety subjects, whereas, Martens (1969), and Quarter and Marcus (1971) found no interaction between anxiety level and performance under audience conditions. Vaught and Newman (1966), however, did find low anxiety subjects (as measured by Manifest Anxiety) making fewer errors than high anxiety subjects on a steadiness test when competition exaggerated the test conditions. In a timing task, Martens and Landers (1969), on the other hand, found no interaction between anxiety level, competition, and failure.

It is thus evident that the information on anxiety level, performance, and competition conditions is far from clear. Considerable research still needs to be done. A further attempt to provide some understanding on how competitiveness is related to one's personality structure can be found in the chapters dealing with personality.

SITUATIONAL COMPONENTS OF COMPETITION

Group Cohesion. Of immediate practical interest is the question as to whether intra-team competition (teammate rivalry) should be fostered in order to facilitate team performance. Traditional points of view have tended to support the assumption that cooperative groups are more efficient and productive than groups with internal competition; that is, that maximum team harmony is needed for maximum productivity. Recent research has questioned this premise. Hans Lenk (1964), for example, demonstrated that intra-team rivalry was successful with the German World Champion rowing team. Rivalry between the rowers on this team was fostered and then successfully turned outward as the team members integrated into a cooperative "skill" unit. Luschen (1970) suggests that the team may have been even better without such internal conflict, but the coach of this team was obviously of sufficient stature to channel this teammate rivalry into a greater individual production as well as a team effort. Klein and Christiansen (1966), in another German study, however, found a definitive need to maximize team efficiency, by being cooperative in a basketball team. In this study, it was found that, in the face of a strong opponent, team members passed the ball to disliked teammates as well as liked teammates.

Though these aspects of competition and cooperation within sports teams are, at present, relatively confused, and certainly in need of research, several factors are of particular interest. First is the view supported by Frankenburg (1957) and Rose (1956) that groups in conflict and competition with others probably develop a higher *solidarity* among group members and a more differentiated social structure. Satisfaction, pressure toward achievement and high productivity are factors continually operating within groups engaged in competition. The question here is whether essentially cooperative rather than internally competitive groups will be more productive. Though Deutsch (1949) feels harmony is required for efficiency, Luschen (1970) feels in-group competition may provide an additional high stimulus for better achievement. Luschen makes the following, very interesting, case:

1. If internal rivalry is fostered within a team, it is important that the conflict is closely regulated. This was obviously the case in the German rowing team where the coach was of sufficient stature to handle such intra-group competition. This is a common occurrence in our North American team sports such as football and hockey.

2. If the reward system includes both group *and* individual prizes in a team sport, then competition within the group can be expected to occur. When the pay-off is a share in the group reward, more intra-group cooperation results. Teams involved in competitive sports, as contrasted to groups participating in recreational-type sports, usually operate on the basis of higher extrinsic rewards. When this occurs, individual team members can be expected to try for a personally higher proportion of the rewards than other individuals, especially their opponents but even their teammates.

3. To control internally destructive competition for extrinsic rewards, a mounted effort must be made to emphasize and

strongly reinforce *intrinsic* rewards such as satisfaction, fulfill-ment, and self-actualization in athletes participating in team sports. Though this is difficult in our current competitive sports world, there is no doubt that more emphasis should be placed on individual achievement and satisfaction than on winning.

4. Luschen feels that sports teams are "open systems." The stronger the opponents, the higher the caliber of competition, the more important achievement becomes. There results a constant pressure to perform better than one's teammates in order to avoid being replaced by a "second stringer." This directly engenders competition rather than cooperation with one's teammates.

5. The optimal amount of internal rivalry would seem to de-pend on the nature of the sport, the ability of the coach to handle his players, and the personalities of the coach and his players. Sports requiring a high degree of cooperation for success (*e.g.*, basketball, hockey, tennis doubles) could be expected to mani-fest more team harmony than sports depending solely on indi-vidual talent (*e.g.*, wrestling, gymnastics, golf). Also, the per-sonality traits of the individuals involved in a particular team would have a determining influence on whether cooperation rather than internal rivalry was predominant.

6. Success is definitely a "controlling variable." Team co-operation decreases suddenly when a team starts to lose. Players start to go "on their own" more in order to reap what little status is left when team failure starts to occur. Success, on the other hand, generates even more team cooperation.

7. If the cultural system within which the group is operating heavily endorses competitive behavior, then in some situations, such as sport, where cooperative behavior would be more effec-tive, one can find intra-group competition. If group solidarity is valued, cooperative behavior within small groups or teams will be highly valued and reinforced. In more primitive societies where *no value* is placed on individual performance, internal cooperation is predominant. Even in our highly competitive Western culture we find subgroups such as sports teams (or street gangs) which have a past history of intra-group cooperation, and which, consequently, are less effective or productive when in-ternal rivalry is introduced.

Generally speaking, in sports situations where the elements of cooperation and intra-group competition are likely to be op-erating, the teacher or coach must be very clear regarding several factors as they affect group cohesion. One must be aware of the extent of interdependence necessary between players for team success, and of the extent of mutual liking for each other that exists between the players. One must understand that dislike, conflict, and competition, however, do not necessarily negate team effectiveness as long as the structure of the reward system for both individual and team alike facilitates performance in the end.

Competition as Conflict. Conflict is a social process which emphasizes and encourages the perceived and real differences between people, while at the same time minimizing what they have in common (Ulrich, 1968). When competition is taken out of a rules and regulations context in which fair play for the competitors is important, open conflict results. War and revolution are examples of open conflict, and sometimes, unfortunately, so is competitive sport. When competitive sport is used to demonstrate ideological, racial, cultural or ethnic superiority it becomes very much a debilitating process; it becomes conflict. Almost all forms of conflict can be linked to societal problems, and though some of these problems (*e.g.*, the place of the Negro in American society) have little hope of immediate resolution, they can be seen to be far more than just competitive in nature. Competition in sport, in some instances, comes close to being conflict. The "win-at-any-cost" philosophy carries within it the seeds of its own destruction simply because it implies an operating outside of the rule structure if necessary. One must realize that conflict engenders hatred, resentment, and implicit destruction, and, in this sense, has no place in sport. If conflict rather than competition is encouraged, then one is risking the very social system one is attempting to establish. Instances of this happening can be seen in the riots accompanying sports events throughout the world and within the actual structure of some games, in which the rules are being stretched or even ignored (*e.g.*, professional hockey).

Competition as Frustration. When two people or two groups are engaged in trying to achieve the same reward and that reward is so defined that a disproportionate share will result (*i.e.*, competition), then automatic frustration will occur in the loser. Still further frustration occurs when the loser is required to act like a sportsman and conceal his anger (Layman 1970). Even for the winner, competition is frustration, because his opponent is constantly attempting to block or thwart his goal-directed behavior. Frustration in sports is thus at its maximum when competitors are nearly equal in ability and skill. In this context then, competitive sport must be viewed as operating continually in a milieu of individual and group frustration. As we will see later, such frustration is directly related to aggression in sport. Frustration, only indirectly related to the relevant competition at hand, is also present from external sources. Frustration emanating from long arduous training and practice, or frustration caused by social events outside the sport, is quickly manifested as anger or aggression during the game and instead of being released (*i.e.*, catharsis) during the contest may even be increased, depending on the circumstances. That sports competition allows for the release, and consequent reduction, of tension due to frustration is a myth. Extreme frustration as a result of losing in competitive sport is both an immediate and a lasting thing and, in many cases, only serves to stimulate even higher levels of subsequent frustration. When frustration is viewed as any interference with a goal-directed response, the analogy to competition is direct. This is exactly what happens in competitive sport.

Overview

People compete in sport because of the reward structure it possesses and because of the opportunity to evaluate their competence in interacting with one's environment. Both direct and indirect modes of competition are available to each person, and one chooses or selects those competitive situations which are most attractive for him personally. Though traditionally our culture has emphasized supremacy rather than the pursuit of excellence, there are many competitors in sport to whom the contest is primarily a personal test. The satisfaction one receives from successfully competing, though strongly endorsed by our Western culture, probably has its roots in the innate or inherent structure of the human species. Man has had to struggle and compete since his earliest days, and it is this natural, primitive urge that causes him to compete in our now modern and civilized society. To ascribe any specific answer to the questions of why people compete or why competition is important in our society would be fruitless. Rather, the point of this chapter has been to provide some insight into the broad psychological scope of competition and competitiveness.

Though competitive athletics, especially for young children, have come under a great deal of criticism recently, it is not competition *per se* which is responsible but rather the misguided and misapplied value systems which accompany it. Rather than allowing competition to be the province of the contestants for purposes of challenge, struggle, and fulfillment, sports competition has been taken over and exploited by agencies external to the sport itself. This exploitation of sport by the media, big business, and political systems has simply served to detract from or thoroughly eliminate the positive values which competition possesses for the individual. Sportsmanship, fair play, respect for one's opponent, and equal struggle within the rules *are all values still revered and adhered to by the large majority of athletes themselves*; it is the external agencies who have attempted, successfully in many instances, to ridicule and negate such values by justifying the premise that winning is the only important thing. The individual athlete or participant is *fully aware* that there are many other things in competitive sport that are just as, and maybe more, important than supremacy over an opponent. Though sports competition has a slightly tarnished image at the present time, when handled correctly by the people involved, it can still provide people of all levels of ability with the opportunities to seek out the reinforcements attractive to them and gain certain measures of self-evaluation.

CHAPTER 5

THE UNDERLYING PERSONALITY DIMENSIONS OF SPORT

Personality, though a highly ambiguous term which is difficult to define, has become a viable and useful concept for describing and categorizing behavior in physical activity and sport. The reason for this is that personality, in its broadest context, can be interpreted as representing the *total psychological structure* of the individual. The personality of a person is an integration or merging of all the parts of one's psychological life — the way one thinks, feels, acts, and behaves. It is this combination that characterizes or distinguishes a person from other people and that represents the more permanent or enduring aspects of one's behavioral patterns. In general, a person's personality is judged on the basis of the ways he interacts with other people in various situations and how they, in turn, view him. A person, for example, may project to other people a very competitive or aggressive personality, or he may be very friendly, or retiring, or self-confident. Such attributes become even more consolidated into a person's psychological structure when other people react to him in such a way as to reinforce those traits which are typical of him. When a person acts very aggressively in most situations, people view him as being aggressive; he, in turn, notes that they think he is aggressive, and thus, gradually, he incorporates aggressiveness into his personality. Though such general descriptions of personality are useful in understanding the surface behavior of people, a more in-depth analysis is necessary if we are to gain insight into why people behave the way they do. The important questions are not so much that a person *is* aggressive, or friendly, or competitive, but *why* he is aggressive, friendly, or competitive.

These are *first-order* questions which require a fairly comprehensive understanding of the more distinctive personality theories available in the literature.

THE DEFINITIVE NATURE OF PERSONALITY

Hall and Lindzey (1970) submit that personality is defined by the particular conceptualizations and formulations used by each personality theorist. That is, the description and explanation of personality is always a function of the particular bias or orientation of the theorist himself. As no one theory is all-inclusive, this is a strength rather than a weakness of personality theory. In the following four chapters the reader will be presented with four major types of personality theory in order that he may choose from such representative positions those particular aspects which are intuitively and logically attractive to him. For each of these positions one specific theory is presented as being the most representative and as having the most relevance for understanding behavior in sport and physical activity.

Generally, people regard personality as a collection of *traits* which everyone is said to possess to a greater or lesser degree. Everyone, for example, can be hypothesized as possessing the trait of *self-assertiveness* with the differences between people being in terms of how much or how little of this trait they exhibit. Someone, therefore, who is said to possess this particular trait in abundance is termed "self-assertive," while someone who does not is termed "shy" or "timid." In this sense, then, to define personality is to list the number of traits which people possess and the degree to which each individual possesses each trait. Such an approach is completely inadequate, because it fails to take into account traits which are either dynamic or structural in nature, and it fails to include the manner in which these traits are organized and integrated into a functioning whole.

Gordon Allport, in 1937, reviewed some fifty definitions of personality and attempted to combine the best features of each by defining personality as:

The dynamic organization within the individual of those psychophysical systems that determine his unique adjustments to his environment.

Although he later modified this definition (1961), by substituting "characteristic behavior and thought" for "unique adjustments to his environment," Allport felt that several of the elements in this definition are of particular interest when attempting to understand the nature of personality. The term *dynamic* implies that the psychological structure of each person is in a constant state of change and development, while at the same time there exists an integration or organization of these changing aspects into a functioning unit. Cattell (1966) also emphasizes the term by stating that *dynamic traits* are concerned with causing the person to act toward some goal. The phrase *psychophysical systems* serves to remind the reader that no clean dichotomy exists between the mind and the body when dealing with human behavior; rather, they are "inextricably fused into personal unity." The word *determine* implies that one's personality consists of decisive tendencies that act in a purposeful manner to change one's environment. With respect to the term *adjustment* Allport feels that a person not only adjusts or submits to his environment but also acts to master and control it in a manner characteristic of him alone. This is a straight emphasis on the *individuality* of personality, and Allport goes to considerable lengths in his theorizing to state that no two people think or behave exactly alike. Thus, no two personalities are the same. Such a view is crucial for understanding behavior in sport. All too often too much emphasis is placed upon the similarities between athletes and participants and not enough on their differences. The coach and teacher must understand that each child or adult they come in contact with is a unique personality and must be treated as such.

Guilford (1959) also emphasizes the fact that each and every individual is unique. He defines personality as: "An individual's unique pattern of traits." Everyone makes a different impression on other people, everyone adjusts to circumstances differently, everyone behaves differently in various situations, and the organization and integration of traits in each person varies to a greater or lesser degree. Guilford claims that within the individual differences which exist one finds the key to personality, and that personality is best understood by comparing the differences between people.

Hans Eysenck's (1960) definition of personality can be paraphrased: the more or less stable and enduring organization of a person's character, temperament, intellect, and physique, which determines his unique adjustment to the environment. Though this supports the concepts of uniqueness and adjustment, Eysenck introduces two terms (character and temperament) which most personality theorists tend to avoid. The reason for this is that *character* has strong ethical connotations which imply that a particular *code* of behavior exists in people's actions. One has a "good" or "bad" character, but only a certain kind of personality. When sport is said to "build character," the reference is invariably directed toward the desirable habits, traits or characteristics which a participant or athlete develops. Though undoubtedly in some cultural settings certain personality traits are more highly valued than others, one is advised to avoid explicitly value-oriented judgments when referring to personality. *Temperament* is another term which is difficult to define. Generally, a person's temperament refers to the biological and physiological dispositions he has toward certain events, objects, and other people. It usually refers to his emotional nature (Allport 1961) and the type of *moods* which are characteristic of him. Though the constitutional psychologists, such as Sheldon, have based most of their theorizing on the basis of temperament, the strong biological overtones of the term have tended to push it into the background of personality theorizing.

One of the most recent and more comprehensive definitions of personality is that of Salvatorre Maddi (1968):

> Personality is a stable set of characteristics and tendencies that determine those commonalities and differences in the psychological behavior (thoughts, feelings, and actions) of people that have continuity in time and that may or may not be easily understood in terms of the social and biological pressures of the immediate situation alone.

Several aspects of this definition are meaningful for understanding the nature of personality in physical activity and sport. First is the fact that Maddi states that *both* similarities and differences exist between people. In sport the study of personality has been mainly directed toward identifying those traits athletes have in common. The objective here has been to determine *representative types* which are most characteristic of certain sports or activities. Attempts to identify a football player type, for example, have hinged on demonstrating those personality traits that football players share with each other. Though such an approach is useful for establishing operational baselines from which to do further analysis, it has the disadvantage of ignoring, or not being able to explain, all the differences in personality that manifest themselves in *any* group. The analysis of individual differences in personality, on the other hand, does permit one to observe actual overt behavior and identify the connection between certain traits and behavior. The best example of this is that people act quite differently in a particular sports situation which, on the surface, seems to be the same for everyone. If the cultural context can be assumed to be similar for everyone, and some people act differently from others, then the reason probably lies in the individual differences in their personalities. It is also of interest when certain people act the same way in obviously different situations.

Maddi (1968) also feels that the personality changes only very gradually, if at all. Practically all the theorists in the personality field sooner or later agree on the relatively permanent and stable features of personality. To look for changes in personality as a result of participating in physical activity or athletics, therefore, would appear fruitless. Repetitive behavior in man is one of his most enduring characteristics, and once you have a reasonable understanding of a person's personality, your chances of predicting his behavior are much better. An understanding of personality, however, is only useful when considered *in context.* Analyzing personality out of context is useful only for comparative purposes. If one wants to know why a person behaves the way he does in a basketball game, for example, then his personality must be examined as function of his thoughts, feelings, and actions toward sport in general, and toward basketball in particular. Such an aspect is constantly demonstrated by people who behave in athletic situations in a manner totally different from that in ordinary or "normal" situations. Related to this is the assumption that personality is a *dynamic* rather than a static structure. It is constantly operating to attain goals, satisfy needs, and interpret both instincts and one's environment. It functions continuously to interpret reality as it relates to a person's needs, interests, and attitudes toward life. Finally, personality can be visualized as having both surface and inner characteristics. Surface personality traits do not always express what lies deep within the psychological structure of the person. Maddi (1968) makes a useful distinction here by suggesting that personality can be viewed as having an inner *core* and an external *periphery.* The core of personality refers to the inherent attributes common to all men which exert a constant, very strong influence on behavior. The periphery of personality refers to those attributes closer to the surface of behavior, which are learned rather than inherent, and which are more concrete than abstract. A later chapter on the personality trait structure of athletes deals almost exclusively with the periphery of behavior. The periphery of the personality, especially as it is expressed in terms of traits, deals mainly with the differences between people.

As the newborn child grows, develops and progresses toward maturity, he develops along several basic dimensions which are intricately related to each other at all times. These dimensions can be expressed as a person's *physical, motor, intellectual, emotional, social* and *psychological* developmental patterns. In order to understand why individuals act, think and feel the way they do in various situations, we must have some insight into the major influences which have an effect on the development of a person's personality and, consequently, his behavior. The teacher and coach are constantly presented with a *fait accompli* in the personalities of the children and young adults with which they come in contact. People are the way they are and though, in some instances, certain modifications do occur, the child's psychological structure is fairly well established by preadolescence. Therefore, to have the utmost beneficial effect on a child's behavior, a teacher or coach must "work with what is there" in such a way as to provide the child with a maximum opportunity to realize his own potential. To achieve this, he must be aware of what factors have influenced the formation or development of the personalities that confront him. These influences are best covered in the context of the issues and controversies they represent in current psychological thought. It is to this end that the following sections are directed.

THE ISSUE OF HEREDITY

The personality a child brings to any sports situation is undoubtedly partially grounded in his evolutionary heritage. Most theorists, in fact, tend to agree that a *genetic blueprint* of an instinctive nature probably underlies all behavior. There is controversy here as to the *extent* this inherited nature actually affects overt behavior. This is particularly true in sport and physical activity, where constant reference is made to the "instinctive" behaviors of athletes and other participants.

An organismic view of personality assumes that each individual possesses certain attributes, traits or qualities which are rooted in his biological constitution rather than in his environment. Though the role of heredity in current personality theory tends to be minimized, most theorists are reluctant to dismiss it entirely. The attractiveness of each person entering the world with a genetic blueprint, upon which is stamped later environmental modifications, is hard to ignore. Some people, such as most of the psychoanalytic writers, Sheldon with his constitutional psychology, and Cattell with his source traits, tend to support the general view that biological instincts directed toward self-preservation and reproduction underlie most of man's basically animal nature. Man's competitive and aggressive nature in sport, for example, is usually interpreted as being more instinctive than learned. His needs for exploration and sensory stimulation, for example, are invariably explained as emanating from instincts present at birth, and probably form the basis for later drives directed toward competence and physical activity. To illustrate this a reference can be made to Jung (1929), who stated that man brings into the world with him certain "ancestral experiences" inherited in the form of what he calls *archetypes* representative of a racial memory that has been repeated time and time again down through man's evolutionary history. This is a position implying that actual cultural characteristics are passed on from one generation to another. These characteristics are considered to combine with actual nature of the world to produce predispositions in the individual to act in certain ways. Numerous archetypes are believed to be present at birth, residing in the person's subconscious. For example, the archetype of *power* is seen as producing, in some people, a personality directed toward gaining ascendancy over other people. Such a predisposition can be seen to operate in sport when athletes or coaches are involved primarily because of the opportunity provided to gain control over other people. Various coaches, and some athletes, quite obviously use sport as a vehicle for their power needs, and such behavior can be interpreted as stemming from experiences deeply rooted in man's ancestral past.

Sheldon's (1942) constitutional psychology, which states that body structure has crucial importance as a primary determinant in behavior, also has a basic hereditary orientation. His contention is that body structure is inherited, and that it silently underlies behavior (*i.e.*, one's personality, to a greater or lesser degree, is directly a function of one's physique). Sheldon has identified three primary components of body build and has related a type or representative temperament or personality to each one. Cerebrotonia, related to ectomorphy, is characterized by restraint, inhibition, isolation and self-consciousness in people. *Somatotonia*, related to *mesomorphy*, implies personality traits such as love of adventure, risk taking, and a need for violent muscular activity. *Viscerotonia*, related to *endomorphy*, is characterized by sociability, love of comfort, and affectionateness. Sheldon provides a scale for the three temperament dimensions containing some twenty defining traits for each one. He thus suggests that one's personality becomes partially rooted in the type of body structure inherited from one's ancestors. Subjective observation tells us that this is probably quite true. Vigorous, active children who participate in sport *usually* have physiques strongly oriented toward mesomorphy and their personalities are usually similar. Also, there is a reasonable realization that extremes in certain physiques are accompanied by fairly consistent distinctive personalities (*e.g.*, the short jockey and the very tall basketball player).

Dollard and Miller (1950) also suggest that people come into the world already equipped with certain behavioral mechanisms consisting of: 1) specific responses to highly specific stimuli; 2) innate hierarchies of response patterns which are elicited only by certain stimulations; and 3) a set of primary drives, seen as strong internal stimuli connected to known physiological functions. Such inherited equipment is seen as not only activating behavior but also directing it, and, depending on the particular individual, certain patterns of behavior begin to develop directly from the date of birth. The designation of high and low active babies is an indication of such an occurrence. Long held thought that some boys and girls are athletic in their response patterns from a very young age would seem to be supported by such a view.

A case, therefore, can be made for connecting the development of an individual's personality to heredity. To what *extent* environment rather than heredity influences personality is, however, a more difficult question. Generally, the position taken is that genetic factors provide the *limits* within which development takes place, but that particular environmental conditions are the primary causes of certain kinds of personality traits emerging within these limits. When athletes come from athletic families, it is probably due to a combination of the traits which they do inherit from their parents and the particular family environment.

EARLY EXPERIENCES IN PERSONALITY DEVELOPMENT

Though most theorists acknowledge the importance of early experiences in the development of personality, they generally maintain that behavior is better understood and accounted for in terms of contemporary or current events. It is thought that an individual's personality is generally independent of previous experience, that it is a function of contemporaneous factors, and that behavior is mainly developed in an interaction with objects, events and people in the present. This is an important factor when attempting to understand behavior in physical activity and sport because, if a person is acting in a certain manner, one must have some idea whether this behavior is caused by the specific situational conditions operating at that time or whether it is due to early developmental experiences in the individual's past life. Again the answer is probably a combination of the two, but some insight into early personality development would seem to be necessary at this point.

Adler (1927) felt that three important factors in early life strongly influence some children into "faulty life styles." These factors (organic inferiorities, pampering, or neglect) were seen as causing the child to feel inadequate and inferior in their ability to face life. He supposed that children develop incorrect conceptions of life which result in faulty life styles when they are badly treated. Spoiled children, in particular, fail to develop any social feeling for others simply through a strong despotism caused by being completely self-centered.

For Freud, the first few years were considered all-important in the formation of personality. He believed that children pass through a series of "psycho-sexual" stages of development during the first five years of life in which the dynamics of their personalities undergo significant differentiations. From age five or six until adolescence, these dynamics stabilize in a period of *latency,* only to erupt again during adolescence. It was his opinion that each of these major stages of development (oral, anal, phallic, latency and genital) represented a specific kind of conflict between the sexual instinct and society. Within each stage, particular types of defense mechanisms were hypothesized as being effective in resolving these conflicts and that specific character or personality types developed out of these resolutions. Thus, an overall kind of personality is generated by the successes and failures which the child has in coping with both his sexual urges and the demands of society. Too much frustration *or* indulgence of the child's wishes at any of these stages is hypothesized as causing *fixations* which are portrayed later in the adult personality.

Sullivan (1947), whose *interpersonal* theory of personality revolves around the importance of social processes, states that the study of personality is the study of interpersonal relations between people. From birth, the child is immediately a part of these interpersonal situations, and his personality development depends on and reflects his successes and failures in relieving tension generated from various organismic needs and from anxiety over security in life. Sullivan, in delineating six stages of personality development (infancy, childhood, the juvenile era, preadolescence, adolescence and late adolescence), suggests that, though heredity and maturation provide the biological underpinning of personality, it is the culture operating through interpersonal relations that enables the person to reduce his tension and satisfy his various needs. For Sullivan the two major influences on personality development in childhood are: 1) the educational influence of anxiety, which forces the child to *discriminate* between whether an increase or a decrease in tension is attractive, and 2) the constant *trial* and *success* that occurs in a child's life which tend to stamp in those behaviors which result in pleasure. Though Sullivan is not a great believer in the early setting of personality, he does feel that personality undergoes change as interpersonal situations change.

All three of these views provide relevant information. Children who have developed faulty life styles because of either real or imagined inferiorities, will approach sport participation with a definite fear of failure in mind. Children who have been over-indulged or frustrated at home will develop strong passive or destructive types of personality which will hinder their enjoyment of and involvement in sport. These traits are usually manifested in attention-getting behavior, laziness, stubborness, and rebelliousness. It is also obvious that sport is a constant series of interpersonal situations. A child's personality from the outset will develop according to how well he handles tension arising from anxiety resulting from fear of failure or injury, and how smoothly his various trials and successes in sport occur. Sport provides an excellent testing ground for the child for developing a personality sound enough for the realities of life. Though usually too much is made of this utilization of sport to build "character," the fact nevertheless remains that the anxiety-provoking situations that occur in sport are powerful and determinative in developing certain personality traits in young children.

THE LEARNING PROCESS IN PERSONALITY DEVELOPMENT

Several personality theories heavily emphasize the importance of learning in the development of personality. This is contrasted with theories that consider personality to be mainly a function of one's heredity, unconsciousness, maturation or self-actualization. At issue here is the importance of an understanding of learning processes in understanding the acquisition of personality. If personality is a function of learning experiences, then the situations one comes in contact with in sport settings will alter or modify one's personality. If, on the other hand, personality is a stable structure, and relatively impervious to change, then sports experiences will have little effect. Allport (1937), for example, though highly critical of the universal claims normally made by most learning theorists, has proposed *functional autonomy* as a basic structure in a person's behavioral development. This principle derives from the realization that what in infancy is a mere striving toward a simple biological goal, develops into a fully autonomous motive that continues to energize and direct behavior long after the biological need is important. Though the individual begins life as a biological organism directed toward tension reduction, he gradually learns about himself and develops motives independent of those which originally motivated his behavior. This is what Allport calls the acquisition of functional autonomy. The mature individual in life, and in sport for example, is thus seen as possessing a set of congruent and organized traits which are conscious and rational. His behavior is a function of his goals and aspirations which can be achieved in many settings, one of which is sport. The motives which dominate behavior, even though originally founded in biological terms, thus are learned.

Cattell (1966) also identifies certain kinds of learning which he deems influential in the development of personality. These he describes as: 1) *classical conditioning,* which underlies the attachment of emotional responses to environmental cues; 2) *instrumental learning,* which establishes particular kinds of behavior directed toward goal-attainment; and 3) *integration learning,* which involves the acquisition of abilities necessary for maximizing long-term satisfactions through the periodic suppression or expression of certain constitutional traits. For Cattell, the learning of personality is a multidimensional modification of response patterns in multidimensional situations. This is a view which involves both the changing of personality traits due to ordinary adjustments in life and the analysis of these adjustments by people when faced with real-life situations and conflicts. According to Cattell, people handle conflicts in their lives by choosing various *adjustment paths* (*e.g.,* aggression, sublimation). Such adjustments affect and modify one's personality traits.

Though Cattell's exposition of personality traits, conflicts and adjustments is highly complex, one specific piece of information is particularly relevant. He believes that personality traits are divided into *surface* traits or overt clusters of variables, which go together, and *source* traits, which are seen as being the underlying variables which influence the surface manifestations of personality. The surface traits are further categorized as being composed of *attitudes* (specific interests in particular situations), *ergs* (biologically based drives), and sentiments (acquired attitude structures). Sentiments are seen as the result of experience and sociocultural influences, acquired as opposed to being constitutional, and organized around important events, objects, or people in one's psychological environment. Sentiments, thus, are learned.

Among the many sentiments identified by Cattell and co-workers is that labeled *sports* and *games*. People, in effect, acquire dynamic traits specifically related to sport which causes them to feel and react in a manner probably different to the way they act toward other important objects in their environment. The experiences and conditioning a child undergoes in sport thus modifies the basic *ergs* in such a way as to establish certain dynamic traits in his psychological structure. For example, athletes participating in competitive sport nowadays tend to have an *attitude* strongly oriented toward winning. Such attitudes are gradually acquired (*i.e., sentiments*) through the conditioning which they undergo throughout their sporting careers via the media, spectators, friends, coaches and parents. This conditioning, and it is a massive, continuous type of conditioning, directly influences and modifies such inherent drives within the person as his aggressiveness, competitiveness and dominance desires (*i.e., ergs*), which in turn contribute to consolidation of various sets of personality traits which are highly loaded on success in sport. The desire to win, determination and emotional stability are just a few of the traits identified in athletes who are successful, and a case can be made, by acknowledging the Cattell thesis, that these are mainly learned.

Miller and Dollard (1941) and Skinner (1969), however, offer an even more attractive illustration of the incorporation of learning theory into the acquisition and development of personality. Though this emphasis has been already thoroughly covered, in Chapter 4, some additional comments are of particular interest. Dollard and Miller's interest in learning theory centers around the concept of *habit,* which is seen as the link between stimuli or cues and various responses or response patterns. They feel that such habits are formed or learned by constant associations between both external and internal stimuli and overt responses. They also suggest that such habits are acquired and extinguished under certain conditions. Personality is seen as consisting of these habits, and these authors feel that a person's personality depends on his continued response patterns to unique events in his life. It is also stressed that particular emphasis should be directed toward the importance of *verbal* stimuli and the responses made to them in the formation of a person's habit structure.

In addition to such manifest stimuli, Miller and Dollard make a point of also stressing that some habits involve internal responses which themselves elicit internal stimuli which have drive characteristics. Such secondary drive acquisition is an important part of one's personality, since most of the dominant motives in a person's life are of an acquired or secondary nature. It is these acquired drives, such as *fear,* that impel most of a person's behavior. They are seen as being related to primary drives only in crises where the cultural influence on behavior has broken down or is nonexistent. This position is further emphasized by the realization that the reward structure of our society is also mainly secondary in nature. Primary reinforcement, such as food to satisfy hunger or water to satisfy thirst, just does not account for much instrumental behavior anymore. Rather, the reinforcements in daily life can be seen as being originally neutral events which have acquired reward significance through consistently being connected to primary reinforcements. Secondary reinforcement eventually serves to reward behavior in and of itself alone. Achieving excellence in sport, for example, is an acquired drive, as is gaining recognition or prestige, or satisfying affiliation needs by making the team. And, though the reinforcement of such behavior can be explained as being related to such primary drives as the need for physical activity or bodily satisfaction, the major portion of the behavioral reward structure in sport can be seen as being culturally determined and acquired or learned by the individual in a secondary fashion.

Skinner's (1969) view of learning in the acquisition of personality rests on the premise that human behavior is basically a function of the individual's environmental history, his present environment, and the environment in which his species evolved (*i.e.,* the person's genetic endowment). Skinner's concept of learning centers on the basic principle that *behavior is affected by its own consequences.* He feels that there exist certain classes of responses that do not fit into the usual classical conditioning paradigm, that such responses are usually spontaneous and voluntary, and occur with a frequency that appears to depend on what subsequently follows them. Also, the strength of these responses appears to increase when they are followed by reinforcement. These responses thus become *instrumental* in changing one's environment which, in turn, affects the reoccurrence of those responses. Reinforcement thus becomes connected to the responses rather than to the stimuli. For example, a boy can be taught to be aggressive in sport simply by positively reinforcing every aggressive response that he makes. If his aggressiveness takes on elements of dirty play or unfairness, we can *decondition* these elements of his aggressiveness out of his behavior by *not* reinforcing those particular instances of behavior. When reinforcement is *contingent* on the response, then the response will reoccur. The more a response occurs, the stronger it becomes, and the more it becomes a part of the individual's personality. The development of personality thus becomes a function of the settings, the behaviors and the consequences of those behaviors throughout a person's life, and through the effects of various reinforcement contingencies operating in each setting (such as sport), the personality becomes consolidated. What the person brings to each new situation has been shaped by prior consequences and is what Skinner calls "random." It is also important to realize that what may reinforce one person may or may not reinforce another. The key to understanding a person's personality, then, lies in observing his behavior over a period of time.

It would appear, then, that at least several prominent psychologists suggest that the learning process is an integral part of personality acquisition. This has particular importance when one considers the question of whether participation in sport changes a person's personality. As we will see later, the research delving into this issue is conflicting. Nevertheless, one point in particular seems to be of relevance here: that children participating in sport will acquire certain behavioral patterns specific to the sports settings they encounter if the reinforcement contingencies are strong and consistent enough to condition certain responses. Also, it would appear that independence from various primary drives is attained through the establishment and consolidation of more socially oriented motives and secondary drives. Certain personality traits can be learned while participating in any endeavor, including sport, but this acquisition is dependent on a highly complex interaction between each individual's genetic endowment, his previous and current environments, and his own particular behavior patterns. In addition, it would appear that personality changes occur only over a fairly significant length of time, and that these changes are probably just modifications of surface traits, not the actual changing of deeper source traits.

THE SOCIAL CONTEXT OF PERSONALITY ACQUISITION

The social and cultural settings within which an individual's personality develops undoubtedly have deep significance. There is relatively little doubt in modern psychology that man is chiefly a product of the society in which he lives, and that his personality and behavior are social rather than biological in nature. In these terms, man is seen as a social being, motivated primarily by social needs and desires. Man is thought to recognize his own personality mainly *as he relates to others*, through being socially cooperative and competitive with others and by eventually placing social welfare above his own selfish instincts. Any understanding of personality, then, must always be considered in the light of a person's social background, his social environment, and the current social processes which are operating in his society. This is particularly true when one attempts to understand behavior in sport. Almost without exception, sport situations are social situations. The dimensions of personality thus become inherently social dimensions, and one realizes that an understanding must be achieved in terms of the specific social context.

Adler (1927) assumed that it is *social interest* that shapes man's nature. He felt that man does not become socialized simply through mere exposure to other people and various social institutions, but that a social interest is born within him and is later integrated into his personality *through* his relationships with other people and *through* the particular society within which he lives. Thus, behavior is socially determined and the influence that a person's family has on the development of his personality is given considerable emphasis. This influence is referred to in terms of the *family constellation* and the *family atmosphere*. The former refers to the sociological facts, such as a child's ordinal position in the family, the absence of a parent, etc., as they influence each person in the family. The latter term refers to the emotional relationships that exist between family members. Cooperative atmospheres of mutual trust, respect, and love, for example, are seen as promoting active and constructive personality traits, whereas the opposite kind of atmosphere encourages distrust and destructiveness in the child.

Adler also hypothesizes the existence of a *creative self* in people. This is a highly individualized and subjective psychological system which interprets life in meaningful terms for each person. The self acts to create fulfilling experiences in one's life if no other experiences are to be found. And, finally, Adler, and only a few others, began the significant break away from the

Freudian emphasis on the sexual instinct. Adler felt that man is unique in that all of his behavior bears the stamp of his own distinctive traits, motives, interests and attitudes. The distinctive style of a person's life is mainly motivated through social interest, and sexual interest plays only a minor role. In fact, sexual interests are seen as being determined by a person's life style, and not vice versa. The one basic force in a person's life thus becomes a drive toward superiority or perfection, which arises out of real or imagined physical and psychological inferiorities. Participation in sport can be seen as part of each person's attempt to become a functional social individual; by being a part of sports groups and teams or by engaging in such a widespread socially acceptable institution as sport, the person is exposed to other people. This exposure is seen as being the main influence on the development of personality.

Miller and Dollard (1941) also feel that no analysis of personality is valid without being familiar with the reward structure operating within the culture. Two people in what is seemingly the same social situation can be expected to respond differently to the same stimuli simply because of the tremendous variation possible between the thousands of stimuli and their responses. For one boy, the roar of the crowd during an athletic contest may be extremely rewarding, for another it may have no effect whatsoever. The type of reward and the responses to be rewarded are particularly influential in determining what kind of behavior occurs. Different cultures and different social groups emphasize different reward structures. Altruistic or cooperative behavior, for example, is heavily rewarded in such cultures as the Hopi Indians and the Eskimos, but is of secondary importance to competitive behavior in Western urban cultures. The groups in which the individual behaves are even suggested as possessing *group personalities* caused by the social-personal relations between their members.

Cattell (1948) refers to these group personalities as the *syntality* of a group. He feels groups within which an individual's personality is developing produce effects in three different ways: 1) sometimes a deliberate effort is made to mold specifically desirable traits (*e.g.*, aggressiveness in sports groups); 2) accidental effects due to ecological or situational factors (*e.g.* athletes develop strong emotional attachments with each other when faced by the periodic crises that occur over an athletic season of play); and 3) as a result of behaviors either purposely or accidentally established. Further modification of behavior occurs in order to satisfy specific motives of the group (*e.g.* in sport an *esprit de corps* is important for success in that it facilitates individual achievement motives operating within the team). Cattell feels that group syntality exists with such social groups as the family, peers, school, political parties, occupational groups, and one's country. Subjective observation indicates athletic teams as also possessing such group personalities, especially those teams which manifest the traits of pride, aggressiveness, and cohesiveness.

To interpret individual personality, one must perforce have some insight into the group personality. To accomplish this, one must have some idea as to the *roles* demanded of the individual by each particular group. In sport, for example, the role of *dedication* is usually demanded of the athletes participating on a particular team. When this exists, one must realize that dedication will be incorporated into the individual's personality structure and appear in his overt behavior as a natural part of his psychological makeup. A great deal of research into the personalities of athletes, for example, has shown extreme contamination by these *group role* influences. It is highly doubtful that timidity or shyness will manifest itself when evaluating athletes simply because of the strong negative connotations these traits have for sport.

To take this social psychological view of personality to the extreme, one could agree with Sullivan (1947) that personality is only a hypothetical construct having no form of its own other than as what occurs in interpersonal relationships. With this in mind, the study of personality in physical activity and sport becomes the study of patterns which characterize the complex interactions of the personalities existing within a particular situation or "field." Not only must one be aware of the kind of personality the athlete himself exhibits but also one must have some idea of the type of influences the personalities of the boy's coach, his teammates, close friends, and family will have on the boy himself. And overlying this is the influence generated by the particular group personality which is operating. Football teams, for example, probably exhibit different kinds of group personalities than do track and field teams. Such contamination predicates the analysis of interpersonal situations if one is to understand the personality structure of the individual.

Overview

The foregoing has been a brief overview of the important issues underlying an understanding of personality theory as it applies to sport and physical activity. To understand personality one must constantly take into account the whole individual. Analysis of only parts or segments of one's personality, when taken out of context, distorts any understanding of the totally functioning individual. Although the nature of scientific analysis necessitates the investigation of discrete variables in controlled situations, an understanding of the total "picture" is necessary for this information to be of any practical use. For example, the evaluation of a person's self-sufficiency is useless unless it is related to what he does and the way he behaves in certain situations. The particular trait must be seen in conjunction with the other dominant traits of his personality, and the manner in which the person's self-sufficiency influences his behavior can only be understood against the fabric of his other actions, thoughts, and feelings. Knowing a particular individual is self-sufficient is not enough. We must have some knowledge of the environmental context in which this self-sufficiency is operating. Is he competitive? Or is he cooperative in nature? Altruistic? Authoritarian? Does he tend to be a success in sport? A failure? All behavior is interrelated and must be understood in these terms. The segmentation of behavior and personality is valuable only when the perspective is broad enough to account for indirectly and directly related factors such as one's environment, one's characteristic behavior, and one's relationships with other people.

THE PERSONALITY TRAIT STRUCTURE OF ATHLETES

INTRODUCTION

The major research thrust into the personality of athletes has been aimed at the identification of personality *traits*. These investigations, using mainly group personality tests, have been directed toward determining which traits correlated most highly with outstanding athletic ability in high school, college, national, and international competitors. Though the numerous traits identified in these studies are naturally restricted to the kinds of tests used, a fairly comprehensive picture of the athlete's personality trait structure has begun to appear. The purpose of this section is directed toward outlining what is meant by the term "trait" and the conceptual significance it has for better understanding the personality structure of people who participate in physical activity and sport.

As was seen in the previous sections, personality is a highly complex construct that has various meanings and interpretations. One of the more seemingly simple ways of identifying personality, however, is by describing it in terms of a person's personality traits. A personality trait is generally considered to represent the characteristic tendency a person has for acting or behaving in a certain way. If a person is aggressive, for example, he is said to possess the personality trait of aggressiveness to a greater or lesser degree depending on the frequency and intensity of his behavior. Thus, if one can accurately identify which traits exist within a person, and to what degree he possesses each of them, it is thought that one can proceed to predict how the person will act in the future, or at least be able to explain his current behavior. If the means for accurately identifying these traits are valid and reliable, then the observer possesses a powerful instrument for analyzing human behavior. Unfortunately, though, too little thought has gone into understanding what is being measured when we evaluate the personality traits of people. Too often, intuitive jumps are made between very ordinary information and highly complex behavioral explanations without realizing the limitations or restrictions that many of our personality inventories possess. To partially alleviate this problem, it is suggested that some basic understanding of "trait psychology" is necessary.

UNDERLYING DIMENSIONS OF PERSONALITY TRAITS

It is increasingly obvious that the coaching and teaching of children engaged in sport must be oriented toward the *individuality* they display. Nowhere is this more obvious than with individual differences in personality. Though most psychologists are still not in agreement as to what personality actually is, consensus is being reached on how to measure it. And it is with the concept of *traits* that most of the evaluation is proceeding. The reason is that this approach lends itself to a rough kind of quantitative scaling. A coach, for example, can say with a certain amount of confidence that one player is more self-confident, or aggressive, than another player. It is because of such practical application that measurement of *single* traits has predominated and become most popular. Though hundreds of tests exist for the measurement of personality traits, the major positions have been those of Gordon Allport and the factor analysts Guilford and Cattell. It is through Allport's various distinctions that a general conceptualization of the term trait can probably be best achieved.

Allport (1961) defines a personality trait as a *neuropsychic structure which renders stimuli into functional equivalents and which initiates and guides consistent forms of behavior.* A trait, in this sense, refers to those traits which are common to a number of individuals. Traits which are specific to the individual are called *personal dispositions* by Allport and have much the same definition as traits. Dispositions are concerned with the person's "unique patterns of adjustment" which distinguish him from other people. Among the traits which exist in a person there is considerable variation in the degree to which each trait drives the person to action. Some traits, such as achievement-related ones, exert explicit motivational states in the individuals, whereas others have little effect. Traits actively create situations within which they themselves become operable. That is, a person who is highly emotional, for example, does not passively wait for emotional stimuli to appear; rather he actively seeks and initiates emotional situations. This is partly the reason why traits and dispositions cannot be observed directly but must be inferred from overt behavior.

Allport also discusses the *independence* of traits and dispositions, *i.e.*, to what extent does each trait operate without any influence or contamination from other traits? He feels a trait is not necessarily restricted to operating in rigid independence from other traits, but operates more in terms of *focusing* upon a particular aspect of life around which the influence of the trait has its most significant effect.

Allport feels that traits admittedly influence one another and have no clearly distinct limits from each other, but nevertheless are identifiable by their *focal qualities.* For example, though the traits of sociability and extraversion may seem to be quite similar and may be observed to seemingly operate together, they actually have different focal qualities; sociability operates more in terms of a need for affiliation with others and extraversion is more directed toward outgoing and volatile behavior regardless of other people.

Also of importance here is the question of *consistency* in traits and dispositions. Most people generally accept that a personality trait implies consistency in behavior from time to time and from situation to situation. Pure observation shows us that such a thing just does not exist. A boy who scores high in self-confidence, for example, is not *always* self-confident. He may exhibit confidence on the football field but not in social situations or in the classroom. He may be confident for a period of time then lose his confidence because of some occurrence, and exhibit a complete lack of self-confidence therewith. What, then, does a high score on self-confidence mean? Allport suggests two reasons for the inconsistencies of traits. First is the fact that inconsistencies probably occur because there are multiple, overlapping traits simultaneously active in any situation, and consistent behavior is highly unlikely when a high degree of conflict results between them. Secondly, personal dispositions (*i.e.*, individual traits) are so *unique* to the individual that what appears externally as inconsistent behavior may not be, in fact, inconsistent to the person involved. Thus, what appears to be inconsistent behavior may actually be a uniquely organized internal consistency.

Allport constantly cautions that not every (if any) personality is perfectly integrated. Conflicts, clashes, and repressions occur constantly between personality traits, and these usually appear on the surface as inconsistent behavior. What is important, he feels, is the realization that even though exact correspondence between measured traits and actual behavior does not always exist, there is the existence of a subtle congruence that appears in the various behavior patterns of people and that it can be detected through measurement or evaluation.

The personality trait concept is also very much a part of Hans Eysenck's (1967) theory of personality. In Eysenck's views, personality consists of a hierarchical structure of personality factors. At the top of this hierarchy are broad, general dimensions called *types*. Personality types are composed of *traits*, which in turn are made up of *habitual responses*, which are composed of *specific responses*, the behavior actually observed. Eysenck hypothesizes three broad personality dimensions: *neuroticism-stability, extraversion-introversion*, and *psychoticism*, which are evaluated and measured through a personality inventory.

J. P. Guilford (1959) also views personality as organized into a hierarchy. The four levels of factors in Guilford's schemata are called *types, primary traits, hexes* (specific dispositions like habits) and *specific actions*. Guilford's dimensions of personality are termed somatic, temperament, motivation, ability, and pathological. Both these schemas represent attempts to organize or structure factors which have been identified in factor analysis studies. As will shortly be seen in a thorough analysis of Cattell's structure of a personality hierarchy of factors, the description and definition of the factors involved in these various levels and dimensions is peculiar to the particular theorist. In both of these schemas it is the specific, concrete actions of a person or his responses to test items that represent the nature and degree of the particular personality trait being evaluated. Individual differences in a personality trait are manifested in the degree to which people possess the trait; not whether they possess it or not. This is why most traits are *bi-polar, i.e.,* one possesses a certain amount of the trait along a continuum ranging from a maximum to a minimum. For example, if one is very low on "tough-mindedness" he will automatically be very high on "tender-mindedness." The traits interact and integrate with each other to give a more general picture of the person's personality type. Whether or not traits are changeable through specific environmental influences (such as participation in sport) depends mainly on what kind of trait it is and where it lies in the structural hierarchy of a person's personality. Generally speaking, traits are relatively stable and impervious to modification except over a fairly lengthy period of time. With the above background in mind, we can now proceed to Cattell's theory of personality.

A thorough analysis of Raymond B. Cattell's theory of personality is particularly pertinent at this point for two reasons: 1) it is a fully comprehensive analysis of the *trait* approach to personality; and 2) a great deal of the research done on the personality profiles of athletes and on participants in physical activity has utilized the 16 Personality Factor Test. We thus have, on one hand, a well-thought-out theoretical position while, on the other hand, we have a considerable amount of empirical data that is particularly relevant to sport. Such a situation should allow us to identify exactly what the concept of personality traits means and how it relates to a better understanding of behavior in sport and physical activity.

Cattell, like Eysenck and Guilford, has used a straight factor analytic approach to the analysis of personality. What this means, essentially, is that one attempts to identify those psychological factors which are responsible for either a person's performance on some task or his behavior in particular situations. This is done simply by obtaining a large number of performance or behavior scores from a large number of people on various tests, inventories, questionnaires, or rating sheets. Through factor analysis the researcher then identifies what underlying factors contribute to, or are responsible for, the variation in the obtained scores. This is a clear attempt *to link* performance or behavior measures to the theoretical constructs described as factors or traits.

Factor analysis begins with a complete set of intercorrelations between all the scores on questions believed to be measures of, or related to, the (personality) factors under consideration. A successful analysis results in the "isolation" of a number of factors or components which are said to account for the major part of the content of the tests analyzed. Factors represent clusters or groupings of tests based on high intercorrelations between scores on a number of tests. From this grouping of intercorrelations a *factor score* is obtained; that is, an average score is taken from only those scores which correlate highly with each other. When the factor score is recorrelated with the individual test scores the *factor loadings* of each test on the factor score is obtained. This represents the correlation of each test with a factor. Those test questions or items which tend to fall (correlate) on the same factor (those with high factor loadings on one factor and little or zero loadings on another)* are then examined *subjectively* to see what they have in common. From this judgment, a

---

*When the factors identified are required to be uncorrelated with each other they are termed *orthogonal* (*i.e.*, at right angles to each other) factors. When correlated factors are allowed to emerge, the method is called an *oblique* factor analysis.

factor is then "named" or labeled in terms of the common requirements assumed. Thus one can obtain performance scores from instruments evaluating a large area of behavior, such as personality, and identify how much of the performance on each of these tests is accounted for by a number of common factors underlying the performances. The factor analyst then proceeds to compute an index of how much of the performance on each test is accounted for by the common factors. This is called the test's *communality* (h^2) and turns out to be the sum of the squares of the test's factor loadings.* Though this is, at best, only a brief and superficial explanation of a complex statistical method, it does lead us into a realization of what Cattell and his associates have done in identifying the first-order factors or traits which he feels constitute a person's personality.

The basic structure element in Cattell's theory of personality is the *trait*. A trait is a structural entity, inferred from and expressing the characteristic and relatively permanent features of behavior. It represents the individual's broad reaction tendency that is regular and consistent over time and across situations. Traits vary. There are traits which are common to all and traits which are unique to the individual. There are traits which are constitutionally determined and traits that are environmentally determined. Though many distinctions between kinds of traits are possible, two are of particular importance.

First is the distinction between *source* and *surface* traits. A surface trait is seen as expressing a cluster of characteristics or behaviors that appear to go together. Though surface traits tend to be more appealing because they appear as direct manifestations of overt behavior (*e.g.*, aggressiveness), the relationships among the characteristics of a surface trait are highly complex. This is due to the fact that they do not always vary together and do not necessarily have the same causal root. For example, a person's aggressiveness in sport may not be matched by his aggressiveness in social situations, and the two manifestations of aggressiveness may have been developed through different developmental patterns. Surface traits are a function of the interaction between various source traits, and it is from this that they probably attain their relative instability. *Source* traits represent the associations among behaviors that *do* vary together to form unitary, independent dimensions of personality. It is these traits that correspond to the factors identified in factor analysis.

---

*For a criticism of the factor analytic method in physical education, the reader is referred to Alderman, R. B., and M. L. Howell: The generality and specificity of human motor performance in the evaluation of physical fitness. *J. Sports. Med. Phys. Fit.* 9:31–39 (March), 1969.

Traits are further distinguished by Cattell into *dynamic, ability* and *temperament* traits. This resembles the traditional psychological distinction between connation, cognition and affection (Horn 1966). That is, *dynamic traits* are expressed in situations where impetus toward some goal is involved and where the situations vary in incentive value with respect to various motivational states (*i.e.*, the connotations of the goals vary from situation to situation). *Ability* traits are concerned with situations that vary in complexity and involve thinking. They are related to the efficiency of a person's goal-directed actions. *Temperament* traits explain *how* a person does things and are probably, because of this, the most representative of personality. These are the traits that are related to the energetic and emotional behavior patterns of people. Cattell also refers to temperament traits as *stylistic* traits.

Dynamic traits are further divided into *attitudes, ergs* and *sentiments*. An *attitude*, as defined by Cattell, is an interest of a specific intensity in a particular course of action toward some object; it indicates the readiness to act in a certain direction in a given situation. For example, the attitude of a young athlete of "I hate playing football" indicates an intensity of interest ("hate") in a course of action ("playing") toward an object ("football"). In sampling the total attitude universe, Cattell identified some 200 different kinds of attitudes that people might possess. He also identified some 72 different ways in which the presence or strength of any one attitude could be expressed. Each attitude was also hypothesized as having an integrated or *conscious* component as well as a less integrated or largely *unconscious* component. To discover what kinds of attitudes exist Cattell devised tests and administered them to large numbers of people. A factor analysis of the resulting scores resulted, as we already know, in the identification of some 16 different factors which Cattell separated into two categories—ergs and sentiments.

Ergs, best considered as being dynamic source traits, are seen as representing innate, biological drives such as anger, sex, hunger, aggression, etc. Cattell has established seven such ergs: sex, gregariousness, parental protectiveness, curiosity, fear, self-assertion, and narcissism.

Sentiments, also dynamic source traits, are environmentally determined attitude structures which are acquired by the individual. Sentiments cause people to select and direct their attention toward certain events or objects and cause them to feel about them in the way they do. Sentiments revolve around the important cultural objects in a person's life such as sport, politics, God, mother, and, most important, *one's self-identity.*

All the various dynamic traits interrelate in a pattern of what Cattell calls *subsidation* and are represented in a "dynamic lattice" (see Cattell, 1950, p. 158). Subsidation is a term meaning that certain elements of one's personality are subsidiary to others or serve as means towards particular ends. Attitudes, for example, are subsidiary to sentiments, which are subsidiary to ergs, the basic drives underlying personality. The *dynamic lattice* is simply a pictorial representation of the motivational structure of the personality and shows how an individual may express a variety of attitudes toward a particular object or event.

Cattell has defined personality as "that which predicts what a person will do in a defined situation." To do this, Cattell has devised a *specification equation,* which is a device constructed for the purpose of predicting the response of a person on the basis of his personality traits, each weighted by their relevance in the particular situation. Thus, the specification equation gives expression to personality factors as they enter into specific situations. The behavior of the individual in a situation, such as competitive sport, thus depends on his stylistic or temperament traits (the 16 primary factors of the 16 PF test for example) and on the attitude (ergs, sentiments and motivational components) relevant to that situation. The concept of the specification equation gives a quantitative expression to the complexity of such interactions in any situation and, by doing so, has obviously interesting possibilities for analyzing behavior in sport.

ASSESSMENT OF PERSONALITY TRAITS

Before reviewing the personality traits that have been identified as having some relationship to athletic participation, a brief description of the personality tests and inventories most often used in the past is outlined in the following section. These descriptions should provide the reader with the further understanding necessary for interpreting and evaluating the findings of research studies dealing with the personality dimensions of athletics and sport.

The Edwards Personal Preference Schedule (EPPS). This test was designed to evaluate the relative strength of fifteen of the manifest needs outlined in Murray's system of human needs. The fifteen variables assessed are:

Achievement	Succorance
Deference	Dominance
Order	Abasement

Exhibition	Nurturance
Autonomy	Change
Affiliation	Endurance
Intraception	Heterosexuality

and

Aggression

Each of these needs is represented by nine statements in the test, and the entire schedule consists of 210 items or questions, with items from each scale being paired off twice against items from the other fourteen. This procedure of pairing items against each other is an attempt to yield an assessment of the relative strengths of competing needs within the person.

The Minnesota Multiphasic Personality Inventory (MMPI). This inventory contains 550 items or statements which the subject evaluates as being true or false with respect to himself. These items cover various life experiences common to everyone, including somatic experiences, family relations, social-political attitudes, sexual attitudes, mood-tone, and beliefs. Scales arising out of these items evaluate the following personality structures:

Hypochondriasis
Depression
Hysteria
Psychopathic deviation
Masculinity-femininity
Schizophrenia
Hypomania

These scales were constructed on the basis of performance of patients in various psychiatric diagnostic groupings and are purported to give an accurate measure of the strength of certain trends or components of personality recognized in the psychiatric literature. This is essentially a tool designed for the skilled psychiatrist.

The Eysenck Personality Inventory (EPI). This instrument is designed to measure the two pervasive and relatively independent dimensions of *Neuroticism-Stability* and *Extraversion-Introversion* as identified by Eysenck. Neuroticism refers to general emotional instability and the individual's predisposition to neurotic breakdown under stress, while extraversion refers to the uninhibitive, outgoing, impulsive, and sociable inclinations of a person. The test is useful in personality counseling and educational guidance. Each of the two dimensions is measured by means of 24 questions, to which the subject answers "yes" or "no." A response distortion or lie scale is also included to identify false responses. Parallel forms (A and B) are available for retesting situations. Test time is approximately ten minutes.

The California Psychological Inventory. This instrument was specifically designed to evaluate the personality dimensions of "normal" people in a variety of situations. Eighteen dimensions are assessed by an inventory of 480 statements which the subject evaluates as being true or false with respect to himself. The 18 dimensions are grouped into four major categories as follows:

1. Measures of poise, ascendancy and self-assurance:
   Dominance
   Capacity to status
   Sociability
   Social presence
   Self-acceptance
   Sense of well-being

2. Measures of achievement potential and responsibility:
   Responsibility
   Socialization
   Self-control
   Tolerance
   Good impression
   Communality

3. Measures of achievement potential and intellectual efficiency:
   Achievement via conformance
   Achievement via independence
   Intellectual efficiency

4. Measures of intellectual and interest modes:
   Psychological mindedness
   Flexibility
   Femininity

The Cattell 16 PF Questionnaire. The 16 primary factors identified by Cattell are described as being functionally independent and psychologically meaningful dimensions of a person's personality. The test itself has two forms (A and B), each of which contains 187 items or questions. Each item represents a statement such as "I like to watch team games," which is responded to in terms of three possible answers—yes, occasionally, or no. The subject is assured that the experimenter is aware that the items are too short to be very specific and he is encouraged to answer in terms of the "average" game or how he responds in most situations such as those described in the items. This test is, in a sense, a personalized interview. It is structured on a "forced response" basis but is voluntary and open since the subject knows it is a personality test. The test yields scores on each one of the 16 personality dimensions, which are then plotted on a "profile" sheet for evaluation. Each one of these scales or dimensions appears to have adequate, though not exceptional, split-half reliability, and the main evidence for validity lies in the factor analytic construction of the test, *i.e.*, many of the factors correspond to factors derived from rating and experimental data. The raw scores of each individual on each scale are converted into *sten* scores in order that they can be compared to scores obtained by other people in some defined population (*e.g.*, adults, college students, males). The 16 primary factors can be described as follows:

PRIMARY FACTORS

A.	Reserved	vs.	Outgoing
B.	Less intelligent	vs.	More intelligent
C.	Lower ego strength	vs.	Higher ego strength
E.	Submissiveness	vs.	Dominance
F.	Prudence	vs.	Impulsiveness
G.	Expedience	vs.	Conscientiousness
H.	Shy	vs.	Venturesome
I.	Tough-mindedness	vs.	Tender-mindedness
L.	Trusting	vs.	Suspicious
M.	Practical	vs.	Imaginative
N.	Forthrightness	vs.	Shrewdness
O.	Placidness	vs.	Apprehensiveness
Q_1	Conservatism	vs.	Radicalism
Q_2	Group adherence	vs.	Self-sufficiency
Q_3	Low self discipline	vs.	High self-concept control
Q_4	Relaxed	vs.	Tense

PERSONALITY TRAITS OF ATHLETES

An athlete can best be defined as any individual actively participating in competitive sport, where sport is considered as an *institutionalized game* (viz. Loy, 1968) requiring the demonstration of physical prowess. Research studies in the physical education literature dealing with the relationship of personality to athletics usually attempt to demonstrate the following facts:

1. That certain personality traits are consistently identified

from study to study as being significantly different for athletes when compared to non-athletes. That there are, in fact, certain personality traits which distinguish the athlete from the non-athlete or the outstanding athlete from the average athlete. Some studies have even attempted to demonstrate an "athletic personality." With respect to the above, Kroll (1967) contends there is a possibility that some discrete set of personality factors exists which is related to causing *some* people to select and participate in sport. He feels that perhaps these people possessing the strongest and most "fortuitous" combination of these "salient" personality factors tend to persist in sport and become successful as outstanding athletes. Demonstration of this point of view, however, is still relatively confused.

2. That participation in competitive sport influences and modifies a competitor's personality structure. Very little "hard" evidence of this exists.

3. That certain "personality types" gravitate toward certain kinds of sports—that there is a "football type" or a "basketball type" or a "wrestler type," etc. Investigations along this line have also attempted to discover whether or not certain kinds of personality traits consistently appear in athletes participating in specific sports. Kroll (1967) again contends that while there seems to be no pattern which enhances entry initially into a particular sport through modification of existing patterns of personality or attrition of inappropriate patterns only those individuals possessing "suitable" personality patterns tend to persist and become successful athletes.

Regardless of the differing degrees of success in demonstrating the above facts in the research reported in the literature, there remains a strong intuitive feeling among many people that a significant relationship between athletics, physical activity, and personality *does* exist and, if it does, may provide an important key for unlocking many of the behavioral problems which exist in sport today. Cooper (1969), for example, feels that some sort of complex of personality factors must be functioning that compels "an individual to join and work with a team, with its regular practices, leadership, and peer involvements and continuity over time." He also states that such factors related to participation in competitive sport may well be different from the general psychological needs related to ordinary physical activity. A perusal of the following information on personality traits indicates that a fairly coherent picture of the athlete is beginning to emerge. This picture is presented in terms of the personality factors which seem to be significantly different for athletes.

Sociability

Consensus is being reached on the fact that athletes tend to be outgoing and socially confident to a significant extent. Demonstration of this trait is evidenced by the findings of Carter and Shannon (1940), Biddulph (1954), Marks (1954), Werner (1960), Ruffer (1965), Schendel (1965), Groves (1966), Werner and Gottheil (1966), Behrman (1967), and Ikegami (1970). Sociability, though quite a broad construct, has the following characterizations:

A sociable person is warm, good natured, easy going, ready to cooperate, attentive to people, soft-hearted, kindly, trustful, adaptable, and warm hearted.

Such a trait indicates that the person is willing to accept expedience in most situations, such as often crop up in athletics, that he has a marked preference for situations involving other people, and that social recognition is important for him. It is an important trait for athletes in that it implies being generous in relationships with teammates and that criticism from without will be accepted in good faith. Because of a fundamental willingness to compromise, such people probably are less dependable in meeting obligations imposed on them.

This factor bears obvious similarity to Cattell's (1950) factor A (cyclothymia), Thurstone's schedule F (friendly), and the combination of Guilford's (1959) scales for objectivity, agreeableness, and cooperativeness. It is also, quite obviously, related to the *trust* personality trait identified by Tutko and associates (1969) in their Athletic Motivational Inventory. The personality trait of trust, as it appears in athletes, for these investigators, is characterized by the acceptance of people at face value, by freedom from jealousy, by the ability to get along with teammates, and by ignoring the ulterior motives of other people in personal relationships. The factor also bears a surface relationship to one's *need for affiliation*; especially in terms of social bonds or contacts and reciprocal relationships which some people desire. Further research is needed, however, to determine in what direction this factor is operating. That is to say, does participation in athletics cause, develop, or permit sociability in the athlete—or, is it just that non-sociable individuals are screened out of athletic participation at an early age? Another question of pertinence here is how highly does sociability load on outstanding performance, *i.e.*, must one be sociable to be an outstanding athlete?

Dominance

Again, there is little doubt as to whether dominance is or is not a trait constantly identified in athletes. Booth (1958), Merriman (1960), Werner (1960), Tillman (1964), Johnson (1966), Werner and Gottheil (1966), Bruner (1969), Singer (1969), and Kane (1970), to mention a few, have all identified the significant appearance of a factor labeled *dominance* in competitive athletes. These studies have found athletes to be characterized by dominance in their life situation and to exhibit dominance in athletic achievement. The factor of dominance is a broad construct generally denoting:

Self-assertiveness, self-assurance, toughness, hardness, unconventionality, and competitive aggressiveness.

Dominance is strongly linked in people to a need for power which is characterized by the desire to influence or control other people and one's environment. It is inherently linked to the ability or capacity for directing and controlling other people through subduing, persuading, seducing, or commanding them. The desire for dominance invariably is traced to a desire *to master* not only one's environment and other people but also oneself. Dominance is characterized in athletes by self-confidence, extreme assertiveness, boasting, conceit, aggressiveness, vigor, force, egotism, unhappiness, an insensitivity to social disapproval, unconventionality and a tendency to extra-punitiveness. In young athletes, dominance is manifested by extreme talkativeness and attention-getting behavior. Related behavior patterns in athletes strong in this trait are quarrelling with others, heckling of opponents, sarcasm about rules, independence, non-cooperativeness, self-sufficiency, and "unshakableness."

There is a strong link between dominance and masculinity and sexual expressions in animals, and there is good likelihood that the trait is also sex-based in humans. Cattell (1957) feels that the factor shows "considerable hereditary determination between families but also a marked environmental determination of individuals within families"; *i.e.*, the origin of the factor is equally determined by heredity and environment. Cattell's factor E, incidentally, provides a measurement of this dominance trait. Dominance is best considered as a *dispositional* trait, based on self-assertion, and innately directed toward mastery of one's physical and social environments. The trait probably underlies Tutko's (1969) characterization of *aggressiveness* in athletes. That is, aggressiveness in the athlete is characterized by the importance of winning to the boy, the ease with which he is aggressive, his concern for not being pushed around, his liking for physical contact, his argumentativeness, and his speaking out when he is angry. There is little doubt that people possessing an abundance of this trait will find sport, and especially high-pressure competitive sport, a convenient and attractive vehicle for expressing this tendency. But again, it is difficult to know whether or not a selection process is operating — is it that sport attracts dominant individuals? Or is it that non-dominant children are gradually screened out over the years?

Extraversion

Extraversion has been found to be highly related or supportive to dominance and sociability in athletes and sports participants by Sperling (1942), Tillman (1964), Ruffer (1965), Whiting and Stembridge (1965), Werner and Gottheil (1966), Bruner (1969), Kane (1970) and Ikegami (1970). Extraversion is a construct evolving out of Jung's (1933) early designation of the two major attitudes of personality: the extraverted attitude, which orients the person to the external, objective world, and the introverted attitude, which orients one toward the inner, subjective world. Eysenck (1947), whose development of the two broad personality dimensions of neuroticism-stability and extraversion-introversion provides the major underlying theoretical structure of this trait, describes extraverted individuals as:

Outgoing, impulsive, uninhibited, involved in group activities, sociable, friendly, craving excitement, and having many social contacts. They stick their necks out and take chances, act on the spur of the moment, are optimistic, aggressive, lose their temper easily, laugh a great deal, and are unable to keep their feelings under control.

Eysenck feels that extraversion is at best a behavioral description of personality, but that it does possess biological causal source implications. He believes that extraversion can be explained at the neural level in that his extraversion-introversion scale reflects the strength of the excitatory-inhibitory functions of the central (cortical) nervous system. He has recently (1967) proposed that the extraversion-introversion dimension also involves the reticular formation and associated reticular-cortical loop systems of the brain stem (refer to Diagram 10).

It is through the linkage of the reticular formation and hypothalamus with personality dimensions that Eysenck believes differing personalities will reflect their positions on a *level of arousal* continuum. For example, cortical excitation in response to external stimulation (*e.g.*, a tension situation in sport) is postulated as being higher in introverts than in extraverts. This is because he sees introverts as having "weaker" nervous systems than extraverts. Conversely, it is believed that inhibition will be higher in extraverts because of their "stronger" nervous systems.

The reason for this is that the weaker nervous system is more sensitive and begins to respond at stimulus intensities which are ineffective for strong nervous systems. This results in the weaker system's responses being closer to the maximum level of responding than those of a stronger system through the stimulus intensity continuum. Eysenck feels that this represents the cortical *supremacy* of introverts as producing a constraint of their behavior in accordance with conditioned and learned patterns of responses that lead to the emergence of those personality traits characterizing introverts; conversely, the absence of such supremacy leads to an absence of such constraints and to the emergence of extraversion traits.

The fact that dominance as a trait continually appears in the personality evaluations of athletes has two particularly interesting implications for motor or athletic performance. First, for example, Eysenck expects extraverts to have low tolerances for sensory deprivation and higher tolerances for physical pain because they have higher thresholds of arousal. If this is true, it would explain why athletes are, in fact, highly physically active and relatively tolerant of physical pain. Without high thresholds of pain tolerance most athletes would be unable to push themselves into the "high pain zones" required in many endurance events and in the hard physical training programs required for skill perfection. Second are the *arousal* level implications.[*] That is, it is generally accepted that an optimal level of arousal, stimulation, or activation exists in each person where his performance is maximal. This is usually represented by an inverted U curve relationship as seen below:

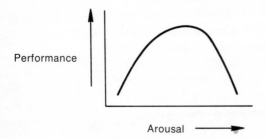

This is a simple representation of Duffy's (1957) proposal that as a person's level of arousal increases, performance increases, up to an optimal point, after which further increases in

---

[*]For a more comprehensive discussion of level of arousal and performance the reader is referred to the section on Arousal in Chapter 4, The Psychology of Competition.

level of arousal result in a deterioration of performance. Eysenck has taken this basic premise, related it to his personality variables, and stated that if extraverts do, in fact, have stronger nervous systems, which have higher thresholds to stimulus intensities (*i.e.*, arousal), then they should be able to handle higher levels of arousal before their performance deteriorates. This is undoubtedly true in outstanding athletes. The ability to withstand the extremely high levels of arousal caused by intense competition and the usually higher vociferous spectator reactions, without a consequent drop in performance, is the hallmark of a successful athlete. A partial explanation for this ability to withstand pressure may lie in Eysenck's neural explanation of extraversion—a trait that continually crops up in athletes.

Self-Concept

Several kinds of identifiable personality traits revolve around what could be considered the athlete's *self-concept.* Traits such as self-confidence, self-assurance, self-assertiveness, self-esteem, self-regard, self-consistency, self-enhancement, and self-respect all evolve out of this elaboration of a person's self-image or self-concept. Self-confidence, for example, has been identified as being high in athletes by Johnson, Hutton and Johnson (1954), Groves (1966), Kroll (1967) and Brunner (1969). In addition, Wilkin (1964) and Schendel (1965, 1970) found athletes to have high senses of personal worth and high self-concepts. What does self-concept mean and what are its implications for understanding behavior in competitive athletes?

An overwhelming body of research is beginning to appear that consistently indicates a high relationship between the concept a person has of himself and his achievement in life, especially school achievement. The major premises underlying this information are that the manner in which a person sees himself is a product of how others view him and that these perceptions are the *major* products in his various achievement behaviors. That is, if you think you are good, and you perceive others as thinking you are good, then you *will* be good. This emphasis on the person's perceptions differs substantially from the psychoanalytic (the unconsciousness of behavior) and behavioristic (observation of overt behavior) positions in that it attaches major significance to *personal awareness* as a determinant in human behavior. Such a position is generally termed a "perceptual" approach in that it stresses the person's *perceived world* rather than the objective or *real* world.

Though no consensus exists as to the exact definition of the term, generally speaking, the *self* is considered as consisting of:

1. How a person *perceives* himself.
2. What he *thinks* of himself.
3. How he *values* himself.
4. How he attempts through various actions to *enhance* or *defend* himself.

(Symonds 1951)

The term *self* is generally defined as being bidimensional. The first dimension, *self-as-an-object*, deals with the person's attitudes, perceptions, thoughts, feelings, and evaluations of himself as an *object*. The second dimension, *self-as-a-process*, deals with self as a "doer" and considers it a *function* of thinking, perceiving, evaluation, and remembering. The concept of *self-as-an-object* is generally known as a person's *self*, whereas the concept of *self-as-a-process* is referred to as the *ego*. That is, self refers to a person's conceptions of himself (his self-concept) and ego refers to a group of psychological processes connecting the person's perceptions of the world with reality. Though there is some evidence (Rentz and White 1967) indicating that these two dimensions are not completely independent, there is little doubt that there is considerable interaction between them. For example, if a person's *ego* is competent in coordinating his inner demands with the constraints and restrictions of external reality, then he will think highly of himself and thus have a strong *self*. Also, if one thinks highly of himself his ego processes are likely to function more efficiently. Such interaction manifests itself in successful achievement. With a strong self-concept base the individual will be more confident, assured and assertive in his actions with other people and in the endeavors he undertakes. This is fairly obvious in the self-confidence and self-assurance displayed by successful athletes and in the results of evaluation of their self concepts.

Characterizations of self-confidence and self-assurance in athletes are expressed in behavior as

cheerfulness, resilience, toughness, placidity, expedience, carelessness, vigor and energy, fearlessness, and self-secureness

The athlete exhibiting these traits tends not to be fatigued by exciting situations, feels quite adequate in demanding and crucial situations, is not easily downhearted or remorseful, prefers excitement, noise and people, and is not likely to be a hypochondriac. Cattell's factor O (guilt proneness) and Tutko's traits of self-confidence and guilt-proneness, can be seen as probably surface measures of the strength of one's self-concept. Athletes high in self-confidence and *low* in guilt-proneness do not tend toward what is called a "depressive-anxiety" syndrome; *i.e.*, they are not easily upset and they do not tend to turn inward their frustrations, anxieties, fears, and emotions.

Though the identification of self-confidence and self-concept in personality trait evaluations of the athlete has been initially established, little or no research has proceeded toward investigating the relationship between self and athletic achievement. This could be a fruitful and interesting area of research for students of athletic performance and behavior. Three categories of inquiry, in particular, have exciting potential: 1) the relationship between self and success in sport; 2) how the successful athlete views himself; and 3) how the unsuccessful athlete views himself. Considerable parallel research in education and psychology has been directed along these lines in investigating self-concept and academic achievement, and the results are more than encouraging in terms of direct application for teachers and students.

Conventionality

Werner (1960), Schendel (1965), Werner and Gottheil (1966), and Kroll and Crenshaw (1970) all have found athletes to be highly conservative and conventional in their responses to social situations. The trait expresses itself in behavior such as:

Being alert to the proper way of doing things; being very practical in most situations; narrowing of interests to immediate problems; being realistic, dependable, and sound; being concerned and worried about issues.

People who score high on this trait have high feelings of responsibility for practical matters which are reflected as "seriousness." Athletes high in this trait, though they will probably lack creativity, will try to do things as correctly as possible and will probably place the needs of the team above their own. In this sense, the trait is closely linked to Tutko's characterization of *conscience development* in athletes.

Mental Toughness

Tough-mindedness has been identified as a personality trait of athletes by Werner (1960), Werner and Gottheil (1966), and Kroll (1967). That it hasn't appeared more frequently in investigations is a surprise, especially when one considers that its converse is "tender-mindedness." Successful athletes supposedly are thought of as being not only physically tough, but mentally tough as well. The reason for this originates out of the realization that top level sport is a ruthless, cold, and hard business, where there is no place for the tender-spirited. Tutko's characterization of this trait indicates that the "mentally tough" athlete:

> Can take rough handling; is not easily upset about losing, playing badly, or being spoken to harshly; can accept strong criticism without being hurt; and does not need too much encouragement from his coach.
>
> (Tutko *et al., AMI* 1969)

Cattell (1957) refers to this trait as *Harria* (Factor I-), in which the emphasis is more on "tough realism." Here the trait is seen as being manifested in realistic, self-reliant, cynical behavior. Cattell feels the trait represents some sort of "tough, practical, mature, masculine and realistic temperamental dimension" (Cattell 1964). Evidence (Cattell *et al.,* 1955) also indicates that the trait tends toward being culturally or environmentally determined and is *not,* as many people might think, constitutional or temperamental in origin.

Emotional Stability

Conflicting results occur with respect to the emotional stability of athletes. Whiting and Stembridge (1965), Booth (1958), Hunt (1969) and Kane (1970) have all found athletes to be emotionally stable and to exhibit low levels of anxiety, whereas Johnson, Hutton, and Johnson (1954), Ruffer (1965) and Ikegami (1970) have found the opposite. Emotional stability in athletes is characterized by:

> Maturity; stability; quiet realism; the absence of neurotic fatigue; placidness; unaffectedness; optimism and self-discipline.

Emotional instability is characterized by:

> A low tolerance of frustration; immaturity; unstableness; high excitability, evasiveness; worriedness; and neurotic fatigability.

It is generally felt that high emotionality is related to, or described best by, Eysenck's "general neuroticism" and that emotional stability is grounded in what Kane (1964) calls "personal integration" or a mature *control* of one's emotions. Though many different descriptions and analyses exist regarding emotion and emotionality, Hans Eysenck's dimension of neuroticism-stability is probably the quickest and easiest way to present the trait in an understandable context.

Eysenck (1948) states that neuroticism (emotional instability) refers to "general emotional overresponsiveness and the liability to neurotic breakdown under stress." He explains the bipolar dimension of neuroticism-stability in terms of the instability of the autonomic nervous system. He maintains that the autonomic reaction is basically dependent on an individual's constitutional structure, which mediates the strength of the sympathetic (*i.e.*, voluntary) reaction to incoming stimuli. Although there seem to be characteristic ways in which various individuals react to this sympathetic stimulation, and the way in which control is indicated by the parasympathetic system, Eysenck nevertheless considers the autonomic nervous system to be the most likely basis for individual differences in emotionality. This is essentially an integration and conceptualization of earlier thoughts by Jung (1929), Pavlov (1927) and Hull (1943), who suggested that variations in the strength of the *excitatory* and *inhibitory* functions of the nervous system could account for temperamental differences in human personality.

The level of emotionality in athletes, then, is to a considerable extent rooted at the constitutional, neural levels, *i.e.*, the inhibitory or excitability of the autonomic nervous system. This constitutional basis (genetically based) is reflected in the everyday behavior of the individual. In the case of neuroticism, this appears as high emotionality, or emotional instability. On the basis of related evidence, high emotionality in athletes would appear to indicate three things: 1) because neuroticism has virtually a zero relationship to intelligence, achievement by highly emotional athletes in sport is due to something other than intelligence; 2) neuroticism is probably related to successful athletic performance through its manifestation in *persistence;* and 3) high anxious subjects show high speed of learning and superior performance in relatively simple tasks, or in complex tasks where faulty associations have not been present.

Though numerous other traits have been claimed as representing significant aspects of the athlete's personality, they have not as a rule had the same kind of consensus as the aforementioned factors. That is, depending on the traits which the specific test identifies, certain significant differences crop up occasionally in independent studies, usually with respect to differences between athletes and non-athletes. In order to minimize this apparent diffusion or scattering of traits all over the place, several investigators have attempted to organize the information into meaningful structures of the athlete's personality. The three most interesting of these attempts are those of Kane (1964), Tutko, Lyon, and Ogilvie (1969), and Cooper (1969).

Kane (1964). Kane suggests that a process of *selection*, on the basis of those personality traits required for athletic success, functions as higher levels of athletic achievement are reached. That is, those youngsters not possessing (or not manifesting) traits such as aggression, dominance, persistence, etc. generally drop out of highly competitive sport, or, worse still, are selected *out* by their coaches up through the years as not having the "desirable" traits for success. What this means is that when athletes are given personality evaluations in their adult years, only those possessing certain traits remain. The others, especially the independent, unconventional, or radical "troublemakers" tend to be factored out of the system. However, regardless of what selection processes do or do not operate, certain personality dimensions in athletes do consistently appear. Kane has factored these dimensions and their characterizations as follows:

I. Personal integration: Persistence and a high control of emotions.

II. Extraversion: Surgency.

III. Tough mindedness: Realistic aggression, self-sufficiency, and a cool-reserved outlook.

IV. Radicalism: Free thinking, experimental outlook, and practical, direct approach to life.

V. General abstract ability.

VI. Ruthlessness: Shrewdness, conscientiousness, and a persistent, energetic efficiency.

Tutko, Lyon, and Ogilvie (1969). Probably the most interesting, and certainly the most prolific, people investigating the personality profiles of athletes are Bruce Ogilvie and Tom Tutko at San Jose State College, California. It is their contention that successful athletes tend to share certain traits that typify athletic achievement and, with this in mind, they have, after many years of measuring and evaluating athletes' personalities, designed a personality questionnaire specifically directed toward the evaluation of personality profiles of athletes. This questionnaire, the Athletic Motivational Inventory (AMI), consists of 190 items, to each of which the subject has a choice of three responses. The AMI gives a nine-point scaled measurement for the individual athlete on each of 11 personality dimensions divided into two general areas. These are briefly as follows:

I. Desire Factors: Those factors which relate to an athlete's expectations from athletics and willingness to work toward fulfilling these expectations.

1. *Drive:*
The desire to win or be successful.
2. *Determination:*
Not giving up easily. Exhibiting persistence.
3. *Aggressiveness:*
A state of placing sole importance on aggressiveness in order to win. Argumentative, dislikes being pushed around, and loves physical contact.

II. Emotional Factors: Those factors which are concerned with the individual's personal attitudes and feelings toward himself, his coach, and to how he is being coached.

4. *Leadership:*
The desire to be able to influence one's teammates to do things in one's own way.
5. *Coachability:*
The capacity for respecting his coach and accepting his advice and instruction.
6. *Emotionality:*
The degree of emotional stability which the individual possesses.
7. *Self-confidence:*
The degree of self-assurance in his ability which the athlete possesses.
8. *Mental toughness:*
The degree of insensitivity the individual has to criticism, playing badly, or losing.
9. *Conscientiousness:*
The ability and capacity for doing things properly.
10. *Trust:*
The ability to accept people at face value and not look for ulterior motives in the way people act toward him.
11. *Guilt Proneness:*
The degree of responsibility one possesses for one's actions.

Cooper (1969). Lowell Cooper, in a review of the literature on personality and athletics, feels that although the picture is not perfectly clear as to how psychological factors relate to athletic activity, a fairly coherent picture of the athlete is emerging. He describes this picture by grouping those personality factors which appear to be indicative of the athlete as follows:

1. Outgoing and socially confident.
2. Outgoing, socially aggressive, dominant, and possessing leadership qualities.
3. Higher social adjustment, self-confidence, and having social prestige and status.
4. Low anxiety and high emotional stability.

5. Less compulsive.

6. High physical pain tolerance level.

7. Low femininity — high masculinity.

Cooper suggests that although the literature tends to show no intellectual differences between athletes and non-athletes, in the area of intellectual functioning, when it specifically pertains to achievement, athletes do appear to score higher than non-athletes. He also feels that although a few contradictions to the above do exist, the picture is nevertheless fairly consistent.

Overview

In this section, an attempt has been made to describe those personality traits which are consistently identified as loading on successful athletic performance. A reasonably coherent picture of the personality trait structure of the athlete has been presented and, with this in mind, several observations should be made at this point:

1. A personality *trait* is best understood as being a surface or peripheral expression of some deep-seated, inner psychological tendency. It is usually descriptive of the overt behavior that we can see and identify.

2. Personality traits are only *partially independent* of each other. They are related to a greater or lesser degree because they all emanate eventually from a common core of personality within the person. It is because of this that *isolation* of them is extremely difficult (and highly improbable).

3. Some traits tend to cluster together into what are generally referred to as *types*. This is because they are related or "loaded" on common elements. Little success, however, has been attained in identifying an "athletic" type of personality. The reason for this is probably because, like motor skills, personality traits tend to be "test specific."

4. The identification of personality traits in athletes is strictly a *function of the tests used*. That is, when athletes are identified as being "conventional" it is probably because the particular instrument used in the study measured conventionality. If it hadn't, then conventionality in athletes would not have appeared. This is not to say, however, that athletes are not necessarily "conventional." To determine whether or not they actually are, however, requires deeper research into the concept of conventionality and the ways it relates to athletics. Generally, this

remains to be done with *all* the personality traits that have been identified in athletes.

5. The discussion of whether or not traits are genetically or environmentally based is, at this point, only of academic interest. The teacher and coach receive in their students and athletes already reasonably consolidated personalities. Depending on the degree to which each trait is consolidated in the personality, certain patterns of behavior can be influenced or even partially changed by the coach. Those traits which seem to be more constitutional or biological in nature will be less open to such influences.

6. Traits are culturally modified. Traits such as dominance in men and femininity in women, for example, receive massive reinforcement from their society and result in fairly restrictive behavior patterns.

7. Generally, the data do not support the hypothesis that specific athletic experiences cause changes in personality traits, particularly in a positive direction (*e.g.,* Werner & Gottheil 1966). This is not to say, however, that behavior patterns remain unchanged; rather, the traits as measured by personality tests appear to be relatively uninfluenced by participation in sport.

8. Generally, the data also do not support the hypothesis that various sports can be distinguished on the basis of different personalities; that athletes with certain personality traits tend to gravitate toward specific kinds of sports (*e.g.,* Lakie 1962). This is also true with respect to hypothesized differences in the personality traits of athletes involved in individual versus group or "team" sports. Singer (1972) rightly feels that the failure of these hypotheses probably rests, at this time, on poor, inconsistent methodology.

9. The personality profiles of athletes based on the measurement of personality "traits" do not increase our knowledge of the dynamic tendencies which move people to action. They do not give us a picture of the "whole" person, just segments. Also, little attempt is made to show how these traits integrate with each other to cause overt behavior.

CHAPTER 7

THE DYNAMICS OF PERSONALITY IN SPORT

Preface

Any understanding of personality is inadequate unless it is related to the actual manner in which people lead their lives and why they behave the way they do. As the underlying dimensions and characteristics of personality can be likened to its structure, then the integration and functioning of these attributes can be considered as the *dynamics* of personality. It is not enough just to know what personality *consists* of, one must also know how this psychological structure materializes into effective and vigorous action. Though structure naturally goes hand in hand with function, an explanation of the nature of human life in psychological terms is still at the center of considerable controversy. It is the purpose of this chapter to explore three of the major viewpoints or categories of personality theory and present them in such a way as to clearly identify their contributions to better understanding behavior in physical activity and sport.

INTRODUCTION

Why people behave the way they do in real life will always be a mystery to mankind. Nevertheless, considerable insight into this behavior has been gained over the years through the efforts of many social scientists, philosophers and scholars. Out of these efforts have come several fundamental structural outlines upon which one can build an understanding of human behavior. Salvatorre Maddi (1968) suggests that most personality theories can be grouped into three general categories, or what he calls "models." He has termed these categories the *conflict, fulfillment,* and *consistency* models of personality, and has developed them in terms of the kinds of major *forces* existing within man that drive him to action, that constitute the way he feels and thinks, and that cause him to behave the way he does. It is his premise, and ours, that such an understanding of the psychological dynamics of people should increase our insight into human behavior, and it is also

153

proposed here that if we can understand behavior in real or ordinary life, it is but a short step to understanding behavior in physical activity and sport.

THE PSYCHOSOCIAL CONFLICT OF PERSONALITY

In this view of personality it is assumed that life is a conflict and compromise between the selfish desires of the primitive inner self of man and the strong, extensive social controls emanating from society. Most representative of this viewpoint is the theorizing done by Sigmund Freud (1908, 1913, 1920, 1930, 1943) and other psychoanalytic writers. Each person is seen as being constantly and inevitably in the grip of two strong conflicting forces, one of which is forcing him to gratify his individual and instinctual desires, while the other is coercing him to obey the demands which society inflicts upon all men. The basic assumption is that the two forces are invariably antagonistic. For Freud, all goal-directed or instrumental (motivated) behavior is directed toward *maximizing* instinctual gratification while, at the same time, *minimizing* punishment and guilt. Such a compromise is necessitated by the inevitable conflict between the individual and society. The success each person has in making this compromise work in his daily life determines his total psychological stability.

In this conceptualization, an individual's personality is seen as consisting of three major psychological systems: the *id*, the *ego*, and the *superego*. All behavior is seen as being a function or interaction of these three systems (see Diagram 12).

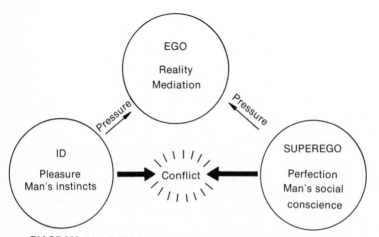

DIAGRAM 12. PERSONALITY AS PSYCHOSOCIAL CONFLICT

The Id.   This is the primitive part of man, the original and ancestral system of his personality. The id is postulated as consisting of one's *instincts*, which have their source in the biological structure of man and from which source they derive their energy. Instincts provide the raw psychic energy upon which the whole personality system functions — and as such they exert a powerful influence on one's behavior. Instincts function according to what Freud termed the *"pleasure principle,"* that is, man's desire to perpetually gratify his instinctual desires, their main aim being reduction of tension (satisfaction). Tension reduction results from achieving one's instinctual pleasures. Freud postulated that all men possess two major instinctual forces: the life instinct (eros), as represented by the sexual drive and its energy, and the death instinct, which he felt, at one time, to be involved with aggression and man's mania for destruction. The sexual instinct was thought to develop to maturity through five basic psychosexual stages (oral, anal, phallic, latent, genital); any overindulgence or restriction of the child's desires at any particular stage resulted in partial fixations. Such fixations were thought to influence later personality traits in adulthood. The death instinct, incompletely formulated by Freud prior to his death, was felt to appear in behavioral manifestations such as suicide, sadism, and masochism.

The Ego.   The *ego* is that portion of the mind that is involved with reality. It is the mediator of the personality and, as a consequence, has as its main function control of the *id*. The ego facilitates or interprets reality for one's primitive self. In this sense, then, its main function is defensive, in that it permits only those instinctual wishes to slip through that will not engender punishment or a feeling of guilt for the personality. The *reality principle* thus is defensive in nature and beneath the level of consciousness. The ego distinguishes between the internal subjectivity of the mind and the cold reality of the external world.

The ego operates on the basis of *secondary process* thinking — realistic thinking. The objective of the ego is to block the release of tension until an object appropriate for need satisfaction has been found. The ego sets up a plan of attack and then tests it to see if it will work. For example, the boy who desires friendship will be aware of several ways in which he can find it (one alternative may be playing on a team). He then makes a choice and proceeds to find how he can attain the friendship he desires. This is called *reality testing* and is the province of the ego. The ego thus has control over the higher cognitive powers of the mind to perform its functions and, in this sense, controls one's actions by selecting only certain instincts to be allowed satisfaction. The ego thus integrates the clashes between the id and the superego in an executive manner. Thus, when a boy indulges in extreme aggressiveness in football, he is doing so because his ego has made a decision that the behavior is acceptable in realistic terms. However, the ego is nevertheless still an extension of the id, with its main function being a realistic integration of the id's desires, not a frustration of them.

The Superego. The superego is that portion of the mind which is one's *social conscience*. It contains all the morals, values, customs, mores, and taboos of society, as interpreted to the child by his parents. Through the superego one experiences *guilt*, an internalized form of punishment. The superego's aim is perfection, not reality or pleasure, and thus represents what is ideal in one's life. It is the portion of one's mind which decides wrong and right, good and bad. One's superego is developed mainly through the actions of one's parents. To obtain rewards and avoid punishments, the child guides his actions along lines provided by his parents, and thus learns what is wrong and what is right. When he does something wrong and is punished for it, then it becomes incorporated in his *conscience*. When he does something right, and is rewarded for it, it becomes incorporated in his *ego-ideal*. His conscience punishes him through guilt feelings, and his ego-ideal rewards through feelings of pride. When one's superego is ultimately formed, self-control is substituted for parental control (Hall and Lindzey 1970).

The superego thus acts to block the sexual and aggressive drives of the id, works on the ego to substitute ideal goals for realistic ones, and drives the individual to strive for moral perfection.

One must not think of these three systems in a mechanistic way. They are not entities which manipulate the personality, but merely names for psychological processes which are differentially involved in behavior. The personality functions as a totality, not as a function of three separate parts.

Dynamics of the Personality. The major overall picture of the functioning of the personality is seen as one of constant conflict between the id and the ego, and as one of *defense*. That is, in people whose personalities contain partial or complete fixations at any one of the psychosexual stages of development, drives are considered as opposition by the ego (reality) to the pleasure seeking of the id. The ego is controlling the demands of the id, and, in defending itself against the strict moral scriptures of the superego, resorts to a number of techniques called *secondary defense mechanisms*. These defense mechanisms plus the id, ego, and superego constitute one's personality. As the whole personality derives its energy from the primitive id, so it is said that chiefly sexual and aggressive urges underlie most behavior. The main achievements in life, regardless of how remote they may seem to such sexual urges, are seen as being the result of efficient camouflaging by the ego of the id's primitive, pleasure seeking drives, in order to sideslip the super ego. Freud felt that practically all this functioning occurred in the unconscious, and only rarely did it appear at the surface. (When it did, it appeared in the form of slips of the tongue, dreams, etc.)

The function of the defense mechanisms used by the ego is seen simply as the effort to displace the instinctive energy of the id toward actions and objects other than the original objects and actions. *Sublimation,* for example, is the channeling of raw instinctual energy into so-called, socially approved activities. *Repression* is a straightforward and active debarring from the consciousness of instinctual wishes and actions of a threatening nature, while *intellectualization* is the substitution of fictitious, socially acceptable reasons for the genuine, instinctual reasons behind one's wishes and actions. *Projection,* on the other hand, is seen as attributing to others an objectionable trait that you yourself really possess. Though space does not permit the analysis of all the defense mechanisms (some 14 in number), certain applications of the Freudian point of view in athletics do now follow.

The Freudian Personality in Athletics and Physical Activity.*   As Cofer and Johnson (1960) so aptly state in their article on personality dynamics in sport, it is unlikely that the pure psychoanalytic position would reflect the direct expression of the various motives people have when they participate in sport and physical activity. Rather, the impetus to sport and physical activity originates more significantly from inherent drives within the person that are more socially oriented. However, as in other areas of psychology, Freudian theory does provide initial starting points for later theorizing, and in play theory this is particularly evident. Some of the psychoanalytic insights into play, games and sports are as follows:

1. Play and participation in sport are generally viewed in Freudian theory to be outlets for the anxiety generated by frustration in the individual. Most of the frustration is derived from the redirecting or virtual blocking of the instinctual energy of the

---

*For a thorough overview of what is basically a Freudian view of behavior in athletics, the reader is referred to Motivations in Play, Games, and Sports (1967), by R. Slovenko and J. A. Knight.

id, and it is in the form of play that this energy is released and enjoyed in socially accepted forms.

2. The types of play children indulge in and some of their play behaviors are thought to represent the particular psycho-sexual stage of development in which the child is having conflict problems. Play, in this sense, is utilized as an analytic tool, used in an effort to discover and pinpoint the causes of troubles or problems in mentally disturbed children. The role of sports is here considered in terms of how these conflicts interefere with the child's enjoyment of sport. This viewpoint, in another sense, treats play as an attempted solution of conflict occurring in the individual's unconsciousness; play serves to act out and recall significant events in the child's past, and enables him to have the illustion of control of the conflict in a derivative form. That is, play is seen as a device used by the child to gain mastery over himself and reality, and the constant repetition of play actions by some children demonstrates this attempt at mastery.

3. In play and sport the instinct toward mastery in children is evidenced. The child finds in sport and play the opportunity to challenge his intellectual, emotional and physical capacities by testing and perfecting his own particular skills at progressively higher levels. In a sense, such behavior may represent the simultaneous statement and symbolic fulfillment (Waelder, 1933) of a wish for an individual child. (A little boy, visualizing himself as Bobby Orr, scoring a goal into an empty net in his backyard).

4. Some children who in reality are forced by their environ-ment to take unwelcome, passive roles may, during play or sports participation, assume active, controlling roles. This is an attempt on the part of the child to come to terms with himself by sym-bolically representing himself as someone he would like to be. Play and sports permit children to depart reality temporarily and center their fantasies around objects which have a direct connec-tion to reality. (Boys act out the desirable roles of the sport's heroes in their games).

5. Menninger (1942) defines play as a pleasurable activity where the means are more important to the individual than the end. This is a view important for its implications regarding the fun element of play. Play is better understood in terms of uncon-scious motivations when the pleasure derived is more important than the participant's stated or explicit motives in playing. That is, play is regressive in nature in that it enables a person to return to the pleasurable moments of childhood, when he was allowed to do what he pleased. In this sense, play permits the person to indulge in and enjoy minor victories that are not available to him

in real life. Menninger has, also, always held that play permits the release of repressed aggressions. He feels that play and sport are symbolic battles full of organized aggression and which have the value of being socially acceptable forms of aggression.

6. Sports are primarily the most prominent form of play and physical activity in *adolescence* and, as such, are inextricably linked with the major psychological tasks which the adolescent must achieve in order to attain adult maturity. Tasks such as the achievement of self-identity, separation from the family, and ego mastery over intensified sexual and aggressive urges are the major ones confronting the adolescent, and it is partially through sport that such special needs as these are illuminated and satisfied. The enthusiastic acceptance of competitive sports appears quite emphatically during adolescence and seems to correlate with the individual's search for identity and attempts at ego mastery. The early adolescent tends to feel sexual tension as a force acting *upon* him rather than outward *from* him and that the gradual integration of sexuality into one's self becomes a prime involvement during this stage of development. The need to find ways of integrating one's sexual drives and of mastering one's aggressive urges finds its expression in sports participation. During early adolescence the child is apprehensive about these sexual and aggressive urges, and uncertain about his control over them and about his capacity to fulfill overly perfectionistic ego-ideals. Thus the tension rises and its release comes mainly in the form of fantasy, usually and especially, symbolic. Here, sports provide a socially acceptable means for expressing and releasing this tension. Aggressiveness in adolescent sport is obvious to all of us and is readily recognizable. The strong competitive urges of adolescence can be, and are, expressed in competitive sport in forms just as strenuous as one could wish, with the clear recognition that one's opponent is striving just as totally. Yet, as Porter (1967) observes, "in victory there can be exhilaration without guilt, and in defeat, disappointment without rage or shame — since no *real* injury has been dealt or received." Sports thus offers the adolescent acceptable forms of release for the tensions within him caused by the intensified drives of this stage.

PERSONALITY AS SELF-ACTUALIZATION

In contrast to the Freudian conflict position are those theorists (Rogers, Maslow, Adler, White, and Allport) who feel generally that only one great force is operating in a person's life. Here, the assumption is that a person's life is concerned with the increasing manifestation or expression of this force, and that any conflict that occurs in a person's life indicates a failure in living. Probably the most representative position in this sense, and that which has the most direct significance for sport, is that of Abraham Maslow (1970).

The major premise underlying Maslow's position on personality and motivation is that man's basic nature is one of *inherent goodness,* and that his personality develops as a result of an active, dynamic effort to *realize* or *actualize* his inherent potentialities. Maslow visualizes life as consisting of two great mutual forces: the push to satisfy the basic needs necessary for physical and psychological survival; and the push toward the actualization or fulfillment of one's inherent potentialities, *i.e.,* the meta-needs of justice, goodness, beauty, order, etc. The actualizing tendency is seen as *growth* motivation, directed toward enhancing life and making it worthwhile, whereas the survival tendency is viewed as *deprivation* motivation, which is concerned mainly with the maintenance of life. It is visualized that the satisfaction of one's meta-needs can follow only after one's basic survival needs are met. Thus, the two great forces do not operate in conflict with each other, but rather in an hierarchical manner.

Maslow's (1970) belief is that man has needs, capacities and tendencies which are biologically or genetically based, some which are common to all men, some of which are specific to the individual; that there is for each of us a genetic blueprint which determines or structures our particular capabilities. This dimly realized blueprint is developed from within the person, and not from shaping caused by external forces. The individual's development to maturity becomes the actualizing of common and special capacities inherent in his basic nature. Self-actualization thus becomes the healthy development of one's inner nature, which, according to Maslow, is good rather than evil. Anything which disturbs, blocks, twists, or frustrates this development is bad or abnormal and results in psychopathological tendencies or behavior. Maslow feels also that this inner feature is delicate and fragile, and extremely susceptible to habit and cultural pressure; but though in some cases it is denied or repressed, it persists forever in the person.

If personality, as a construct, can be viewed as a combination of structural entities (*i.e.,* traits, characteristics, etc.) and dynamic tendencies (*i.e.,* goal-directed thoughts, feelings, and actions), then Maslow's position would indicate that the personality is composed of a hierarchy of needs in a constant state of being satisfied, blocked, or repressed (see Diagram 13). This is a dynamic rather than a strictly static view of personality and, in

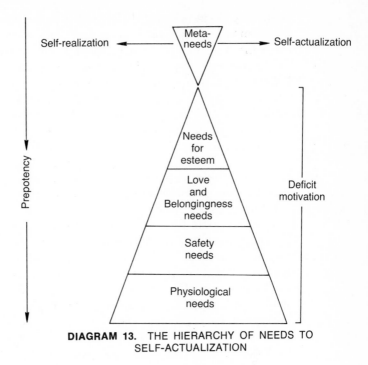

DIAGRAM 13. THE HIERARCHY OF NEEDS TO
SELF-ACTUALIZATION

this sense, revolves around the two major tendencies operating within the person's psychological structure.

Maslow's theory is not the typical "drive-reduction" theory of human behavior. The goals themselves are emphasized rather than the reduction of tension associated with the drives towards these goals. This is essentially a humanistic approach which emphasizes the totality or wholeness of life, and in which the end rather than the means is important.

Of central importance in Maslow's theory is the concept of instinctoid* needs, *i.e.,* the relatively weak inherent needs within each of us that are the combined result of one's nature and nurture — the accumulated product of one's evolutionary inheritance and one's accumulated learning. These needs are best considered as latent predispositions which, because of their weakness, are not universally reflected in human behavior as in animal behavior where they are stronger, but which *do* become manifest under appropriate cultural, environmental and specific situational conditions. These instinctoid needs are arranged in a

---

*The term instinctoid need is seen as representing a stage of internal deprivation determined in the main by one's hereditary background, *i.e.,* the goals, goal effects and goal-directed drives are basically instinctive in nature.

hierarchy of prepotency; *i.e.*, in order for a higher level of needs to become manifest or appear, the previous lower-level needs must first be satisfied. It is best *not* to view this hierarchy in an "all-or-nothing" fashion but rather to view it generally in terms of increasing non-satisfaction at successively higher levels in the hierarchy. That is, overlaid on this hierarchical system are *individual differences* (people will differ in the required amount of need satisfaction at each level) and *cultural factors* (depending on the particular culture, certain needs will be more important or salient than others) which will influence the salience of particular need levels in particular or specific ways. Certain types of cultural conditioning can take place in individuals so that they can ignore lower needs and concern themselves with the higher needs, *e.g.*, people in India and China involved with Yoga and Zen Buddhism. Also, although there is a tendency to move up the hierarchy toward wholeness and uniqueness of self, such progress is not necessarily automatic. There are safety or regulatory mechanisms in people that make them afraid to take chances, to gain freedom or independence, and that make them cling to current gains.

There are four levels of lower or *deficit* needs that involve the individual in physical and psychological survival: *physiological* needs, *safety* needs, *love* and *belongingness* needs, and *esteem* needs. At the base of the hierarchy, and most prepotent, are one's *physiological* needs. These include the needs for food, air, water, vitamins, minerals and other elements. Extensive deprivation of one or more of these needs causes a total loss of interest in *any* of the other needs existing in a person. This is what prepotency means — a lower need is stronger than a higher need simply because it dominates the organism in obvious ways when both needs are simultaneously frustrated. A completely hungry person will think only of his hunger and food to the complete exclusion of everything else. However, even though such needs are the most prepotent, they are the least instrumental in affecting human behavior in Western society because their satisfaction is virtually automatic. That this is so strengthens Maslow's view that *when* physiological needs *are* completely satisfied, at once higher needs emerge and dominate the life of the individual. This view releases man from being only a tool of his basic needs (a position taken by many theorists), and permits the realization that the gratification of more socially oriented needs and goals is the predominant feature of human motivation.

When physiological needs are met there emerges the next level of needs, roughly categorized as *safety* needs. These are the needs for security, stability of one's life, dependency on others, protection, order, regularity, freedom from fear and other anxieties, etc. People who live predominantly at this level of need satisfaction are obsessed with seeking a warm, comfortable, undisrupted, routine, predictable life with freedom from unexpected and unfamiliar situations. This is a need level at which the infant child operates for a significant period of time. And if his safety needs are *not* met satisfactorily he will continue to operate at this level until they are. There is, however, a need for predictability, to a greater or lesser degree, functioning in all of us which, as we will see later, is a determinant in play, games, sport and physical activity.

Once the "lower" need levels are satisfied, people tend to become preoccupied with "higher" needs, the first level of which are *love and belongingness* needs. It is at this point in the hierarchy that psychological survival starts to become predominant over pure physical survival. Here, people seek affectionate relationships with each other, seek to join groups, and deeply miss an absent friend or relative. Love needs involve both the giving and receiving of affection and at this level seeking an identity or place in the family constellation becomes imperative. Loneliness, ostracism or rejection are felt quite sharply at this point in the hierarchy. Maslow feels very strongly that man has a deep tendency to herd, to join, or to belong together (consistent with Ardrey's territorial imperative) and that possibly the increasing contemporary movement toward affiliation with others in the form of T-groups, intentional communities, and growth groups is motivated by a satisfaction of the needs of this level. Quite possibly the strong affiliation motives that youngsters have in wanting to belong to athletic teams and sports groups is also a manifestation of these needs.

Following love needs on the hierarchy are the *esteem* needs. These deal specifically with psychological survival and are the last of the deprivation states. Maslow divides this level of needs into: a) the desire for achievement, independence, adequacy, mastery, success, self-confidence, and freedom, and b) the desire for reputation, prestige, status, or recognition from others. The blocking or repressing of the satisfaction of these needs produces feelings of inadequacy, helplessness, and inferiority. Such feelings give rise to basic discouragement, and one could speculate here that nonsatisfaction of esteem needs in sports participation will result in the child's quitting the activity.

It is thus important to realize that the tendency toward survival (the satisfaction of the four levels of deficit needs) is prepotent over the actualizing tendency. That is, life must be maintained or secured before it can be enhanced. Also, these four levels of needs are seen as deprivation motivation, *i.e.*, the urges that drive the person to achieve certain goal-states that are necessary in order to relieve or reduce the tension or discomfort due to their absence. For example, one is driven to achieve self-esteem because its absence (the lack of a stable self-identity) causes psychological discomfort in the person. Maslow sees satisfaction of the survival tendency as the major task of childhood, and although the actualizing tendency can appear at any point in life, it is more probably most salient in adulthood. Such a view would indicate that the enthusiastic embracing of sport by children is linked more to the survival than actualizing tendency.

On the fifth and last level in the hierarchy are "meta-needs," which are categorized simply by Maddi (1968) as the need for *self-actualization.* The actualizing tendency is seen as growth motivation in the schema and refers to the basic human urges to enrich one's life and enlarge one's experience. Growth motivation does not, like deprivation motivation, involve the satisfaction of deficit states but rather the expansion of one's horizons. Goals are general rather than specific in nature, and an increase rather than a reduction in stimulation and tension is sought by the individual.

Maslow describes the need for self-actualization in terms of the characteristics which he deems are possessed by self-actualized or self-actualizing people. He feels that such people possess distinguishing features which denote whether or not they are functioning at the *meta-need* level of growth motivation. The fully functioning person is thus characterized by the congruence between his sense of self and certain organismic qualities. Briefly, these distinguishing features are as follows:

1. *A realistic orientation* in terms of how one perceives events and other people in one's life. Reality thus is comfortable and not threatening for the person, especially in a cognitive sense. Unpredictability and uncertainty become desirable, stimulating challenges, rather than torture, for this person.

2. *Self-acceptance*, acceptance of other people, and acceptance of one's environment, without even really giving it any thought, characterizes the actualized person. This is not entirely self-satisfaction but is rather a stoic acceptance of one's strengths as well as weaknesses or shortcomings.

3. *Spontaneity, simplicity,* and *naturalness* in one's behavior and inner view of life characterize the self-actualizing tendency. There exists a lack of artificiality or straining for effect, and unconventionality is more an inner thing with these people and does not appear on the surface of their behavior in outrageous forms.

4. These people are *problem-centered* rather than *self-centered*. That is, their concern is for solving problems, fulfilling tasks, having a mission in life, and not being overly concerned with themselves or their own problems. They are not basically ego-centered, *i.e.*, overly concerned with reality.

5. There is a need for *privacy* and an air of *detachment* in the behavior of these people. Isolation is not uncomfortable for them; it is sometimes even desirable. Related to this is their ability to separate or detach themselves from controversy and remain unconcerned by events or occurrences which cause discomfort in other people. Calmness, serenity and aloofness are recognizable traits in self-actualizing people.

6. These people are *automonous* and relatively *independent* of their physical and social environments. They are not dependent for their main satisfactions on other people, their society, or the real world. They are more concerned with their own capacities, abilities, and potentials for enjoyment and fulfillment.

7. A *freshness of appreciation* characterizes their behavior. They have a continuous fresh enjoyment of ordinary events, objects and people that persons who exhibit stereotyped responses do not. They derive strength and inspiration from everyday life.

8. Another feature is the seemingly strange capacity they have to engender *peak* or *mystic experiences* in their lives. The capacity to feel limitless horizons opening up or experience feelings of great power or intense ecstasy characterize these people.

9. There is a deep *identification with mankind*. Identification with other people in terms of affection, sympathy and empathy characterize the actualizing tendency. Maslow feels this occurs in spite of occasional anger or disgust over the behavior of man in general.

10. These people have a need, and a capacity, for deep and *profound* relationships with other people. There is, here, a capacity for eliminating the usual causes for hangups over love, respect and affection for other people.

11. Their *values* and *attitudes* are *democratic* in nature. They have no trouble learning from anyone who has something to teach them. In a humble sort of way, they are capable of realizing how *little* they might know about something in comparison to how much *could* be known, or *is* known.

12. They do not confuse means with ends. They are basically ethical in nature, and do not confuse right with wrong. They find abhorrent the use of means to justify the end.

13. Their *humor* is *warm* and *philosophical* rather than hostile or sick.

14. *Creativity* is an essential part of their nature. Originality,

inventiveness, and a naive way of looking at life characterize these people. This is creativity, not so much in terms of genius, but rather as an expression of a healthy personality; *i.e.,* truck drivers, ditchdiggers, clerks, etc. can enjoy this kind of creativity.

15. There is a resistance to conformity and the ability to *transcend* one's environment. Here there is a capacity to resist the pressures of society and function above or beyond it. There is an inner detachment which enables one to be tolerant of a conforming society but not be a part of it.

In summation, then, Maslow (1968) feels that the tendency to actualize one's inherent potentialities is

... an episode, or a sport in which the powers of the person come together in a particularly efficient and intensely enjoyable way, and in which he is more integrated and less split, more open for experience, more idiosyncratic, more perfectly expressive or spontaneous, or fully functioning, more creative, more humorous, more ego-transcending, more independent of his lower needs, etc. . . . He becomes in these episodes more truly himself, more perfectly actualizing his potentialities, closer to the core of his being, more fully human.*

Self-Actualization in Sport

It is quite possible to speculate that the physical activity, recreation, and competitive sport in which a person engages could, in a sense, reflect the general or basic instinctoid needs operating within him at any particular moment in time. Also, there is good reason to believe that his behavior in physical activity and athletics could serve as an indication of his progress up through Maslow's hierarchy toward self-actualization. His behavior thus would be independent of the type of activity in which he is participating, and his attitudes and interests in physical activity and athletics would be the direct offshoot of the level of basic needs that are important for him at that time. Several speculative implications of Maslow's hierarchy of instinctoid needs, then, are as follows:

1. It is highly unlikely that the lower level of *physiological needs* are reflected to any great extent in Western physical activity and sport. Such needs would be reflected only in fairly primitive cultures, where a great deal of daily emphasis is on actual survival. Activities such as hunting, fishing, archery, shooting, and hiking reflect skills necessary for the procurement of food—

---

*Cited in Wankel, L. M.: A Self-Actualizing Theory of Play. Paper presented at the 2nd World Symposium on the History of Sport and Physical Education, Banff, Alberta, May-June 1971.

an immediate necessity in primitive cultures. The play of children would reflect such needs and the play of adults would be virtually nonexistent; *i.e.*, they would be completely engaged in the work entailing survival.

Initial research done with Eskimo children in a competitive skiing program indicates that their culture has a heavy influence on their athletic behavior. For example, cooperation is more heavily emphasized than competitiveness in Eskimo life and it was found that some Eskimo children found beating each other quite abhorrent. Sports which emphasized cooperation, however, were enthusiastically embraced. Thus, in Eskimo culture, where people must cooperate to survive their natural environment, their play and sports activity reflects their basic needs for physical survival.

2. People operating at a level where *safety needs* predominate would probably participate in physical activities which are safe, highly controlled, predictable and secure. People operating at this level seek an undisrupted routine and predictable life with freedom from unexpected or unfamiliar situations. Thus, people who choose nice "safe" sports such as golf, lawn bowling, and solitary jogging could be considered as reflecting basic needs for safety and security. Also, there is a possiblity that such people use physical activity and sports participation as mechanisms for learning how to control their environment, *i.e.*, a mastery principle. It would be highly unlikely, for example, to think that people who enjoy skydiving or white-water canoeing would be doing so out of need for safety.

3. There is little doubt that many people participate in sport out of a need for affiliation. Various physical activities and many sports are seen as prime vehicles to achieve and maintain social relationships with other people. Sport becomes only a means toward a social end. People who are dominated by *love and belongingness needs* would probably participate in many activities in order to promote social relationships at the expense of achieving excellence in any one particular sport. As has often been observed, many people are singularly disinterested in how well they do in a sport, as long as there exists the opportunity for fun relationships with other people. Only in exceptional circumstances would one expect people functioning at this level to be participating in highly competitive sport. One exception could be the individual who can achieve affiliation with other people only through excelling in sport. Interacting with other people and achieving friendships are the main motives for participation in these people. Kenyon (1968b), for example, found that physical activity as a social experience held a stronger meaning for sec-

ondary school students than did other conceptualizations such as vertigo, fitness, aesthetics, catharsis and ascetics. Again, the basis for such findings could be seen to arise out of fundamental needs for love and belongingness.

4. *Self-esteem* needs, as represented by intense drives for achievement, recognition and prestige, are easily recognizable in the endless hours of dedication and sacrifice devoted to their events by superior athletes and outstanding individuals in other areas of endeavor. Athletics as a vehicle for achieving recognition and prestige is particularly attractive because of its potential for immediate success. Individuals can perfect skills, and achieve success, in sports over a short period of time, and at very early ages not possible in science, arts, and business. Athletic success to satisfy the needs for self-esteem also receives massive reinforcement from society via the media and spectators at sports events. The successful athlete receives tremendous unconditional social approval for his exploits which directly satisfies esteem needs.

5. Wankel (1971) hypothesizes that for those individuals who do reach the *meta-need level* (*i.e.,* who have satisfied all their basic needs) and who are self-actualizing, the distinction between work and play disappears. Such people enjoy and "exist" in their work to such a degree that it, in a sense, becomes "play." Thus, for an athlete, or any sports participant, who is self-actualizing, his involvement in sport becomes justifiable in and of itself—he becomes one with his sport. On occasion, professional athletes have been noted as saying that they derive such enjoyment from sport that they would play for nothing. Though such statements are usually greeted with cynicism and derision, they do indicate that the "oneness" with sport that the athlete has attained represents existence for him. Great musicians and artists have expressed much the same kind of feeling so there is no reason for us not to consider a similar occurrence in sport. Maslow, in this sense, would add the possibility of what he refers to as *peak experiences.* That is, some people can become so involved in their play or sports participation that they completely lose touch with reality—they totally transcend themselves—and though initially their participation was in terms of a lower basic need, they are now so totally involved that they are actually performing at a metaphysical level. Once-in-a-lifetime, extraordinary performances, such as Beamon's long jump at the Mexico Olympics in 1968, might be explained in such terms.

6. The higher needs (love, esteem and meta-needs) are most probably manifested in play and sports which are influenced to a greater degree by cultural and individual differences than be-

havior manifested from the satisfaction of lower needs. Thus games and sports events reflecting the higher needs would exhibit much more variability, originality, and creativity. Games representing or reflecting the lower needs would be constant from culture to culture, from individual to individual, *i.e.*, they would reflect hunting and other food procurement forms of activity. The more complex, highly organized games of our culture, on the other hand, would reflect man's desire for self-expression and achievement. The complexities of our various team sports can be seen as satisfying such needs. The tension and pressure that often accompany such sports will also be part of the satisfaction of the higher needs for increased stimulation and activation.

Summary

Maslow's viewpoint on personality and motivation undoubtedly is attractive in helping us understand why people participate in physical activity and athletics with such enthusiasm and dedication. Simply stated, it would be that the play and sports activities of both children and adults reflect the basic instinctoid needs which are operating within them at any particular moment in time. Maslow considers personality types to be representative of the degrees of particular need satisfactions on a straight-line continuum; *i.e.*, each person can be compared with any other in the degree to which certain needs are satisfied. Such an organismic-holistic view of personality classifies people on a single continuum rather than as the parts, factors, or traits which characterize him and the values which are significant for him.

Individual participation in physical activity and sport can be seen as a function of both the developmental stage of the person and the basic need level in which he is operating at any given moment in time. This is best viewed chronologically. In the infant and childhood years, from ages 2 to approximately 7, children engage in play and game activities which probably reflect the lower need levels of Maslow's hierarchy. Though many classifications of play and games abound throughout the literature, they can be subsumed generally into several relatively distinguishable categories. Children engage in manipulative, make-believe, explorative, creative, symbolic and social types of play and games. Most of these play behaviors are the result of the child's attempting to gain a mastery over himself and his environment, and are thought to serve the function of socializing him. These forms of play can easily be seen to reflect the lower instinctoid needs such as the need for activity and the needs for safety and stability which help him prepare for an effective inter-action with his environment. As the child grows older the com-plexity of his *social* play increases and becomes the dominant form of his physical activity from preadolescence through adult-hood. Social play, or participation in sport for its social experi-mental value, can be seen as a reflection of the child's needs for love, affection, affiliation, and belonging to a group. (For many children, just "making the team" is an important satisfaction.) Sport also becomes very achievement-oriented during adoles-cence and directly reflects the striving of children to satisfy needs for achievement, self-esteem, and recognition. Play and sports participation thus becomes a direct function of the social and achievement needs of each child. Sports participation as a ve-hicle for deliberate self-actualization or self-realization, though occasionally present in these younger years, necessarily requires a certain degree of emotional and intellectual maturity and as such is more likely to occur in later adult life.

PERSONALITY AS VARIED EXPERIENCE AND LEVEL OF ACTIVATION

Almost 350 years ago, John Donne wrote: "No man is an island, entire of itself." All people live in a state of constant bombardment from stimuli in their external and internal en-vironments. We are creatures of our social and physical environ-ments, and the influence of our environment goes a long way in determining the way we act, behave, feel, and think from day to day. Our personalities are to a large extent determined by the type, degree, and variety of stimulation which is generated not only from within ourselves but also from without. One area of thought in psychology views man's behavior as largely a function of the formative influence of feedback from his external world. If the feedback a person receives from other people and events in his life is consistent with what he expected to receive, then a state of homeostasis or quiescence occurs. If the feedback is in-consistent with one's expectancies, then there is a pressure on the person to reduce the tension, anxiety, or discomfort caused by this inconsistency. Life, in a sense, is viewed as constant ef-fort to maintain consistency between feedback and expectancies. Such a general model of personality is called a *consistency* model by Maddi (1968). In Fiske and Maddi's (1961) version of the con-sistency model the emphasis is on the consistency between the degree of bodily tension or activation that is customary for a person and that which actually exists at a given moment in time.

Traditional drive reduction models of human behavior would seem to be inadequate in explaining why some people voluntarily choose to participate in sports activities characterized by high tension, excitement, or arousal. Drive-reduction explanations of motivated behavior are predicted on the assumption that the organism always acts to reduce the discomfort caused by some deficit state or inherent need within it. So that, for example, one participates in sport to reduce his need for physical activity and once he is finished participating in physical activity for a period of time, the need is satisfied and he becomes comfortable; *i.e.*, he acts to reduce his discomfort. However, what is the explanation for people participating in vigorous physical activity and highly competitive athletics because they want to? The possibility has to be recognized that maybe these activities are attractive to some people *because* of the tension, stimulation, activation, arousal, or excitement that they generate. In short, one must consider that some people are actually *active tension-seekers,* and that physical activity and sport are prime means for achieving such goals.

Evidence in physical education is now also starting to appear which characterizes some youngsters (and adults) as being *high-active* people, as contrasted to other children who are said to be *low-active.* The behavior of people who are constantly highly active cannot be explained solely in drive or tension-reduction terms. Some alternative explanations do exist. Berlyne (1960), for example, feels that explorative play behavior in children is caused by the attraction of novelty, change, complexity, and uncertainty in his environment. Though Berlyne feels that a child willingly seeks play situations of high stimulation so as to reduce such stimulation, he does state that such high stimulation experiences are felt as pleasurable. Even suspense, fear, and danger are factors in play engendering such explorative behavior. Dember and Earl (1957) account for exploratory play behavior by postulating that it is an effort to *optimize* stimulus complexity rather than reduce it. They feel that stimulus complexity becomes optimal when it is just *above* the individual's present complexity level, and that play (and probably sports participation) is an attempt by the child to maintain the complexity of the stimuli impinging upon his body at a level which is particularly ideal for him. For one boy, playing sandlot baseball offers enough stimulus complexity, whereas for another, only hyperorganized little league baseball would be attractive. Heckhausen (1964) has also presented an *activation* explanation of play. He states that play is governed by *activation cycles* which consist of alternating drops and rises in the daily tension levels of people. These drops and rises in activation are attributed to what he calls *perceived discrepancies*. These are discrepancies between current and earlier perceptions (novelty), between current perceptions and earlier expectations (surprise content), between parts of the child's perceptual field (complexity), and between different expectations (uncertainty). Heckhausen, like Dember and Earl, feels that there is a motivation intrinsic in the individual which compels him to keep his level of activation at an optimal level, and that movements of short duration toward and away from this optimum are experienced as pleasurable. Generally, play behavior (and probably sports participation) is seen as increasing the child's arousal potential, and, in doing so, compensating for the *lack* of unpredictability, risk, surprise, or danger in his everyday life. This can be viewed as a seeking for variability, or a seeking of tension, through play. If true, play can be interpreted as contributing to, rather than detracting from, a child's level of activation. An attractive conceptualization of this whole idea of *levels of activation* as the prime motivating force in a person's life is formulated in a theoretical structure by Donald Fiske and Salvatore Maddi (1961).

The Concept of Activation

Fiske and Maddi (1961) feel that the core tendency within a person's personality is the "attempt to maintain the level of activation to which he is accustomed or which can be said to be characteristic of him." Activation, in this sense, is described as one's normal level of excitement, alertness, tension, or energy. Its neurophysiological correlate is seen as subcortical excitation, with a focus in the reticular formation of the brain. The emphasis in this view is on the discrepancies that occur between the level of activation customary for a person and the level of activation that exists at any actual moment. These discrepancies are seen as always producing behavior to reduce the discrepancy. For example, when you find a situation too exciting for you, or not exciting enough, you indulge in behavior that makes the situation less or more exciting. Activation can be viewed as the level of excitation or tension that exists within a person.

What determines this level of activation? And what does it, in fact, consist of? Fiske and Maddi describe the *impact* which stimulation has on one's level of activation in terms of its dimensions and sources. The three dimensions of stimulation are *intensity, meaningfulness* and *variation*; the three sources of stimulation are exteroceptive, interoceptive, and cortical.

The *intensity* of stimulation simply refers to its amount of physical energy, so that a siren has more of an impact on you than the ringing of an alarm clock. *Meaningfulness* is that dimension of stimulation which refers to the significance or importance that the stimulation has for you. A siren on a police car may have degrees of meaningfulness for you depending upon whether or not the police car is pursuing you or someone else. *Variation,* as a dimension of stimulation, is interpreted in terms of *change, novelty,* and *unexpectedness.* Variation is referred to as a state: 1) in which current stimulation is different to the stimulation which preceded it (change), 2) in which the current stimulation is unusual, infrequent, or new to the person (novelty), and 3) in which the stimulation received deviates from what you expected it would be (unexpectedness). All three of these dimensions of stimulation overlap and strongly affect a person's activation level.

The sources of this stimulation are characterized as being *exteroceptive* (excitation of organs sensitive to the external world), *e.g.,* a broken shoulder would be a strong source of stimulation; *interoceptive* (excitation of organs sensitive to the internal environment of the person), *e.g.,* a rapidly beating heart from exercise; and *cortical* (excitation directly from the cortex of the brain) *e.g.,* the cognitive interpretation of a traumatic experience.

Thus, the level of activation that exists at any one time in a person is a function of the total *impact* that all kinds of stimulation have on him. Impact is also a function of the intensity, meaningfulness, and variation of these kinds of stimulation. Fiske and Maddi state that activation, impact, and the dimensions and sources of impact are the intrinsic or core characteristics of an individual's personality (*i.e.,* these are aspects common to all people).

Customary Level of Activation. Here the assumption is made that people normally experience fairly constant levels of activation from day to day, and that over a period of time they do, in fact, become accustomed to a particular level of activation that is customary for them. This *customary level of activation* is the result of day to day similarities in the intensity, meaningfulness, and variation of stimulation from all sources in a person's existence; so that a person comes to think of as normal particular degrees and kinds of stimulation that regularly have impact on him. These normal levels of activation are an "averaging-out" of the rises and drops that occur during and from day to day.

It is now hypothesized by the authors that at any particular moment in time a discrepancy may exist between a person's *customary* level of activation and his *actual* level of activation. If a discrepancy does exist, the person engages in impact-modify-ing behavior; that is, if the actual level of activation is lower than his accustomed level, then he engages in impact-*increasing* behavior; when it is higher, he engages in impact-*decreasing* behavior (see Diagram 14). Impact-decreasing behavior is inter-

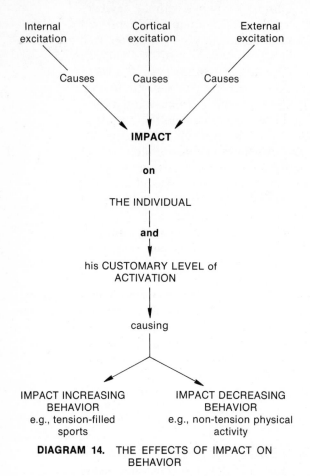

DIAGRAM 14. THE EFFECTS OF IMPACT ON BEHAVIOR

preted, then, as action by the individual to decrease or minimize the intensity, meaningfulness, and variation of stimulation from all sources. Impact-increasing behavior is the converse. Thus, the "consistency" position taken by Fiske and Maddi is that they consider the directionality in a person's life to be governed by his attempts to match up actual with his customary levels of activation.

Anticipation and Correction of Customary Activation Level. A person's customary level of activation is seen as the result of accumulated experience throughout his life. Though there is the possibility of a genetic or inherited influence, it is a person's environment which seems to be the major determinant. This environmental effect probably occurs initially during childhood and, as the patterns of stimulation in a person's daily life occur and recur over a period of time, an individual characteristic curve of activation develops throughout a person's life as he becomes aware (or learns) that he can, by design, control the size of the discrepancy between his customary level of activation and the actual levels of activation that occur in his daily life. He learns ways of ensuring that large discrepancies do not occur. He does this (through habit) by selecting and maintaining certain activities and experiences that match actual to customary levels of activation. He, in essence, *anticipates* beforehand how successful certain behaviors will be in achieving such a match-up and acts in a manner such that he will be successful. Anticipatory processes function so that future levels of activation will neither fall below or rise above one's characteristic curve of activation. So that low-active people, for example, normally behave in such a way as to avoid high-active situations and experiences, and vice-versa.

When anticipatory processes fail in matching actual with customary levels of activation, emergency *correctional* processes are necessary. That is, a person acts to correct the discrepancy that occurs by engaging in either impact-decreasing or impact-increasing behavior. Though Maddi and Propst (1963) feel reducing or augmenting actual levels of activation might cause a distortion of reality, they do feel that these actions are simple attempts to under- or over-exaggerate the real impact of stimulation. This will become clearly evident in some of the behavioral analyses of athletic behavior in the next section.

In summary, then, the position taken by Fiske and Maddi is that a person's personality is largely determined by the success he has in maintaining a match-up between his actual levels of activation and his customary level of activation. They feel that people differ in the amounts of activation which they require for a comfortable psychological life, and that these requirements are reflected by their customary levels of activation. People who require high activation in their life will seek high stimulation intensity, meaningfulness, and variation. People with low activation requirements will fear these stimulus dimensions. It is from these activation requirements that a person's basic personality emerges.

Implications of Consistency for Physical Activity and Athletics. Of major importance here is the possible explanation and further understanding of "high" active people and/or individuals who actively seek tension in their lives — as we all know, the enthusiastic acceptance and pursuit of physical activity and sport by young children has long been universally accepted as reflecting a *need for physical activity.* No explanations, however, other than those having an instinctual basis, have been forthcoming, and, at best, trying to explain some form of behavior as emanating from a basic instinct within the human being has little theoretical, rational, or practical value. On the other hand, if some link can be made between the biological, cognitive and affective mechanisms operating within the individual, the explanation of certain phenomena can be structured in such a way as to further one's insight into what is actually happening. Such is the case with the phenomenon of *high activity* and its relationship to level of activation. The same is true when attempting to explain "tension seeking" in people. There seems to be little doubt that, for some people, sport provides a particular or peculiar opportunity for achieving high states of excitement, stress, or tension. Some basic attraction must exist for people to voluntarily put themselves into situations involving danger, thrills, pressure, and tension for reasons other than just financial remuneration, recognition or prestige. Otherwise, why would a person voluntarily choose to put himself into pressure situations where thousands of people are watching him (a high caliber tennis player in the finals of the Davis Cup) or actually depending upon him to come up with a superior performance (the 100 meter final in the Olympic Games). Money, prestige, and recognition are simply not reward enough (especially in amateur sport) to explain why athletes put themselves in such situations. This is evidenced by the withdrawal of some participants who "just can't stand the pressure" or who are not prepared "to pay the price." Some fundamental affective attraction has to exist for people to skydive, tower dive, surf, bobsled, or race high-speed automobiles. A consistency viewpoint could indirectly explain such a phenomenon.

Simply interpreted in Fiske and Maddi terms, high active children are children with extremely high customary levels of activation. To avoid huge discrepancies between their *actual* and *customary* levels of activation they seek out activities which will provide stimulation high in intensity, meaningfulness and variety. Among activities which provide such stimulation is participation in physical activity and sport. In considering such a hypothesis one can trace the explanation of high activity through the several dimensions of Fiske and Maddi's theory. First, it must be understood that activation in the present sense refers, psychologically, to excitement, tension, alertness, and attentiveness, and neurophysiologically, to cortical excitation. This means that viewing a great painting or listening to a symphony orchestra might raise one's level of activation just as much as participating in an athletic contest. That is, the impact from the stimulation one seeks is a cognitive and/or affective impact, not just the tension developed from physical movement. With this in mind, one can begin to interpret the intense pursuit of sport by children of all ages. The daily existence of school-age children is one of routine which offers little or no excitement—no real impact in affective terms. For some of these children this routine is comfortable and little discrepancy exists between the actual level of activation produced by this routine and their customary levels of activation. For other children (and adults too), however, a large discrepancy does exist, and they act to reduce it by engaging in *impact-increasing* behavior. Some go out for music, some for drama, some for politics, and some choose sport. The particular activity chosen by a child depends on both his anticipatory and correctional processes. That is, he anticipates (usually, but not always, on the basis of past experience) that by participating in football, for example, he will receive the necessary stimulation, in terms of its intensity, meaningfulness, and variation, to bring the actual levels of activation *up to* his customary level of activation.

The high degree of excitement and tension generated in competitive sport, its meaningfulness in terms of the status, prestige, and recognition that accompany athletic performance in our modern society, and the variation in one's routine life pattern provided by competitive sport, all contribute in making physical activity and athletics attractive or appropriate means for increasing the impact of stimulation upon a particular individual. Also, all three sources of stimulation can be seen to be involved—the wildly beating heart and increased expiration from hard physical exercise (interoceptive stimulation), the physical contact and hyper-perspiration (exteroceptive stimulation), and the constant mental excitement and involvement in decision-making (cortical stimulation) all combine to increase the impact derived from participation. The wild fervor with which sport is pursued nowadays, and the increasing significance it has in our society, simply serve to further emphasize its attractiveness and validity as a vehicle for increasing existing actual levels of activation. For many children, in fact, who are introduced to competitive sport at an early age, the excitement and tension of sport become so incorporated into their customary curves of activation that they virtually become addicted to it. Correctional processes function in this context, in such a way as assure the person that the activity he does choose provides the payoff which he expects. That is, a boy will turn out for football because of its potential for high stimulation impact and find that it is actually quite boring and routine; when such a situation occurs he will either quit football and look for some alternative (*e.g.*, wrestling or boxing) or he will try to inject into the game of football a personally higher potential for stimulation, *i.e.*, he will become a "hyper-holler" guy and try to generate within a game an excitement, tension, and stress.

One must at this point realize that the converse of these interpretations is also true. That is, by choosing to participate in sport in order to bring actual levels of stimulation up to customary levels, the person might overshoot and discover that the activity or sport he has chosen provides too *much* impact for him. When this happens, he will correct back by quitting and finding a sport which is more appropriate for his needs, or he will attempt to play a slightly more passive role within the sport he has chosen. This is partially why children (and adults) involved in a particular sport react differently to situations laden with excitement and tension. For those who are seeking high impact, the tenseness and stress connected to crucial moments in athletic contests will be quite attractive, while to those who have lower customary levels of activation the same situations will be quite uncomfortable or threatening. This leads directly to a possible explanation of people who are "tension-seekers."

Until just recently, there was general agreement among various authorities that people participate in sport mainly because of its *cathartic* value. That is, that sports participation provides the contestant with the means for releasing tension built up by frustration occurring in his daily life. Sport, in this light, becomes a tension-reducer. Violence, brutality, and aggression in sport are sometimes explained in these terms. A person who becomes frustrated in his daily life (either from inactivity or the thwarting of particular desires) seeks relief from this tension by going down to the gym, pool, or field, and engaging in vigorous aggressive activity, *i.e.*, by punching a heavy bag, playing squash, or swimming himself to pure exhaustion. Such behavior is said to rid the person of his tensions and return him to a state of quiescence or homeostasis. Though such a model for explaining some behavior in sport is attractive, there remain several important questions unanswered. First, research indicates that people participating in activities which provide outlets for their aggressive tendencies becomes *more*, not less, aggressive.* Second, evidence is accumulating that certain kinds of

---

*See Chapter 10, Aggression in Sport, for a fuller explanation of this phenomenon.

personality types are attracted to different kinds of sport. People high in dominance or aggressiveness tend to choose those sports which will allow free expression of these tendencies, whereas people not high in these traits will choose other kinds of sport. Third, it is reasonable to assume that frustration occurring in one particular aspect of life will only be relieved in that aspect, and not in a totally different part of one's life. If one is frustrated in love, playing football may or may not relieve this frustration; only by becoming successful in love will that particular frustration be minimized. Fourth, if people are all "up-tight" to begin with, why do they choose sports which will simply make them more up-tight? The frustrations occurring from learning or perfecting certain athletic skills can only add to a person's level of tension, not relieve it. If a businessman arrives at the golf course full of tension, then his game of golf will be full of tension, *and* as it deteriorates because of this tension, will become even more tension-filled. Fifth, if people are engaging in sport to reduce tensions resulting from their other pursuits in life, why do they voluntarily choose competitive sports situations that can only provide even more tension? In a slightly different respect, why is it that some athletes purposely choose to participate in competitive situations which they know from experience are normally accompanied by all kinds of pressure, stress and tension? For example, boys who pitch in baseball, goal-tend in hockey, or quarterback in football have to be aware, consciously or sub-consciously, that they will constantly find themselves in pressure-packed situations with everyone depending on them to come through with superlative performances. With such realization, individuals who voluntarily choose such endeavors are obviously certain that the payoff is worthwhile, i.e. that the particular goals which they are striving for are worth the effort. The possibility also exists that they welcome and actively seek the pressure, tension and responsibility that accompany being the "center of attraction." For some boys the possibility also exists that the pay-off for them would be inadequate without this context of supercharged excitement and tension.* This explanation becomes even further weighted with importance when one considers it in the light of amateur sport where the athlete is not paid for shouldering all this responsibility. This explanation becomes even more viable in terms of the "success phobia" identified in athletes by Ogilvie and Tutko (1966). These authors feel that

---

*The same explanation can be valid for the reasons that leading figures in other pursuits such as business, politics, music or drama also find the "spotlight" to be very attractive and worthwhile.

some athletes have a greater fear of succeeding than they have of failing, that being a winner or a champion entails too much responsibility, and that being second or a near-champion is more attractive because one derives most of the prestige and recognition that accompanies success without having its major responsibilities. Such athletes, then, would not actively seek the pressure and tension normally accompanying star status and would make correctional attempts to avoid extremely high levels of activation. One could also speculate that athletes who play well in practice but not in games are doing so simply because the actual level of activation in a practice session matches more closely their customary level of activation. In more specific terms, one might add that the impact of stimulation during a game is too high for such athletes, not only in terms of its obvious higher intensity but also in meaningfulness and variation; *i.e.*, in a game situation it is more important to play well than in practice, and also the unexpectedness and instant change of situations occur more frequently during a game. Such high intensity, meaningfulness, and variation of stimulation can be seen to exceed some athletes' customary levels of activation, resulting in *impact-decreasing* behavior, as exemplified by lack of drive, desire, determination and aggressiveness.

Overview

In Fiske and Maddi's terms, personality identification in athletes and participants in physical activity must be considered in three basic dimensions: one's characteristic curve of activation, the height of this curve, and the anticipatory and correctional adjustments utilized in maintaining a characteristic level of activation. It is through these basic dimensions that the personality differences and similarities between people can be most easily seen.

First, Maddi and Propst (1963) state that the major similarity between people occurs in that their general curves of activation take on much the same shape; *i.e.*, typically, activation rises suddenly after waking, increases gradually to the middle of the day, starts to then decrease gradually until just before bedtime where it declines sharply. Differences between people are hypothesized as being manifested by the different shapes each person's curve of activation might take. We know through observation that some people function more effectively at particular times during the day; in fact, some people are known as day or night people. Such people would show corresponding high levels of active behavior during these time periods and thus provide us with some insight into the makeup of their personalities. On this basis it is foolish to expect all children in a physical education class to be prepared for a high level of activity at exactly the same time on any one particular day. Also, the success of athletic performances may very well be a direct function of the time of day when they occur. Like anything else, however, if a person's behavior sequences vary little from day to day, the possibility exists that a person's curve of activation can be so conditioned that the peaks can be made to occur at appropriate times. It thus becomes important to have some insight into each individual's daily curve of activation so that one can coordinate daily events of major importance with the peaks in a person's curve of activation. This has particular implications for athletes participating in highly organized, competitive sport. It is suggested here that, if competitions take place during particularly precise time periods (such as football, baseball, and hockey games do), then the coach and his athlete must work toward setting up a daily curve of activation which will peak at these particular times. This would require, for many athletes, a changing in their daily habits for each day, not just the day of a game. The implications are also direct for practicing: if skill perfection or learning is going to occur under optimal conditions, then a person's characteristic curve of activation must be taken into account.

The second major dimension of activation as a personality theory refers to the distinction made between *high-activation* and *low-activation* people. This involves the average height of each person's characteristic curve of activation. It is hypothesized that a certain amount of variability exists between people in the average heights of their curves of activation and that this is a direct reflection of the levels of activity that characterize them. That is, people with typically high curves of activation generally engage in *impact-increasing* behaviors, whereas, people with low curves constantly shy away from high impact situations. Again the implication is obvious; children (and adults) in physical education programs and sports situations must be considered in terms of their individual needs for activation. Low-activation people will require different levels and kinds of stimulation than high-activation people, and unless this is realized hyper-level programs or treatments will simply cause low-activation people to engage in *impact-decreasing* behavior, i.e., they will "turn-off" or quit. This is not to say that low-activation people will not participate in physical activity, nor is it to say that low-activation people will not become successful athletes. Rather, it is to realize the importance of fitting individual programs to individual needs as characterized by individual customary levels of activation.

This is further emphasized by the correctional and anticipational techniques used by people to maintain actual activation at a customary or comfortable level. Generally speaking, people are similar in respect to the techniques they use to minimize discrepancies between actual and customary levels of activation, but certain individual differences do exist and these are described by Fiske and Maddi as being dependent mainly on the way individuals define and handle the impact of stimulation. High activation people, for example, seek challenges, are energetic, have voracious appetites, pursue causes, and like action, adventure, and danger. Low activation people, on the other and, negotiate their lives through control, are constant conversationalists, simple and conforming in their tastes, tend to oversimplify their problems, and prefer the familiar to the new.

Maddi generally considers this personality typology to revolve around the three dimensions of impact previously mentioned and that this can be explained by regarding high activation people as approaching (or desiring to approach) intensity, meaningfulness, and variation in stimulation. So, children classified as being *high-active* people would be seen as constantly demonstrating a *need* for high intensity, meaningfulness, and variety in their lives, and that, depending on individual differences, these needs would be manifested in overt behavior. A series of distinctions may well be made along these lines on the basis of the activities that the child chooses to participate in. That is, his choice may largely be determined by the pure intensity of the impact of stimulation he gets from the activity (*e.g.*, competitive baseball vs. sandlot baseball), or its meaningfulness for him (*e.g.*, physical contact sports for the boy who is aggressive), or the variety it provides (*e.g.*, novel sports like skydiving), or a combination of all three. The converse is also true. Low-activation children will be influenced in their choices of activity by the *fears* they have for too much intensity, meaningfulness, and variety in stimulation. Their preferences will emerge as attempts to "match-down" high impact situations to their lower customary levels of activation. They, for example, may prefer soccer to football (intensity) or intra-murals to surfing (variety in terms of unexpectedness). Such speculations in terms of Maddi's personality typology provide possibilities for answers to that most perplexing question in sport: Do certain personality types gravitate toward certain sports?

A further distinction necessary for understanding this ty-

pology is the difference between *external* and *internal* traits.*
Here, the distinction is related to which *sources* of stimulation
the person is oriented toward. That is, whether a person primarily refers to exteroceptive sources of stimulation when regulating
impact (external) or to interoceptive or cortical sources (internal).
The former would, for example, be exemplified by athletes who
seek the sight, noise, and feel of contact or competition in their
external environment, and the latter would focus more on the
internal stimulation caused by the tensions, excitements, or mental stresses reflected through cognitions, mentations, or emotional disturbances. Again, the distinction seems to have immediate implications for better understanding sports behavior. We
are reasonably sure, introspectively at least, that participation in
sport has different *meanings* for different people and that each
internalizes this meaning in a different way. This we know happens, even to the extent of maybe distinguishing between outstanding and average competitors. An athlete, for example,
adjusting to the competitive conditions in his sport will do so
differently if the main sources of stimulation for him are essentially outside rather than within himself. This is possibly why
some athletes perform consistently regardless of external conditions and others seem to need both external and internal stimulation. Some understanding, in these terms, of what "turns people
on or off" would seem to be mandatory for both the coach and his
athlete.

The last distinction of importance in this typology is that
made between *active* and *passive* traits, *i.e.*, for every active personality type there is a passive counterpart. A person with active
traits is typified as being highly initiative, and as constantly trying to influence or control his environment. The person with
passive traits, on the other hand, is seen as being constantly controlled by his environment, and as being indolent, basically lazy,
and nonproductive. Such active and passive traits constantly
show up in the differences between bona fide leaders and fol-
lowers. Maddi feels this activeness-passiveness distinction is
directly reflected by whether a person engages mainly in anticipatory or correctional techniques when adjusting actual levels of
activation. That is, active people anticipate events and prepare
themselves for them, whereas passive people let events occur
and then correct if discrepancies emerge. Again, in athletics and
physical activity we can sense that this distinction has important
implications. Some athletes have a real need for leadership

---

*The term *trait* refers to habitual rather than motivational behavior.

and/or independence, whereas others are constantly avoiding responsibility in any shape or form. People who participate in sport through a basic desire to control not only themselves but also their environment and other people will become *instantly* negative if overcontrolled either by their coaches or through institutionalization.

The child (or adult) who is enthusiastic and keen about participating in physical activity and sport is best exemplified by Maddi's characterization of the *high-activation* person with active and *external* traits. Such a person is always on the go, and is energetic and voracious in his appetites. He attacks the physical and social worlds in a concrete, tangible way and will tend to be quite realistic. He will have a high need for intensity, especially in terms of the action, tumult, and excitement that competitive sport can provide. He is straightforward and commits himself enthusiastically in goal-directed actions. He is people- and object- rather than self-oriented. If he has a high need for meaningfulness, he is usually caught up in causes and social problems. A high need for variety is characterized by adventurousness and curiosity. Although such a characterization of people involved in physical activity and sport is particularly attractive the reader is naturally cautioned that *all* of Maddi's personality types are probably involved in sport, not just *high-activation-external-active* people.

CHAPTER 8

THE UNDERLYING MOTIVATIONAL DIMENSIONS OF SPORT

Preface

Understanding and gaining insight into the manner in which the concept of motivation functions in competitive athletics is probably of more interest (and value) to the student of sport and physical activity than any other single element. The all-pervasive influence of individual and group motivation on athletic and motor performance has long been an interesting, but highly speculative topic of discussion for many years. Analysis, however, of the structure and functioning of motivational processes in sport, games and play has been lacking. The coherence, continuity, and relevance of professional thought has been based almost entirely on subjective, individual speculation. Only in the odd, carefully considered circumstance has there been any analytical thought supported by empirical data. Though a considerable amount of literature exists on motivation, most or all of it does not concern itself even indirectly with athletics. The purpose of this section, then, is to attempt a juxtaposition of the information contained in motivational theory to professional intuitive thought on the subject of motivation in athletics and physical activity. Various theoretical positions on motivation will, therefore, be examined in the light of two objectives: what relevance each theory has for improving our understanding of motivation, and, what practical implications each theory has for providing insight into actual athletic behavior.

INTRODUCTION

The study of human motivation is the study of human action and its determinants. It is concerned with the analysis of those factors which initiate individual action and then direct it toward a particular end or goal. Its scope is the explanation and analysis of why certain behavior is initially selected by the person, why it varies in intensity, and why it persists. It is a search for *why* man behaves the way he does. In this context, then, one can appreciate that fully one-third of all psychological literature is either directly or indirectly related to the topic of motivation. Contained in this vast amount of literature is information relevant to the nature and role of motivation in athletics and physical activity. It is the intent of this section to delve into this storehouse and abstract that information which will provide us with insight and understanding into the athlete and his performance.

Of initial interest is the question, why do people wish to participate in athletics and physical activity in the first place? And once there, why do they continue to pursue athletic excellence or perfection? Various reasons, deeply rooted in the physical, psychological, and sociological structure of each individual must be present in order to explain why one (especially the superior athlete) is prepared to subject himself to the brutal rigors of training and the continuous boredom of practice so that he can suffer the mental anguish and further punishment of his body in formal competition. Though the questions are complex, the answers can possibly be reduced to two broad but basically opposed positions: that the individual athlete persists because he *has* to (that there is an urgent need or compulsion within him to participate) or that he persists because he *wants* to (that he voluntarily chooses to participate in order to minimize certain losses to his psyche, while at the same time maximizing certain gains important to him). Most of our insights into athletic behavior will probably be a mixture of the two positions.

Motivation as a defined term has no fixed technical meaning in contemporary psychology. Over the past two hundred years, it has been used in reference to conceptualizations ranging from a conscious feeling of *desire* to acting as a synonym for *drive* in S-R behavior theory and, for the last 70 years, it has been profoundly influenced by Freud's position that the basic determinants of motivated behavior lie in the unconscious. Motivation as a term, then, has to be interpreted in very broad general terms, *e.g.*, as an arousal to action. The term is probably best used in reference to *the tendency for the direction and selectivity of behavior to be controlled by its connections to consequences, and the tendency of this behavior to persist until a goal is achieved.* In addition to referencing motivation in these terms (the selection, intensity, and persistence of behavior), it should also be considered with respect to its determinants, and the way in which they influence the purposive characteristics of man's actions. Birch and Veroff (1966) neatly categorize these determinants of goal-directed behavior into four broad sources of influence: 1) *availability,* or the extent to which a particular situation makes available a certain kind of behavior; 2) *expectancy,* or the anticipation that engaging in a particular action will lead to a particular goal; 3) *incentive*, the specific consequences that are attached to particular courses of action; and 4) *motive*, the strength of repulsion or attraction to a general class of consequences. These authors state, briefly, that within any one person, at any given moment in time, there exist a number of tendencies toward relatively independent courses of action, and that when a person is *motivated to do something*, it is the result of the strongest of these competing tendencies winning out. So, when a boy turns out for the football team or doesn't show up for basketball practice one day, he is doing so because the tendency to engage in those courses of action won out over other competing tendencies. These courses of action were influenced by the particular situations (availability), what he expected to derive from these courses of action (expectancy), the various incentive values he attached to these courses of action (incentive), and his general basic motives underlying these courses of action (motive). Such referencing of behavior permits us to look at many different isolated actions without losing sight of the basic communality of motivation. Within such a framework, several questions are immediately self-evident and seem to have importance.

First, why do people participate in exercise and sport? Is there some inherent need in the human organism that can only be satisfied by activity or athletic competition? Or is such participation caused by the external pressures of a society which views sport as a proving ground for individual achievement? Or are there specific motives whose direct expression lies only in athletics? Or, possibly, can the partial gratification of needs and interests common to everyday living best be achieved in the playing of various sports? And, in conjunction with the above queries, is it pertinent to ask why some individuals participate in only competitive athletics? What is it that causes people to risk physical injury and bodily harm, to engage in strenuous training over long periods of time, and to suffer the agonies of defeat, when the general attitudes prevailing in our society are almost directly antithetical? If we are indeed becoming a nation of spectators, why are there still individuals prepared to pay the price of participating? Are the rewards really that great? Why do some children pursue athletic excellence with a devotion that drives their parents to despair and distraction? Why is it that, when interviewed, professional athletes who supposedly are concerned with only their financial gain invariably say that when playing ceases to be fun they will quit, or that they play because they enjoy the fundamental exhilaration of the game? And what is it about particular sports that attract different kinds of people? Why do some people select one sport, but not another? Why do some athletes play with an intensity that surpasses even animal ferocity, while others play it quite cool? And why do some athletes continue to play their sport almost up until the day they die? What is it in sport, or in man, that causes such intense and persistent devotion?

A second order of questioning prevails along the general line of attempting to explain why some individuals are *better* than others. Usually, this context deals in reverse with the question of motivation, in that when a person exhibits superiority over another in some sport, and it is accepted that they are relatively equal in physical assets and skill, then it is inferred that the first person was "more motivated" than the other. And if this is true, and we can identify, measure, and control this higher degree of motivation, can we, in the end, manipulate it both extrinsically and intrinsically? Or is the particular above outcome simply the cause of the two athletes being *differently* motivated? Do motivational characteristics differentiate outstanding athletes from others, winners from losers, "clutch" players from "front-runners"? What is it in some athletes that *drives* them to be better than all others? What pressures exist, both internal and external, that cause an individual not to be satisfied until he is a champion? In general, then, why, after electing to participate, do some people feel they have to perform better than other people?

Peripheral information arising out of research in psychology, sociology, and physical education can provide us with some guidelines along which we can speculate on these questions. It is necessary, however, to keep in mind that motivation is a multidimensional consideration. No one general theory incorporates a complete explanation of motivation. Thus, it is necessary to view a number of theories and conceptualizations if we are to shed any light on the questions of motivation in sport.

CONSCIOUS VOLITION

William James (1890), the foremost pioneer of introspective psychology in the late Nineteenth Century, was probably the person most responsible for the transition from a "commonsense" view of motivation to the careful and extensive psychological analysis that exists today. His view that mental states are reflected in conscious actions which are deliberate and selective predated modern thought. His acknowledgment and introduction of concepts such as instinct, habit, and response-produced stimuli set the foundation for later theorizing, and his attempt to explain consciousness as a *steering* mechanism for a complex, nonself-regulatory nervous system was a hypothesis that would be constantly tested down through the years.

James' conceptual view suggested a continuity between the blind reflexiveness of one's *instincts,* the automatic character of *habit,* and the selectiveness of *conscious volition.* That is, people behave according to a combination of habitual patterns that are common to them as individuals and the basic or inherent instincts peculiar to them as a species. This combination of influences is then deliberated upon by the consciousness of the person, and a selection of behavior between alternative goals is made. For James, *instinct* was a person's disposition for acting without regard for the results of his actions and without any previous experience upon which to base his actions. Instinctive tendencies were reflexive and were concerned essentially with self-preservation. *Habit,* on the other hand, he defined as the tendency to act in a certain manner simply because one had acted in that manner in similar previous situations. Habit was a pattern or sequence of actions that "rattled off" automatically when given the initial impetus of volition. *Consciousness* was seen as a selecting agency which was constantly making action choices dependent upon the interests and desires of the consciousness paramount at that moment.

Of particular interest was James' view of pursued pleasure and the pleasure of achievement (Atkinson, 1964). Though probably a forerunner of later "functional pleasure" positions in the psychology of play, James felt that the pleasure of achievement may itself become a pursued pleasure. He observed that in a football game the impulsive excitement of getting the ball into the goal, in most cases, seemed to override the actual success of the performance. That the various situational conditions of the contest arouse one's instincts in a cumulative manner, resulting in pleasure far beyond the mere scoring of a goal. This view strongly orients toward the concept of instinctual pleasure advocated by Freud.

INSTINCTUAL ENERGY

The first major critical revision of conscious volition and hedonism was developed by Sigmund Freud (1943) in the early part of the Twentieth Century, when he recognized that many unconscious psychological processes influence and direct man's actions and behavior. Freud felt that human behavior could be analyzed according to a *pleasure principle,* pleasure now including unconscious satisfaction. He postulated three basic instinctual forces: the life instinct, the sexual instinct, and the death instinct. He ascribed the source of the life instinct to that aspect of a person's metabolism that entails growth, its energy to the tension generated by hunger, thirst, sex, etc., and its aim to the reduction of this tension through food, water, and mate gratification. The life instinct had as its major function survival of the organism. Freud's *sexual instinct* was thought to be present at birth and was considered to pass through a series of psychosexual development stages before reaching maturity in adulthood. A fixation (a lasting attachment) at any of these stages resulted in an adult type or character having the defense and trait characteristics of that particular infant or childhood stage. Each stage represented a period of maximum pleasure through gratification from stimulation of various bodily regions. It was out of this schema that Freud developed the pleasure principle, around which all behavior is centered — the person seeks pleasure which is defined as the reduction of libidinal tension (tension caused by basic primitive urges) through gratification of a drive or instinct. The pure pursuit of pleasure, selfish instinctual gratification, sooner or later, however, has to come into conflict with the similar pursuits of other people. Thus, living in a society of people, it is necessary to modify one's instinctual gratifications. The pleasure-seeking individual is therefore constantly faced with frustration, threats, and punishment unless he can adapt his life to the real world (he must, of necessity, live according to a reality principle).* Freud's third basic instinct, the death instinct, formulated in the later years of his life, was an attempt to explain death which occurs as a result of decision making, *viz.*, murder, war, genocide and suicide. In direct antagonism to the life instinct, the death instinct was thought to have as its aim the biological death of the person and supposedly was thought to also have its source in the biological metabolism of the individual.

As Cofer and Johnson (1960) mention, it is highly unlikely that sports and exercise reflect the direct expression of motives in a psychoanalytic sense. Rather, the impetus to physical activity and athletic participation probably comes from inherent drives within the person that are more socially oriented. However, one aspect of Freudian theory, at this point, which does seem to have direct relevance is the psychological relevance of sports during adolescence.

Perhaps the most important task facing the young adolescent

---

*A thorough discussion of Freudian personality dynamics can be found in Chapter 6, where an attempt is made to clarify the conflict that occurs between the pleasure and reality principles.

is the seeking for and achieving of a stable and appropriate sense of personal identity. Success is dependent upon how well he has met the challenges of other adolescent problems. The principal problem of this stage of development is the achievement of ego mastery over intensified sexual and aggressive drives, so that they can be controlled without being repressed. Equally important is the achieving of independence from the family unit and the formation of a capacity to meet the basic social and sexual needs of adult life. Since sports are the most important aspect of play during this period, it would appear that they provide many opportunities for satisfying many of the developmental needs of the youngster. The active pursuit of competitive sports by adolescents seems to correlate with increasing need for a sense of identity compatible with impending sexual maturation, and to discover acceptable outlets for the high drive energy which grows in intensity during puberty. The typical adolescent faces the problems of two very powerful drives, sexual and aggressive, the first requiring integration into his life pattern, the second requiring ego mastery. Both are important in terms of their social consequences, and it is in sport that the aggressive drive is usually redirected. Preoccupation with the goals of adult fulfillment evoke fantasies of competition in young children, and if the boy wants to succeed then he must contend with the efforts of all other boys and men. Thus, on the basis of individual desires, there is a need to become outstanding and to excel in whatever is accepted as being important in the competition for love and approval. Sports and games permit practice in the acceptable and controlled release of sexual and aggressive strivings in purely symbolic form. Sport provides an arena for the boy's efforts to grow up and hold his own in important areas of endeavor.

INSTINCT

A basic sporting belief is that outstanding athletes act or behave instinctively in various situations. It is usually held that various instincts, such as the competitive and aggressive instincts, are prime factors in influencing successful performance, and that outstanding athletes tend to possess such attributes. These viewpoints, coupled with the historical importance of the concept of instinct in the formation of modern motivational theory, make instinct of central importance.

As previously mentioned, James (1890) defined *instinct* by stating that it is the faculty for acting in a certain way uninfluenced by previous education and without foresight as to what the outcome of the action may be. This clearly differentiates it from *habit*, which is the tendency for a person to act in a certain way because he has acted in that way before. Instinctive tendencies thus become reflexive actions. One acts without any conscious thought, deliberation, or recall. The central aspect of instinct thus becomes one of blind impulsiveness and, as such, has interesting connotations for explaining anger and violence in sport. Explanations of instinctive behavior, however, suffer one important flaw: when a person acts in a certain manner once (*e.g.*, losing his temper during a game), it can be termed instinctive; but if he behaves the same way on a subsequent similar occasion, is it now termed a habitual action? It was this contradiction that caused early 20th Century psychologists to downgrade the importance of instinct in psychological behavior. Darwin commented on this difficulty in distinguishing between habits built up by association and inherited habits. He felt that habits, innate or learned, are adaptive in function, that is, that they contribute to survival. Mcdougall (1908) took this controversy one step farther by stating that all habits arise out of instincts, thus making all behavior basically instinctual.

However, probably the most influential view on instinct was that of Freud's. His view stemmed from the belief that instincts were the propelling forces of personality. In this sense, instinct is seen as a *psychological representation* of inner physiological stimulation. The internal deprivation is called a *need*, its psychological template a *wish*. The wish acts as a motive for behavior: a person wants to do something and he uses this desire as a motive for action. So instincts not only drive behavior and determine its intensity but also influence the selectivity of behavior. In other words, an instinct exercises selective control over a person's behavior by contributing to one's sensitivity for specific kinds of stimulation. For example, a hungry person is more sensitive to various food stimuli—or an athlete who is aggressively or competitively aroused will be more likely to respond to situation stimuli that appear in crucial aggressive or competitive instances in sport. Freud felt that the sum total of all instincts provided the psychic energy in individual motivation.

Instincts, then, if viewed as *persistent internal stimuli* (*i.e.*, as needs), possess four characteristics (Hall and Lindzey, 1970): they have a *source*, an *aim*, an *object*, and an *impetus*. The source is already defined as internal deprivation, a need. The aim is satisfaction of this need—removal of the internal stimulation. The object refers to the thing one must obtain to satisfy the need (in hunger the object is food) and also to the behavior of the person in obtaining the object. Such behavior is usually referred to as *instrumental activity, i.e.,* goal-directed behavior. The impetus of an instinct is its force or strength; it is determined by the intensity of the internal need. This general viewpoint is construed as belonging to a *tension-reduction* model of motivated behavior. The behavior of an individual is therefore activated by an internal deprivation and continues until it is satisfied, thereby reducing the tension caused by the internal irritation. The need for physical activity is usually explained in these terms. The child has within him a strong need for movement which can only be satisfied or removed by vigorous activity. Such a viewpoint places physical activity into the realm of instinct.

Instinctive behavior on the part of athletes during the heat of a game thus becomes very difficult to explain. It depends to a large extent on the particular behavior manifested. If it is a cool, calculated, coordinated act — such as a Mickey Mantle turning at the crack of the bat to run with his back to the infield to the fence — then we are probably talking about an instinct that has become a learned habitual pattern. On the other hand, if it is an explosive, emotional act of anger — where two linemen in a football game suddenly start trading punches — then we are probably dealing with instinctive behavior: the reduction or releasing of tension built up by frustration during the game. No simple explanation is possible.

DRIVE

Drive is normally considered as a contruct concerned with the *impetus to action* or as the *activator of behavior.* Though its initial popularity as a term was originated by R. S. Woodworth (1918), in his book *Dynamic Psychology,* the most intensive use and analysis of the term was developed by Clark L. Hull (1943), in his book *Principles of Behavior.* It was through Woodworth's writings that the concept of instinct was largely replaced by that of drive, and it was Woodworth who made the distinction between the problem of mechanism — how one does something — and the problem of drive — what induces one to do it. Drive, then, is seen as a psychological mechanism directed toward consumatory reactions, that is, reactions which bring immediate and direct value or satisfaction to the individual — such as eating, drinking or scoring a goal. When an athlete does score a goal, or make a basket, he is actually completing a long line of behavioral sequences which were "driving" him to that end.

Motivation, for Hull, was the "striving for goals," and drive was a central concept in his thinking. He felt that the basic principles of learning could explain the growth of habit strength and that this, plus a knowledge of what stimuli are present at any one time, would, in turn, explain the motivated or purposive pursuit of goals. Two variables, habit (sHr) and drive (D), were of central importance to his theory of motivation, the former taking account of learning, the latter dealing with the energy of action. Though he conceived of learning habits as strengthening the connection between stimulus and response, he felt that, for action to occur, some energizing element was necessary—this he labelled *drive*. Drive, then, was the propelling agent, the "vehicle" of action. He proposed that *habit* increases in strength as a function of the number of times that stimulus and response are associated and as a function of the magnitude and delay of rewards connected to the response. *Drive* is derived from internal biological deprivations and intense stimulation. Since 1943, however, considerable modification of Hull's formula has occurred, with the most important addition being (K), an intervening variable referring to *incentive motivation* (Birch and Veroff 1966). His theory thus indicates that two energizing sources, drive and incentive, act on habit to produce action.

In Hullian terms then, *drive* is assumed to arise out of internal biological imbalances, such as deprivations or noxious stimulus events (hunger, thirst, pain, discomfort, etc.), and is postulated to act as an energizer of all habits. Also important in this context is that drive was hypothesized to multiply the strength of all habits as well. For example, all things being equal, if you are achievement oriented in athletic situations that are devoid of pressure (such as a touch football game), then in situations which have real importance attached to them (such as the game to decide the league championship), you will be very strongly achievement oriented. Raising the drive level multiplies all habit strengths. Also, the higher the drive, the greater the persistence of an activity, since the tendency is stronger; this makes it more difficult for competing tendencies to win out. For example, if a boy has an extremely high need for achievement, and realizes athletics are his only real vehicle to attain recognition of his achievement, then it is highly doubtful that he will select alternate courses of action when faced with a choice.

Drives can be either primary or secondary. Primary drives, such as hunger, thirst, and sex, are deprivation states, brought about by withholding some kind of stimulus, such as food, and reduced by providing the organism with the stimulus. Noxious stimulations, such as pain, also act as primary drives. Dollard and Miller (1950), in fact, postulate that any internal or external stimulus, if intense enough, evokes a drive and impels action.

Secondary drives are slightly more complex. A simple paradigm can be used in explanation. A bell ringing initially elicits none of the behavior usually associated with an applied electric shock. However, after repeated presentations of the bell with the shock, the bell achieves the capacity to elicit a number of internal responses associated with pain, similar to those originally elicited by the electric shock—a conditioned response (CR) has been learned or, in experimental language, acquired. In the Hullian system learning has taken place—an associative connection between the conditioned stimulus (the bell) and the response (pain) has been established and is represented by the theoretical concept of *habit*. Once the classically conditioned response is established, the bell *alone* not only elicits internal responses associated with pain but also causes the rest of the behavioral sequence, that is, pain and withdrawal, which were originally only associated with electric shock. This internal pattern of stimulation, in combination with the bell, now acts as a cue to elicit overt behavior. Such behavior is now energized by the drive properties of this internal pattern of stimulation. Since this drive is now elicited by a *learned* response to a previously neutral stimulus, it is known as an acquired or *secondary* drive. In this particular example, this classically conditioned sequence elicited by the bell is distinguished by Dollard and Miller as *anxiety* or *fear*. Thus, fear is a learned response *and* an acquired or secondary drive.

The effect of drives on human behavior thus becomes exceedingly complex by the large number of acquired or secondary drives that make their appearance in a person's life. In fact, in our modern society, secondary drive stimulation, though acquired on the basis of primary drives, essentially replaces primary drives. Acquired drives, such as anxiety, achievement, power, impel most of our behavior. The same can be said for *reinforcement*. Most of the reinforcements we receive in ordinary life are not primary rewards but originally neutral events that have acquired reward value by being consistently associated with primary reinforcement. Cheering of a crowd, status with the group, public recognition—all secondary rewards—serve to very definitely reinforce certain behaviors in the athlete. If closely associated with primary reinforcement, such as a feeling of satisfaction from accomplishment, the drive becomes a strong force in the individual's life.

PSYCHOLOGICAL HEDONISM

Arising from the social philosophizing of the Eighteenth and Nineteenth Centuries, in which the concept of individual liberty was paramount, was the rational hypothesis of *psychological hedonism*. This principle maintained that a person maximizes his gains and minimizes his losses: that a person, in any point of time, is usually confronted with a set of choices which he analyzes in order to decide which course of action does most to maximize pleasure while at the same time minimizes pain, with the decision being the one that is likely to yield the best return. Though elaborate theories were postulated to stress either maximization or minimization, the common thread running through all these viewpoints was that man's actions were conscious and deliberate—that he was a rational animal capable of choosing from a set of alternatives. This was the first real departure from the general view that human action was predominantly instinctual.

The significance of psychological hedonism, that is, that a person chooses those courses of action which are pleasurable to him, is a principle fundamental to physical activity and sport— especially today, when people are doing what they *want* to do rather than what they are *supposed* to do. People are choosing only those activities that are attractive to them in some manner and are disregarding those that are unattractive. When a boy chooses to play tennis rather than golf, or basketball rather than football, then he is, in essence, making a choice in order to maximize some psychological gain which he feels will result for him. The choice is a conscious and deliberate attempt to maximize his pleasure from sport and to minimize its unattractive aspects. Young people, therefore, who are voluntarily participating in large sports programs should be given the opportunity to choose those activities which will maximize for them the particular gains they are seeking. For example, if we sense that a boy is playing football in order to increase his self-confidence, then we err seriously if, for some external reason, we criticize or negate his attempts to build up confidence in himself, *regardless* of the outcome of the game. A coach must be prepared to help each boy maximize whatever gains he is seeking while, at the same time, helping him to minimize whatever losses he might accrue. No one will persist in an activity distasteful or unpleasurable for him. If the individual is allowed to proceed in maximizing a particular gain which has specific attractiveness for him, then he will be fundamentally motivated to continue in that activity.

Winning in sport can clearly be seen in the context of psychological hedonism. Simply stated, winning is more fun than losing. If not because of the tremendous reinforcement of our society toward winning, then simply because man is a competitive animal. Winning becomes an effort to maximize pleasure.

The psychological pain accompanying losing, usually in the form of external disapproval, derision or disgust, is such that a deliberate, intensive effort is made to avoid it. Some boys may *not* participate in sport simply as a way of avoiding the losses or pain which they know accompanies failure. They are, in a sense, minimizing losses by not playing.

NEEDS

Constant reference in the psychological literature to the term *need* necessitates at least brief introduction to the concept. Although many theorists have discoursed at length on the term, probably the most comprehensive analysis in a modern perspective is by Henry Murray (1938), who states:

> ... a need is a construct (a convenient fiction or hypothetical concept) which stands for a force ... in the brain region, a force which organizes perception, apperception, intellection, conation, and action in such a way as to transform in a certain direction an existing, unsatisfying situation. A need is sometimes provoked directly by internal processes of a certain kind ... but, more frequently (when in a state of readiness), by the occurrence of one of a few commonly effective press (environmental forces).

Thus, need is connected to underlying physiological processes in the brain; it is conceived of as being aroused by both internal deprivations and external environmental forces — that the person's activity caused by the arousal of a need continues until the situation has been altered so as to reduce the need. Most needs are accompanied by emotions and feelings, and are usually associated with instrumental or goal-directed behavior designed to produce the particular goal and reduce the need.

Murray states that a particular need can be said to exist: 1) when the end result of a person's behavior can be observed; 2) when a particular pattern of behavior can be observed; 3) when the person selectively attends to or responds to a particular class of stimulus objects; 4) when a particular emotion or feeling surfaces; and 5) when satisfaction or disappointment is expressed when a particular end is reached. For example, a need for affiliation usually involves the following sequence of events (Maddi, 1968): the inner state of a person sometimes involves loneliness and is thus perceived by him: the person must then have as a goal, a state of warm friendly interaction with other people; his subsequent activity then shows a consistent pattern of behavior leading to closer contact with people; and, finally, if certain effects do result from his actions toward closer contact with people, they have to be satisfying to him for them to continue.

Utilizing the above criteria, plus the subjective reports of people dealing with feelings, intentions, and goals, Murray originally formulated a list of some twenty needs. The needs listed were for abasement, achievement, affiliation, aggression, autonomy, counteraction, defendance, deference, dominance, exhibition, harm-avoidance, infra-avoidance, nurturance, order, play, rejection, sentience, sex, succorance, and understanding.*
In order to distinguish between these needs, five general categories are formulated for the reader. First are primary versus secondary needs; primary needs deal with organic events and refer to internal physical satisfactions such as needs for water, food and sex, whereas secondary needs, presumably derived from primary needs, are *psychogenic* and are characterized by a complete lack of connection to any internal organic processes—such are the needs for achievement, affiliation, recognition, dominance, exhibition, etc. Second is the differentiation between *overt* needs and *covert* needs: overt needs (or manifest needs) are those needs that are allowed to surface, that are permitted direct and immediate expression; covert (or latent) needs are those that are generally repressed, hidden, or blocked beneath the level of consciousness. That is, needs which have trouble being socially acceptable, or needs that operate in the context of dreams and fantasy, that cannot be given free expression, are labeled covert needs. Third, there is the distinction between *focal* and *diffuse* needs: focal needs are those directly and closely linked to only a limited and particular class of objects (*e.g.*, the need for athletic success); whereas, a diffuse need is so generalized as to be applicable in any broad environmental setting (*e.g.*, the need for achievement). Fourth, there are *proactive* and *reactive* needs: a proactive need is one generated from within the individual, the result of something dynamic occurring inside the person; whereas, a reactive need is one activated by some external environmental event or object. Fifth is the differentiation between *process activity, modal* needs, and *effect* needs: effect needs are simply those needs which lead to some desired state or goal; whereas, process activity and modal needs are concerned with tendencies to perform certain activities just for the sake of performing them (the need for play is a good example of the latter). Modal needs also involve the desire to do something with a specific degree of excellence or quality (such as the need to perform a gymnastic stunt correctly).

Though Murray accepted the fact that a hierarchy of needs

*All illustrative list of these twenty needs and their definitions can be found on pp. 176–177 in Hall and Lindzey (1970).

probably exists (with certain tendencies taking precedence over others), he made sure to point out that these needs do not operate in complete isolation to each other, nor do they operate independently. He also emphasized the importance of effective or significant determinants of behavior in the external environment of the individual (*i.e.,* Murray's concept of "press"). He felt that a "press" is a property or attribute of an environmental object or person which facilitates or impedes the efforts of an individual to reach his goal. For example, it is far harder for an athlete who has a high need for aggression to satisfy this need in a golf match than it is in a football game. The "press" in one situation is far different than in the other.

Finally, Murray conceived of the individual as being launched into action by a complex set of motives or needs, and that when a need is aroused, the individual is in a constant state of tension until it is satisfied (straight tension reduction theorizing). The individual eventually learns to attend to objects and perform acts that he has found in the past to be associated with such tension reduction. Murray even went so far as to note that some people not only learn behavior aimed at tension reduction but also engage in acts which lead to the development of tension, so that they can subsequently enjoy the reduction associated with them. This is a direct forerunner of Fiske and Maddi's position on "tension seekers" (Maddi 1968), a concept with considerable attractiveness in athletic participation and which is discussed in the previous chapter.

MOTIVE

Broadly interpreted, *motivation* can refer to the general level of arousal to action in an individual. The *motives* that an individual possesses, then, become the specific conditions attached to particular courses of action and their consequences that result from this arousal. Motives are the latent, relatively stable dispositions a person has toward certain classes or groups of consequences. In this sense, a motive is a personality characteristic involving a persistent or constant desire to either approach or avoid a particular course of action. For example, the motive for achievement is usually described as a latent personality characteristic involved in the intense and persistent desire to achieve in competitive situations. The motive a person has for something, then, is the tendency within him either *to do* that something or *not to do* it. A tendency is a psychological entity that determines a person's thoughts, feelings, and actions directed toward goals and/or certain kinds of behavior. A *motive,* then, can be defined as a latent, relatively stable personality characteristic which causes a person to be either attracted or repulsed by the consequences of particular courses of action; it is a tendency within the person directing his thoughts, feelings, and actions toward the service of goals or functions.

Consequently, a *drive* can be considered to be the initiator of some action in order to satisfy a *need,* with the *motive* determining the strength of attraction or unattraction to the consequences of that general action. Athletes who have needs for achievement, then, not only exhibit high drive for success in achievement settings but also develop strong motives for achievement. The intense striving for achievement becomes part of their personality makeup, just as it does in successful businessmen, artists, and scientists.

INCENTIVE

Incentive is a concept which Birch and Veroff (1966) define as the character of a goal-activity, which in turn is the reason for goal-directed activity. That is, the consequences of particular actions have incentive value to the individual. This causes the individual to indicate, through his behavior, the degree of attractiveness or unattractiveness that these consequences have for him. If he consistently approaches or consistently avoids specific consequences, then they are considered to have either positive or negative incentive value for him. The incentive value of a consequence is an important determinant of the strength of a goal-directed action. For example, the consequence of winning in athletics usually has high positive incentive value, and strongly affects the desire of an individual to participate — on the other hand, if the anticipated outcome is losing, then the consequence has negative incentive value and the person will tend *not* to participate. Most situations in sports and athletics possess these expectancies for either positive or negative outcomes, and there is no doubt that they cause conflicts in the individual as to whether he should participate or not.

Though it is difficult to attain accurate *absolute* measures of the incentive value of certain objects or various outcomes, it is possible to detect relative differences in incentive value between events. Winning in a championship game will have more positive incentive value to a participant than winning in an exhibition game; making the varsity team will be more attractive to the aspirant than making the second team. Achievement, success, excellence, prestige, recognition, and power are all goals thought to have positive incentive value in sports. Physical injury, pain, social isolation, inadequate reward, and fear of failure can be considered as events having negative incentive value. Whatever their sources, consequences with positive incentive value contribute to the tendency to do something; negative incentive value consequences contribute to the tendency *not* to do something.

Overview

Several basic psychological principles which underlie motivation theory have been presented in this chapter. The selection of these principles was deliberately oriented toward providing the reader with concepts relevant to the specific motivation systems presented in the next few chapters. It was also the purpose of this chapter to present those aspects of motivation which seem to have particular significance for understanding the motivational behavior of people participating in physical activity and sport.

For example, we must not make the mistake in physical education and sport of assuming that people participate solely because of some unknown, unconscious, instinctual need. Rather, it is important for one to realize that the conscious deliberation, or free will of the person reinforced or initiated by some general, secondary drive is probably closer to the answer. Motivation thus becomes a combination of both conscious and unconscious instincts, needs, and drives. Maslow (1970) illustrates the importance of this view when he states that man must be considered as an integrated, organized whole, not as a collection of parts working independently of each other. People choose to do certain things and do them for a multitude of simultaneously conflicting and congruent reasons. The same reasoning naturally holds true for sport — very rarely can we trace a particular action to a single origin or cause. A grasp, however, of concepts such as needs, drives, and motives must certainly enable us to better understand the complexities of the multiple motivations that exist in man. If, as Maslow (1970) states, instinct can best be defined as a motivational unit with its root source in heredity, then we must be prepared to accept the possibility that, in man, instincts gradually become submerged in the common everyday actions of people by a variety of individually and culturally determined drives, needs, and motives. We will see, however, that some behavior in sport seems to have no basis for explanation other than instincts rooted in our heredity. Ardrey (1966), for example, thoroughly discusses aggression in instinctual terms.

An attempt will be made in subsequent chapters to present motivation in sports as a combination of a series of general motive-incentive systems which, though rooted in traditional or historical instinctual patterns, are both individually and culturally determined. An attempt will also be made to clarify a distinction between need, habit, and motive; that is, though the terminology refers to "motive" systems, an intuitive association with basic "need" systems is evident.

The aforegoing chapter, then, dealing with the analyses of conscious volition, instinctual energy, needs, drives and motives is oriented toward considering man as a whole, not as specific parts of a larger entity. The objective was, and is, the understanding of behavior, not its dissection. When a person chooses to play a certain sport, his decision is the result of many psychological processes, not just one or two. Thus, the attempt made in this chapter was to show that motivated behavior is the *sum total* of instincts and needs, motives and drives, conscious and unconscious forces, and a function of what one expects to gain from participation in sport.

ACHIEVEMENT IN SPORT

Preface

Preface

A theory which seems to have considerable intuitive attractiveness and relevance when attempting to explain motivational factors in athletics and physical activity is the concept of need for achievement or achievement motivation. The reason for this viewpoint is simply that a great deal of emphasis in sport is placed upon competing against some standard of excellence, and this is the exact focus of achievement motivation theory. Whether the standard of excellence is internalized (*i.e.,* a person's personal level of aspiration) or whether it is external (*i.e.,* a generalized goal set by one's culture or simply the outcome of competing against other people) is unimportant when one realizes that constantly attempting to achieve certain goals in life is a fundamental aspect of human life. In a society which places high value on success, in athletics, where intense emphasis is placed upon winning, and in ordinary motor performance, where attaining a higher level of proficiency is desirable, the importance of the basic need for achievement is quite obvious. With these connotations in mind, it would appear an analysis of achievement and its relation to physical activity and sport should be undertaken.

INTRODUCTION

The theory of achievement motivation, developed by Mc-Clelland, Atkinson and associates (1953), attempts to determine the direction, intensity, and persistence of behavior in a specific and limited context—that is, behavior or performance in a pure achievement setting. The theory is intended to be applicable *only* when the person knows this performance will be evaluated (by himself or by others) in terms of some criteria or standard of excellence, and that the outcome of his performance will be either favorable (success) or unfavorable (failure). This is a theory concerned with *achievement-oriented* performance (Atkinson, 1964) and, though it has historical derivations in the works of Hull, Tolman, Lewin, and Murray, most of the formulations have arisen out of research dealing with the need for achievement, anxiety in test situations, and level of aspiration. The theory is well-substantiated by empirical evidence related to achievement oriented behavior.

As mentioned already, achievement motivation deals generally with the need for competition with a standard of excellence accompanied by (and supposedly welcomed) the realization that the consequences will either be success or failure. Several factors are conceptualized as influencing such a psychological state in the individual. Achievement-oriented behavior seems to have a definite correlation with how much pleasure children derive from success in achievement activities, and achievement-oriented behavior also seems to be inversely related to anxiety in achievement settings. Atkinson (1964) cites research studies by Winterbottom (1958) and Raphelson (1957), which suggested first, that children high in need achievement usually experience more pleasure in success than those low in need achievement, and, second, that need achievement scores were negatively correlated with a "physiological symptom of anxiety," as indicated by performance on Sarason's Test Anxiety Questionnaire (1952). Two situational variables were also hypothesized as helping to account for the above relationships between performance, anxiety, and need for achievement. First was the *expectancy* of success and second was the *incentive* value of that success to the performer. In these terms, it was emphasized by McClelland (1961) that, for achievement motivation to be present, the person must be conscious of being responsible for the outcome of his actions, that he must know immediately whether he has succeeded or failed, and that some risk or probability as to the outcome must be present. The analogy to athletic competition is almost perfect: the typical athlete is usually fully conscious of the fact that he alone is responsible for how well he performs, he knows immediately (through his own perceptions and the feedback from teammates and spectators) whether he has failed or succeeded in his particular endeavor, and there is always present in sports settings an element of risk as to the outcome of his performance. The major contaminating factor of this analogy is that, for some people, sports competitions may not be *pure* achievement settings — the individual may be largely motivated by reasons other than achievement. However, with the above in mind, it is then assumed that, as a result of the person's past experience in settings or situations similar or identical to the one that now confronts him, his expectancy of success (or failure) will be very strong, moderate, or weak. (It is natural to assume, for example, that outstanding athletes have strong expectancies of success in most of their athletic confrontations.) This strongly influences how achievement-motivated he will be. The second influence on his level of achievement motivation is the incentive value attached (by him) to the outcome of his performance. If, on the basis of his past experience, he has established how important certain kinds of success are to him, then his pride of accomplishment will strongly affect the incentive value he attaches to certain successes. Thus, a difficult goal would seem to have more incentive value to a person with a high pride of accomplishment than would an easy one. This, in turn, affects his motive to achieve, which, in turn, affects his performance. It is often said in athletics that an athlete must have great pride in his ability to do well if he is to be highly motivated—in an achievement context this is probably quite true. This speculation leads directly to the necessity for some explanation of the achievement motive.

APPROACH AND AVOIDANCE MOTIVES FOR ACHIEVEMENT

McClelland (1951) defines *motive* as:

> ...a strong affective association, characterized by an anticipatory goal reaction and based on past association of certain cues with pleasure and pain.

Briefly, what McClelland means here is that a person has a motive for something whenever some cue or stimulus arouses in him an anticipation of some imminent change in his psychological state that is going to bring pain or pleasure. A tightness in the throat and a rapidly beating heart just prior to a game, for example, serve as cues that some radical change in events is imminent, and these cues are largely formulated on the basis of past experience. The person's anticipated change in state (that he will do well or poorly) also comes out of past experience with similar or identical situations, and this anticipation contributes to both the content of the motive and its intensity. For the anticipation of a change in state to be properly identified in motive terms, there must be an expectation of either an increase in positive or negative effect. *Motive*, then, is a *state of mind* aroused by some imminent change that serves as a cue—a change in the person's psychological state that is going to be pleasurable or unpleasurable. McClelland makes the assumption that the individual proceeds to act on a motive in such a manner that he successfully achieves pleasure or avoids unpleasantness. If the person acts so as to bring about an anticipated change in pleasure then he is said to be operating on the basis of an *approach motive*. If he acts so as to avoid unpleasantness, then he is operating via an *avoidance motive*. McClelland feels that the content of any motive which the person possesses contains these two aspects. So, if an athlete, for example, has a high motive for achievement, his state of mind immediately prior to most achievement situations is such that he anticipates success and that his success will provide him with pleasurable satisfaction. The desire to achieve then, or the desire to be successful, is thus connected to a pleasurable outcome, and is a function of his past experience in similar situations.

A second focus which McClelland details is the linking up of these two types of motives to a person's need for achievement. He contends that both an approach and an avoidance version of this need must be considered. The *approach version* of the need for achievement (which Atkinson, 1957, refers to as the "hope for success") involves the person's reacting to cues that tell him a competitive situation exists and that the outcome will be successful, and thus pleasurable, by throwing himself actively into the contest. The high need for achievement possessed by most outstanding athletes thus expresses itself both as a need for competition and as a need for success and pleasure. Thus, if a person consistently experiences, or actively seeks, a large number of competitive situations in his career as an athlete because he has high expectations of success with its strong concomitants of pleasure, then there is gradually developed in his personality makeup, a strong *motive* for achievement (more precisely, a strong "approach" motive for achievement). The need for achievement thus underlies the motive for achievement which only becomes consolidated in a person's personality if, in competitive situations, he constantly succeeds and experiences pleasure. The goals of competition, success, and pleasure combine to motivate a person to achieve.* The converse holds just as true in athletics. The *avoidance version* of the need for achievement is best described as *fear of failure*. In this version, an anticipated negative change in state causes the person to avoid his anticipation becoming a reality. If a boy is motivated by a fear of failure, it can be hypothesized that a cue or stimulus exists which tells him a competitive situation is imminent; this brings to mind an expectation of failure and its negative concomitants and causes the boy to resort to avoidance actions. In athletics, for example, the boy who has experienced failure in the past, anticipates more failure in the immediate situation, and thus chooses not to participate at all. In encouraging very young boys and girls to participate in sports, a definite attempt must be made by adults and coaches involved in the program to reduce negative connota-

---

*It is fruitless, then, for coaches and significant adults to expect boys with a past history of failure in sport to bring with them a high motive for achievement. They may have a high *need* for achievement, but their motive to achieve and their expectancy of success are probably quite low.

tions usually associated with failure. If this is not done, those young participants who do not succeed will slowly build up a strong motive for *not* achieving in competitive situations. Such a motive manifests itself in young children in terms of quitting, withdrawal, or rejection of the sport. Overemphasis on winning in age-group sport causes more children to quit than to continue, and in the vast numbers of children who are "turning off" sport there are likely to be countless potential champions whose ability has not yet had a chance to mature.

What effect do these two motives have on the person's general behavior? There is little doubt that the arousal of such motives causes an increase in the amount and intensity of a person's behavior, which subsequently leads to an increased performance output. According to McClelland, motives also serve to orient, direct, and relate various aspects of a person's total behavior. The effect is to organize, or focus, a person's actions. This is easily seen and understood when one observes high achievement motive athletes singlemindedly pursuing their objective of excellence in sports. In addition, motives serve to *sensitize* the person to more and varied cues and stimuli in his environment, especially cues indirectly related to the motive under consideration. An athlete who is strong in achievement motive is more sensitive to advice and information that can help him to succeed than one who is low in motive strength. Such boys are extremely responsive to coaching and aid of any sort simply because the focusing or concentration of their psychological energy toward achievement makes them sensitive to fringe cues. Approach and avoidance motives are, however, affected differently by this focusing and sensitization of behavior. Approach motives lead to an anticipation of how gratifying success will be, which causes an intense concern over how best to organize for successful performance. Avoidance motives lead to a state of mind overly obsessed with all the possible obstacles one has to overcome in achieving a particular goal. Such obsessions express themselves in frustration, dissatisfaction, and anxiety. This kind of behavior is difficult to deal with because it is mainly rooted in the person's imagination and is only slightly concerned with present reality.

McClelland is a consistency theorist.* A consistency view of motivation in life emphasizes the importance of the emotional and mastery experiences a person seeks in interacting with his environment. More specifically, the viewpoint hypothesizes that for each individual there are particular kinds of information and emotional experiences which are best for him alone, and thus he

---

*A thorough analysis of consistency theorizing is covered in Chapter 7, under the concept of Activation.

acts, thinks, and feels in those ways which will provide him with those experiences. Motivational behavior, then, is determined more by feedback from this interaction with the external world than by any inherent or fundamental attributes which the person possesses (Maddi 1968). McClelland sees people as craving small amounts of unpredictability in their lives so as to avoid boredom, while eluding large amounts of unpredictability in order to offset fear or specific threats. People, generally, like a little risk but not too much.

McClelland's view of general motivation, then, is that people tend to *minimize* large discrepancies between what they expect to happen and what *actually* happens, while *maximizing* small discrepancies between their expectations and actual occurrences. These discrepancies produce the emotional state in a person that provides the energy and direction for motivated behavior. Only large discrepancies result in emotional discomfort, frustration, and fear (*e.g.*, a boy wants to make the high school basketball team but cannot because he is too small), whereas, small discrepancies result in pleasure and satisfaction (*e.g.*, a boy wants to shoot par golf and is steadily approaching this goal with each round even though he has not yet shot par). In context then, in order to develop strong motives for achievement in young children, parents and other significant adults must help children to arrange their experiences so that small rather than large discrepancies predominate; that is, demands should be placed on the young athlete or performer as long as they are not too great for him to handle. This will ensure that the child learns and consolidates approach behavior. If the discrepancies are too small, however, the child is likely to become indifferent or bored. Consistency, in this sense, is the degree of relationship between what the child expects of sport and what he gets. If he gets what he wants, whether it be satisfaction, fun, or a sense of achievement, he will continue to participate — if he doesn't he'll quit and turn to something else. Every child naturally wants to become better in his personal athletic performances and is willing to accept small discrepancies between the skill level expected of him and his actual ability; however, if the discrepancy becomes too large (if he clearly recognizes that he is at a competition level too high or too low for him), then he loses interest.

THE THEORETICAL CONTEXT OF
ACHIEVEMENT MOTIVATION

Achievement motivation is directly related to those achievement-oriented performance situations in which the person *knows* that he will be evaluated (either by himself or others), that competition will be present, that there is some risk as to the outcome, that the outcome will be either favorable or unfavorable to him, and that the excellence of his performance will be judged. This basic conceptualization is directly relevant to athletic competition where a zero-sum, finite game situation is invariably present; that is, the player either succeeds or fails, wins or loses. As has been mentioned, the achievement motive can be considered to be a general, but peripheral, personality characteristic involving an intense and persistent desire to achieve in a competitive situation. It is related to one's disposition toward striving for success, toward competition, and toward public evaluation.

This theory postulates that in an achievement situation, such as athletic competition, two kinds of variables operate. First are the achievement-oriented motives that a person brings to each situation, these motives being fairly specific dispositions which the individual has learned and incorporated into his psychological structures over the years. These dispositions are relatively stable and permanent. In the McClelland framework, there are two kinds of achievement motives which are hypothesized as working simultaneously against each other within the individual, and which are elicited in any achievement situation. These motives are referred to as M_s (the motive to achieve success) and M_{af} (the motive to avoid failure). The individual is thus presented not only as constantly being confronted with a desire to be successful in attaining a particular goal but also as forced to face the possibility of failure. These two general motives are conceived as existing to a lesser or greater degree in everyone, and are mainly the result of the person's past experience in similar or identical situations. They are general conditions which a person carries with him from situation to situation.

The second set of variables operating within this framework are referred to as *situational* variables. These vary and change according to each specific situation and, in turn, affect the strength of the achievement motives. Related to the motive to achieve success (M_s) are situational factors designated as P_s, which indicates the probability of success or the individual's *expectancy* of success, and I_s, the attractiveness of success or its *incentive* value. Conversely, related to the motive to avoid failure are P_f, the probability or expectancy of failure, and I_f, the unattractiveness or incentive value of failure. Each of these situational factors combines multiplicatively with its corresponding motive to give the sum or total tendency of a person to either approach success in an achievement setting or to avoid failure. This is represented in the following diagram.

$$T_s \quad = \quad M_s \quad \times \quad P_s \quad \times \quad I_s$$

| The tendency to approach success | Motive to achieve success | Probability of success | Incentive value of success |

$$T_{af} \quad = \quad M_{af} \quad \times \quad P_f \quad \times \quad I_f$$

| The tendency to avoid failure | Motive to avoid failure | Probability of failure | Incentive value of failure |

The above formulation is relevant only in those achievement settings where the individual's *primary* motives are achievement oriented. Each person approaches performance situations carrying different combinations of several different kinds of motives, for example, affiliation motives, aggression motives, power motives, and, unless the situation is extremely *pure* only to achievement, these other motives will contaminate the effect which the achievement motive has on performance. Pure achievement settings are relatively rare and are usually found only in rigidly controlled experimental research settings. However, one can speculate that athletic competition comes as close as any to satisfying achievement requirements in real life.

This is clarified somewhat by McClelland (1961), when he emphasizes that three fundamental considerations are necessarily present in achievement motivated performances:

1. That the individual willingly accepts the responsibility for the outcome of his performance, whether he is successful or not.

2. That explicit knowledge of results is available, that is, the person knows how well he has done.

3. That some degree of uncertainty is attached to the success or failure of the performance.

As a result of past experience in situations similar or identical to the one that confronts the performer at any time, his expectancy of success will be strong, weak, or medium. The stronger he thinks the probability of success is (up to a point), the stronger will be his tendency to approach the situation with a desire for success, or the stronger is his motivation. Conversely, the stronger his expectancy of failure, the weaker his motivation. Theoretically, in a pure achievement setting $P_s + P_f = 1$, so that if an individual is 90 per cent sure of success, he is only 10 per cent sure of failure. If an athlete has a past history of winning, or if a performer has always had success in executing certain tasks, then his expectancies of success in new but similar situations are usually quite high. Confidence is quite naturally based on how well one has done in the past, and is very much a determinant in the level of motivation of individual athletes and performers.

Conversely, situations in which individuals have strong expectation of failure based upon a past history of failing or losing in similar situations will influence them to enter or approach new situations with low tendencies toward success. This perhaps provides a partial explanation for "losing streaks" and "slumps" that athletes and teams undergo from time to time. If an athlete has had a bad run or series of performances (in which an objective evaluation would state that he has been failing), then his expectancy of success in subsequent games or contests requiring the same skilled performances will gradually be weakened, and as his level of motivation is directly tied to his expectancy of success, one could speculate that the individual's level of desire will be low. Some coaches, when trying to pull an athlete or a team out of a slump, go back to fundamentals in an effort to get the person doing something which he can succeed at. This builds up his confidence and indirectly starts to raise his level of expectancy of success in subsequent performances. There is little doubt in the minds of some physical educators that simple to hard progression in the learning of complex stunts is by far the best way to keep young performers interested and motivated in achieving high levels of skill. In terms of motivation theory, they are simply building up the individual's expectancy of success.

In terms of the other situational variables in this schema, the incentive value which success holds for the person, one must anticipate how much pride a person has in achieving certain goals. If achievement is extremely attractive (has a high positive incentive value) to the individual, then, multiplicatively, his tendency to approach success is strengthened. On the other hand, if failing in a task or performance has very strong concomitants of censure and social disapproval, then the high *negative* incentive value of failure will cause the person to avoid failure at the risk of not achieving success. So again, like expectancy, the two tendencies tend to simultaneously detract from each other in purely achievement situations. Athletes, one can be sure, are very aware of results concerned with success or failure of their particular performances. As a result, they approach each situation in athletics fully aware of what *both* success and failure mean to them individually. Consequently, the attractiveness of success on one hand is weighed against the unattractiveness of failure on the other, and some sort of balanced tendency results. Generally speaking, $I_s + I_f = 1$, so that if a boy feels that the attractiveness of succeeding far outweighs the unattractiveness of failing in a particular task, then his total tendency to approach success will be greatly strengthened. This is particularly true in athletics, in which the boy is likely to assess the potential value of accomplishment only in terms of success and ignore the possibility of failure completely. An additional factor in this interpretation is the differential value certain kinds of achievements possess. We normally expect extremely difficult tasks to have much more incentive value than fairly easy ones and that athletes take considerable pride in accomplishing the "impossible" when performing during competition. One could generalize here by saying the more difficult the task, the more positive incentive value usually attached to it, and consequently, the higher the total achievement motivation of the person. Atkinson (1964) feels that this sort of interpretation has some legitimate theoretical significance, having specific and testable implications when one considers the assumption, arising out of work by Escalona (1940) and Festinger (1942) on level of aspiration, that accomplishment of difficult tasks is more attractive than success in easy or trivial ones. Though difficulty of task plays a slightly more complicated role than this, this is an assumption on which many coaches constantly proceed—that a boy takes greater pride in the successful accomplishment of more difficult performances. Roughly speaking then, I_s, the incentive value of success, is inversely proportional to P_s, the probability of success.

LEVEL OF TASK DIFFICULTY AND ACHIEVEMENT

Individuals, when confronted by tasks of various difficulty, will choose those of intermediate difficulty when their achievement motive is strong. This development has been observed in experiments involving college students and their stated levels of aspiration.* Subjects in this kind of research consistently choose levels of aspiration that fall between what is so obviously easy that success is certain and what is so obviously difficult that failure is certain. These results are normally considered in the light of research findings that indicate college students as a subpopulation with extremely high needs for achievement. This is further confirmed in research on small children who, high in need achievement, choose tasks of intermediate difficulty. The reason for this is obvious. Individuals who are high in achievement motive are very oriented toward performing successfully any tasks which they take on. Because of this, they are not too likely to choose tasks involving a high possibility of failure,

---

*For a thorough discussion of the concept of level of aspiration, please refer to Level of Aspiration and Achievement in this chapter.

whereas, because of their strong achievement motives, they are also not likely to choose tasks that are ridiculously easy (there is satisfaction of their need for achievement in doing something everyone can do). Consequently, they choose the intermediate difficulty tasks. If athletes and children in physical education classes can be assumed to have higher than usual needs for achievement, then we can expect them to also choose intermediate level of difficulty tasks *if* they are given the choice. It would appear to be important, then, that teachers carefully offer to the student those tasks which are of intermediate difficulty in order to reinforce the child's motive for achievement. It is generally assumed that if a child fails repeatedly on a particular task, he will gradually lose interest in it — probably because his expectancy of success is low and the negative incentive value of failure is high, thus lowering his level of motivation.

With athletes, the picture is a little more confused. One would naturally expect superior athletes, or individuals with superior athletic potential, to be interested only in those tasks of extremely high difficulty, tasks which really separate the "men from the boys." One would also naturally expect such individuals to have high needs for achievement, to have high achievement motives. If these two assumptions are valid then it would appear that, in the McClelland schema, athletes and their performances have to be explained in terms of the two situational variables, the expectancy and incentive value of success. That is, outstanding athletes normally expect to do well regardless of task difficulty, and because of this attitude their tendency to approach success is considerably enhanced. The fact that most superior athletes are involved only with tasks having a great deal of incentive value for them (*i.e.*, championship games or events) only serves to strengthen their tendency to approach success. Most athletes are involved in performances requiring only high levels of difficulty and are probably not inherently interested in choosing intermediate or easy situations, where success is partially or wholly guaranteed.

EXPECTANCY OF SUCCESS

The level of an individual's performance has been found to be highest when the probability of success in winning a monetary reward was .50 (Atkinson, 1958). Here, it was observed that performance shows an inverted U curve trend in relation to probability of success if, in addition to the incentive value of the money, there is an incentive to achieve inherent in the competitive nature of the task. This is certainly evident in professional sport. The inherent nature of sport is competitive, and when this is combined with the incentive value of money, most athletes will be more motivated to succeed if they have a 50 per cent chance of success. That is, the caliber of opposition very definitely affects the strength of an athlete's motive to achieve; if the opponent is very weak or very strong, the tendency to be highly motivated to achieve is weaker than if he is of a caliber similar to your own. Occasionally, this will not hold true as in the case of "upsets". When a supposedly weaker individual or team upsets a stronger opponent unexpectedly, one could speculate that the high incentive value of beating a superior opponent combines with the high motivational state of the weaker team to cause the upset regardless of the low expectancy of success. On the other hand, a more reasonable explanation would be the converse: the stronger individual or team has such a high expectancy of success and the incentive value of a win over a weaker opponent is so low that his or their level of motivation is quite low; *i.e.*, they go into the contest overconfident or not particularly concerned about the outcome of the event. Upsets are, of course, quite complicated occurrences, being contaminated by the effects of many different variables, but in motivational terms, this viewpoint has some validity. When there is no expectancy that successful performance will lead to pride of accomplishment because the conditions surrounding the setting rule out the generation of feelings of success, then there is no basis for expecting differences in performance between high and low need achievement people.

Accompanying the general disposition to seek success is the disposition to avoid failure. The motive to avoid failure causes the individual to react to failure with shame and embarrassment; when this disposition is elicited because a task is so obviously difficult and failure is likely, the result is anxiety and a tendency to withdraw from the situation. Again, the degree of antipathy related to failure is a function of the difficulty of the task; that is, if the task is virtually impossible there is little or no stigma attached to failing; however, if the task is simple, then considerable shame or embarrassment accompanies failure. This disposition to be anxious about failure affects all performance situations in which there is evaluation; it threatens the individual, especially those children, in a physical education program who are required to perform in front of a critical audience. An athlete, on the other hand, *knows* that his performance is going to be evaluated by the fans, by his coach, by his teammates, and his friends every time he steps out onto the field, or the floor, or the ice. For some individuals this results in a general avoidance of actions which might result in failure; *i.e.*, the strength of the tendency to avoid failure is a *negative* motivation, a motivation *not* to perform the task. In a real situation, such as an athletic contest, an individual who has a strong tendency *not to* act is nevertheless constrained by other inducements *to* act, so that a highly anxious person, realizing that he must perform regardless of how much he does not want to, will usually set his aspiration level ridiculously high or low. Some children in physical activity classes, because they are nervous about their performance in a motor task, will not even try, or will try something so difficult that no stigma is attached to their certain failure.

Thus, the resulting resolution between a person's tendency to approach success and his tendency to avoid failure are combined to give his theoretical level of motivation for achievement. For example, a coach may have two completely different kinds of boys playing in the defensive backfield of his football team in terms of their tendencies either to approach success or to avoid failure. One type may be the boy who is a wild gambler at heart (or so it appears), a boy who is prepared to take chances on always making the "big play" (making interceptions, tackling runners for big losses, pursuing all over the field), a boy who is solely oriented toward success and who doesn't give much thought to failure or making disastrous mistakes which might result in long runs, passes, or touchdowns through his zone. This kind of boy is positively oriented toward success and is subconsciously or even consciously willing to *risk* failure because he feels the fruits of success are worth it. In achievement motivation terms, this type of individual generally has a high or strong motive to achieve success, he has a high expectancy to achieve success, and success holds a high positive incentive value for him. He thinks mainly in terms of success, and is relatively oblivious of failure. These boys are usually superior performers; they are the players who hope that their opponents will operate in their zones, that they will have the opportunities to make interceptions and great tackles *the entire game;* simply because, if they are getting all the action, they will get the chance to perform well, to succeed, to achieve. On the other hand is the boy who has stronger tendency to avoid failure than to approach success, the type of boy who plays "according to the book." He does exactly what is required of him and makes a determined effort *not* to make any mistakes or not to *look* bad during a game. Because his disposition is toward avoiding failure, he will neither gamble on making the "big" play nor will he take too many chances. He is likely to play pass receivers "loose" rather than "tight" and to be quite content to consistently make the tackle rather than the interception; and very seldom will he be scored upon by letting a pass receiver get behind him. The reasons for this probably lie directly within McClelland's framework of situational variables, in that the boy may lack confidence and, as a result, have a low expectancy of success, *or* the negative incentive value of failure (its extreme unattractiveness) may far outweigh the attractiveness of success (*i.e.*, it is more important to avoid "looking bad" than it is to achieve "looking good"). This is the kind of boy who probably would be quite happy if the opponents never operated in his area of primary responsibility throughout the game.

LEVEL OF ASPIRATION AND ACHIEVEMENT

A major goal of most coaches is to aid the athlete in achieving optimum performance. Similarly, the teacher is concerned with the student's motivation to learn and perform in the physical education class. To attain these ends, educators and coaches employ various motivational techniques, one of which involves the *setting of goals*. Though it has not been established as yet whether goal-setting is effective, whether some types of goals are more effective than others, or whether goal-setting always influences the performer's welfare, there seems to be little doubt that it does exert a strong influence upon both his level of motivation and his subsequent performance. One method for examining such goal-setting behavior is through the evaluation of the individual's *level of aspiration* prior to, during, and following performance on particular tasks, especially in terms of its relationship to achievement motivation.

Generally speaking, a person's level of aspiration concerns his personal expectations, his goals, and the self-demands which he associates with his performance on a particular task. His personal feelings of success or failure are related to his degree of achievement or non-achievement, which in turn affects the goals he deems important and the manner by which he sets these goals. Perhaps most relevant is the knowledge one should have of the motivational effect that the act of explicitly stating a goal has on an athlete's performance. In order to gain some knowledge of the effectiveness of goal-setting as a motivational technique in sport, some understanding of the various goals which athletes have, and the effect goal-setting has in terms of feelings of success or failure is therefore necessary. The conflict a person faces when trying to decide the goals that are realistic for him—whether to attempt performances that are very difficult for him, or whether to simply settle for the easier goals—is very similar to the conflict faced by the typical athlete in competitive sport. Arising out of this psychological conflict are two critical problems which must be resolved by both the coach–teacher and his athlete–student: What factors determine a person's level of aspiration? and what are an individual's reactions to achieving or not achieving his particular stated level of aspiration?

Basic Concepts.   Frank (1935) provides what is generally the most accepted definition of level of aspiration:

> ... the level of future performance in a familiar task which an individual, knowing his level of past performance in that task, explicitly undertakes to reach.

Early studies by Dembo (1930) and Hoppe (1930) were the first empirical attempts to describe and explain the nature of goals, goal-setting behavior, and the dynamics of anger. Information arising from these studies indicated that the degree of a person's satisfaction or dissatisfaction associated with performance on a task is related to his personal level of aspiration, and that people who explicitly state their aspirations tend to be confused between *momentary* and *ideal* goals. It was also felt that goals, as phenomena, possess an inner psychological structure which causes success and failure to be understood as *feelings* aroused by attainment or nonattainment of personal goals, rather than as externally set standards. Goals, to most people, are ends in themselves, not means toward various ends.

The standard technique for measuring level of aspiration revolves around asking a person to explicitly state "how well he intends to do or thinks he can do in a subsequent performance. This technique operates within a typical sequence of events as diagrammed below:*

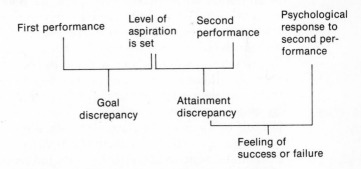

Ideal Goals vs. Action Goals.   From the above sequential series of events, Lewin et al. (1944) felt that the level of aspira-

---

*Adapted from J. W. Atkinson (1964): Introduction to Motivation. Princeton, D. Von Nostrand, p. 97.

tion presupposes a goal which has an inner structure consisting of: 1) an ideal or ultimate goal which the person hopes to attain sometime in the future, and 2) an action or momentary goal which the person tries for because of the seemingly unobtainability of the ideal goal. Level of aspiration, then, is concerned with action goals and is influenced by the relative strength of three basic needs: 1) the need to make the level of aspiration approximate the level of future performance as closely as possible; 2) the need to keep the level of aspiration as high as possible regardless of past performances; and 3) the need to avoid failure. Level of aspiration represents a compromise between a person's *evaluation* of his ability and his *desire* to do well. Frank (1935) felt that stating a level of aspiration is usually a threat to a person's self-esteem because of the open commitment he has to make to future performance.

Also derived from the sequence are two types of discrepancy scores: 1) goal discrepancy, which refers to the difference between a person's level of aspiration and his past performance; and 2) attainment discrepancy, which refers to the difference between level of aspiration and subsequent performance. The former gives one information on how confident a person is and whether he is oriented toward success or not, and the latter tells us how accurate he was in his evaluation of both his ability and his aspirations. The positive attitude toward achievement in our Western culture generally causes people to set levels of aspiration higher than their previous performances. This is especially true of successful, confident, and well-adjusted people. How much self-confidence an athlete possesses would therefore require some understanding of how and where he states his level of aspiration while he is in competition. Both Robinson (1964) and Atkinson (1964) have found that persons with a high need for achievement set moderate, realistic and positive levels of aspiration. And those people who possess a high fear of failure often set their levels of aspiration so low that they cannot possibly fail or so high that there is no stigma attached to failing. In both cases these people are protecting themselves from feelings of failure. By choosing realistic, intermediate goals, a person is exposing himself to the risk of failure. Athletes, then, who set moderate, realistic goals in their events or sports, are portraying high needs for achievement and by doing so, are indicating less fear of failure than if they were always pointing toward something beyond them.

Reaction to Success and Failure. Generally speaking, the research confirms what one would expect: namely, that failure to reach a level of aspiration on subsequent performance leads to a lowering of level of aspiration for the next performance, whereas success causes a moderate rise in aspiration level. This is obvious in athletics, where both individuals and teams after losing several games or events consecutively, tend to set their aspirations lower and show significant decreases in motivational level. In fact, there is evidence to show that continued failure results in withdrawal from sport (this is particularly true with young children) and a subsequent reluctance to strive toward similar goals or explicitly state levels of aspiration again. And avoidance-oriented individuals, who normally have a high fear of failure, continue to set ridiculously low or high goals regardless of their performances. Level of aspiration is a valid index of a person's feelings of success and failure *only* when the person has a free choice of goals; if the goal is set beforehand (as it often is by coaches and parents for their athletes), then the subjective probability of success is a better test of feelings of success and failure. To use goal-setting as a motivational device with athletes, then, one should allow the individual to realistically appraise himself and set his own goals.

Studies concerned with generality and specificity of level of aspiration indicate that not only personality variables (such as need for achievement and fear of failure) but *also* past experiences in specific tasks affect the level of aspiration a person sets. A person with a high need for achievement would always tend to set high levels of aspiration in any task *except* one in which he has a definite past history of failure. It is thus important for the coach to discover any particular areas of weakness which his athletes may have in their past history before jumping to conclusions about a boy's performance. And another factor which has an important effect is the *reference* group within which the person is performing. Individuals will raise their level of aspiration if they are performing below the average performance of a reference group which they consider inferior and will lower their level of aspiration if their performance is better than a group which they consider to be superior. Knowledge of group performance serves as a framework for the setting of level of aspiration in individuals. Again the significance for athletics is almost direct: if the performance of a superior player starts to unexplainably decline, he may be subconsciously "playing down" to the average performance of the team because he fears censure from his teammates.

Whether a person sets his level of aspiration in private or in public also influences how high or low he sets his level of aspiration. People try to avoid the loss of self-esteem when stating their levels of aspiration in front of other people simply because one tends to be sensitive to the opinions of others, and failure in front of them is harder to rationalize. This usually results in higher levels of aspiration being set in public than in private. The reason for this seems to be dependent upon whether or not an ego-involvement is present. When ego-involvement is minimal, levels of aspiration have little motivational significance and are primarily rational judgments of how well the person thinks he will perform. When ego-involvement passes a certain limit, however, defensive considerations become salient and a person's level of aspiration becomes more complex. Hanawalt *et al.* (1943), for example, found that people rated as *non-leaders* in a study generally reported higher goals in a private setting than in a public situation, whereas people rated as *leaders*, and supposedly more ego-involved in a public setting, did the reverse — probably because of the fear of failure in front of the group. Individuals are also less likely to lower levels of aspiration after failure in a public setting because of a greater commitment to the first estimate. Coaches and teachers are advised to refrain from the public setting of goals for their students or athletes simply because of the complex effect it may have on their aspirations, motivation, and performance.

Differential Aspiration.   The standard technique for setting a level of aspiration calls for the individual to make some type of statement of his future performance. People interpret this in three basic ways: 1) they can take it to mean the *minimum* score which they would undertake to better; 2) they can set their level of aspiration at the *maximum* which they *hope* to come close to; and 3) they can set it at a level which they *expect* the average performance to be. "Hope" and "expect" interpretations that individuals make have different effects on stated levels of aspiration and performance. Levels of aspiration elicited by *expect* instructions are more realistic and fluctuate with changes in subsequent performance because they are based on the individual's appraisal of his ability to meet the demands of the task. Using stated level of aspiration as a motivational technique with athletes, then, should be so maneuvered that the athlete is asked what he "expects" he will do. Levels of aspiration elicited by "hope" instructions are based more on the wishes, hopes, and fears of the individual and produce a greater range of individual differences in performance and much larger discrepancy scores. Asking an athlete what he "hopes" he will do in subsequent performances is relatively useless as a motivational technique because of its dependence on the boy's imagination.

Summary.   Both adults and children who participate in athletics and physical activity pre-evaluate their chances for success in any given performance. Success is relative and depends not only upon the person's ability but also upon his evaluation of that ability and what he thinks is a good and reasonable criterion of performance to aim at. What is highly successful for some people is quite inferior for others, so that in stating goals we can come to understand how much and what kind of self-confidence the athlete or performer possesses. Both personality and past experience affect a person's goal-setting behavior and this in turn influences his performance. If coaches and athletes, teachers and students, can together accurately evaluate the individual's goals, there is little doubt that performance can be enhanced.

An individual's level of aspiration reflects how optimistic he is, how realistic he is, and how confident he is about his ability. If it is consistently high and positive, then in athletics the individual is generally expected to do quite well. If it is low or negative most of the time, an effort must be made to analyze the reasons. If level of aspiration is properly manipulated by the coach and the athlete, it can be used as a motivational device to improve performance. In achievement motivation, the explicit stating of goals involves the individual in placing his self-esteem on the line for everyone to see. This is potentially a dissonance-producing situation. The athlete is faced with the knowledge that he may suffer loss of respect and, hence, self-esteem if he fails to reach his stated goal prior to his performance. According to Brehm and Cohen (1962), such a commitment leads to a heightened motivation to achieve and is a specification of the psychological implications of the choice the person makes; *i.e.*, explicitly committing oneself to a goal, coupled with the knowledge that failure will threaten self-esteem, in itself causes the increased motivation. The psychological tension caused by putting oneself "on the spot" is uncomfortable (cognitive dissonance), thus forcing the person to seek relief from the dissonance by actually achieving his stated goal. Goal-setting forces the athlete into commitment, a dissonance-producing situation which forces him to achieve.

In order to improve in athletic performance, one must constantly be trying toward goals that are always slightly beyond one's current ability. Goal-setting puts this requirement into real terms. Setting level of aspiration quite high acts as an incentive in itself, so that successful performance becomes an important end rather than a means toward other ends. Doing well becomes as important as the consequences of doing well. This is doubly important with young athletes because one can remove the concomitant pressure of winning if one can convince the child of the *sole* importance of top individual performance. Such a reorientation of emphasis not only puts motivation into more sensible terms but also directly improves performance. Coaches and teachers in physical activity and athletics must be aware of the importance of putting their performers and athletes into only re-alistic performance situations—those situations in which the child can attain reasonable improvement. Successes which come too easy or repeated failure contribute nothing to either an indi-vidual's level of motivation or his improvement in performance. A close examination of the performer's goal-setting behavior can serve as an accurate indicator of desire for achievement.

Overview

The motive for achievement in an individual is best consid-ered as a dispostion toward competing with standards of excel-lence where public evaluation and self-evaluation of success or failure is immediate. The theory of achievement motivation provides a framework within which two kinds of variables are operating in typical pure achievement settings: 1) the relatively stable achievement motives which a person carries to each situa-tion and 2) the two sets of variables which are specific to each situation, his expectancy of success and the incentive value of that success. A converse situation exists which revolves around the motive to avoid failure, the expectancy of failure, and the negative incentive value of failure. Each of these motives are hypothesized to combine multiplicatively with their correspond-ing situational variables to give both a tendency to approach or achieve success, T_s, and a tendency to avoid failure, T_{af}. The total strength of achievement motivation, T, thus becomes the sum of these two tendencies, $T = T_s + T_{af}$.

One must be careful to consider this theory only in situations in which achievement motives or needs (Willis and Bethe 1970) are primary over other motives and needs. Even in pure athletic settings, other important motives are operating within the indi-vidual, and thus may detract from the strength of his achieve-ment motivation. Such motives as independence, power, ag-gression, and affiliation would tend to complicate and even con-taminate the influence achievement holds for the individual. Other motives such as sensory, curiosity, and competence may even detract from achievement motivation. Atkinson (1964) em-phasizes the importance of the achievement setting being *pure*, but it almost never is. Nevertheless, this conceptualization of achievement has intuitive attractiveness as a base from which to view striving in sport. It is also a mistake to view the achievement motive as being aroused only in certain circumstances. McClelland *et al.* (1953), in fact, hypothesize that a variety of cues may cause the achievement motive to operate. Such cues may be motives or needs in themselves: for example, if a strong power motive is operating in a boy, he may recognize that the best method of gaining influence over other people is through achieving in athletics — thus, a cue which is not primarily achievement in nature, serves to arouse the motive for achievement. A certain kind of specificity does function, however, in that a boy, extremely oriented toward achievement in sports, may or may not be achievement-oriented in other settings such as the schoolroom. Though this is probably a function of the different expectancies and incentives that operate between settings, there is reason to believe that the development of the motive to achieve is highly situation-specific in nature.

There is also some evidence indicating that people having high achievement motives tend to exhibit certain strong personality characteristics (McClelland 1961). They exhibit, for example, patterns of delayed gratification and the acceptance of long term involvements; they are optimistic, conscientious, and ambitious; they work harder when the odds seem to be against them; they exhibit a high degree of self-confidence; and they emerge as top performers when conditions are of moderate uncertainty (Willis and Bethe 1970). All these traits or attributes have been identified in personality research on athletes, and it stands to reason that athletes *must* be able to defer gratification and enter willingly into long-term involvements if they want to develop their skill level to championship caliber. They *must* be conscientious, ambitious, and optimistic in order to withstand the long-drawn-out boredom of training and the agony of injury and defeat. Without these qualities, most athletic careers would never get off the ground. Every time an athlete enters competition, a milieu of uncertainty as to the outcome exists — thus making a positive reaction to it a necessity. If, in fact, a causal relationship exists between these attributes and the motive for achievement, it is a highly important relationship to understand.

Also important is the discussion by Willis and Bethe (1970) of the premise that situations involving competition and achievement, which produce strong emotional involvement, tend to yield individuals high in achievement motive. This premise is based upon the assumption that emotional arousal is primarily responsible for the development of various motives. There are certain types of cues which release diffuse and covert responses rather than clear, observable behavior, and changes in the manner in which some people adapt to these specific cues seem to result from corresponding changes in the person's emotional state. If this premise is valid, then, the more meaningful an emotional occurrence is to a person, the more adaptable he is to various cues in achievement settings, and the more likely he is to develop a strong achievement motive. This links high emotional involvement directly to achievement in performance settings. If an athlete can derive some meaning from his sport in an emotional context, his level of motivation, especially achievement motivation, will indeed rise. Such emotional involvement in outstanding athletes is constantly observed.

As one would expect, the McClelland-Atkinson interpretation of achievement motivation, especially the probability formula, cannot take into account or explain all the various situations that arise in sport. In fact, some parts of the theory are still undergoing considerable modification. However, the theory certainly seems appropriate for gaining some insight and understanding into achievement in sport.

CHAPTER 10

AGGRESSION IN SPORT

Preface

Aggressive behavior is inextricably linked to the violent concept of aggression, a concept which generally possesses distasteful or negative connotations in our society today. It is this value interpretation of aggression that influences almost all literature on aggression, the general viewpoint being taken that aggression is bad and should be controlled. It is not the purpose of this section to make a value judgment on aggression either way; rather, it is an attempt to analyze what constitutes aggressive behavior in athletics, how it comes to exist, and whether or not it can be viewed as a major component in human motivation. As is normal in psychological literature, aggression is a broad hypothetical construct that defies exact definition — however, operationally, aggression can be viewed as *the intentional response a person makes to inflict pain or harm on another person.*

AGGRESSION AS INNATE BEHAVIOR

The basic controversy in human aggressive behavior revolves around whether it is innate, a fraction of our evolutionary heritage, or whether it is acquired, a product of frustration (Ardrey 1966).

Konrad Lorenz, an ethologist-psychologist on staff at the Max Planck Institute for Animal Behavior in Germany, provides probably the most convincing case for viewing aggressive behavior as innate in man (1964). His basic position is that most animals cannot survive without being aggressive, such is the selective value of aggressiveness in the welfare of individuals, populations, and species. Among the obvious values of aggression are the spacing of individuals over an available living area, the selection through competition of the better-qualified males for breeding purposes, and, in a social context, the construction of a formal dominance hierarchy which provides leadership and discipline in which the superior wisdom, courage, experience, and abilities of the group's leaders can be used to the greatest advantage of the entire community (Ardrey 1966). Lorenz supports this view with

225

case after case demonstrating the natural history of aggression in animals in which fighting is more ritualized than it is actual for the simple reason that the individual can then benefit from the values of aggression while the species avoids the liabilities of aggression.

Freud (1913, 1930) postulated that the nature of aggression is innate to man—that it is the outward manifestation of what he termed the *death instinct* in man. Freud's idea of the death instinct was that there is a force within man constantly working toward his total disintegration, which is in opposition to the life forces within him, and which when turned outward against the external world results in destructiveness and aggression. This postulation was partially the result of Freud's attempt to explain the irrational, almost unbelievable hostility that man had directed against man on the battlefields of World War I; a carnage unequalled until the subsequent attempt by Hitler to annihilate the European Jews. The instinct of aggression as the derivative and main representative of the death instinct was made by Freud *after* he had discarded a frustration-aggression hypothesis as being too naive an explanation.

Lorenz, however, turns Freud's position around somewhat when he states that aggression is a *normal,* fundamental instinct, and that the death wish is the neurotic, frustrated consequence of aggression turned *inward.* The Lorenz position is that aggression is healthy, necessary, innate, and eradicable; that ritualizations, displays, and diversions (*e.g.,* athletic competitions) are necessary to absorb our hostile tendencies and direct them toward harmless or constructive ends; and that to deny the innateness of aggression is to ultimately sanction hostility because its root cause is frustration.

This general viewpoint, then, that aggression is natural to man, that it already lies in his fundamental, instinctive nature, and that it is not necessarily based on a drive to self-destruction, has several implications for sport in general, and athletic behavior in particular. First, it would seem to reinforce the view that athletic competition is necessary for man to indulge his aggressive tendencies in a socially acceptable manner.* Such ritualization is said to have a benefit for society in that man is viewed as taking his hostility out on the playing field rather than on the streets. Though sports certainly provide such means, it is quite evident that they haven't served to reduce violence in the streets; displacement of aggression in sports in this way is obvi-

---

*Whether this reduces or increases their aggressive drives is another question and is discussed later in this section.

ously not too successful. Second, though every boy can be said to innately possess aggressive impulses, it is obvious, on a subjective basis, that some are more aggressive than others. Such a differential outcome is most certainly the result of varied environmental modification. Boys having a past history of aggressiveness will behave and perform quite differently from those who do not. Third, the positive connotation placed upon being aggressive in sport can be justified in that a natural instinct of man is being developed and reinforced. Even fighting in hockey is generally condoned as being important for success in that it contributes to team spirit. Also, it is thought that, to be successful, a hockey player must avoid being intimidated. This is especially true in all the physical contact sports.

AGGRESSION AND FRUSTRATION

Although subsequent research failed to completely validate Freud's basic belief that the main goal of most organisms is to reduce tension, and that aggression is simply one form of reducing tension in the system, there were still many people who thought aggression an innate tendency though partly modified in the form it takes through learning experiences. In 1939, however, a group of Yale psychologists formulated the position (based on some of Freud's earlier writings) that aggression was the consequence of frustration, that aggression presupposes the existence of frustration, and that the existence of frustration always leads to some form of aggression (Dollard et al., 1939). Frustration is generated by those circumstances which interfere with goal-directed behavior. This group was interested in reconciling Freudian theory with objective learning theory, but unfortunately overstated their case by hypothesizing that frustration is the *only* cause of aggression, and that aggression *always* follows frustration. On the basis of considerable subsequent research, these hypotheses have been faulted as being too broad. The Dollard viewpoint, for example, would say that a feeling of frustration commonly associates with aggression, partly because it feels like anger, partly because one way to remove frustration is to attack it directly, and partly because frustration of the aggression itself causes even more aggressive behavior. This paradigm would seem to easily explain certain aggressive behavior in sports. For example, when a player is continually prevented from achieving his main objectives during a game (*e.g.*, scoring goals in hockey), he will become quite frustrated or angry—and because he cannot remove this frustration by achieving the original objective he will displace his anger and aggressiveness to a substitute object (such as another player) and attack it aggressively in order to eliminate the frustration. If the substitute object also causes frustration or fights back (as opponents tend to do) then aggression is even more strongly evoked. Aggressive behavior in this kind of situation usually deteriorates into fighting. Fighting in sports as a manifestation of aggressiveness is a waste of both psychic and physical energy, and interestingly does not necessarily alleviate the players' frustration. It is more sensible for both the coach and the player to realize that aggression directly channelled into the actual playing of the game will significantly contribute to more successful performance.

The Dollard paradigm, though attractive, however, is not always or completely valid. For example, as it is true with mice, it is also true that we can train people (and athletes especially) to be highly aggressive by reinforcing their aggression with rewards such as success, approval, recognition, etc. This can easily be done in the absence of frustration. This is aggression determined or caused through learning. Another major weakness of the frustration hypothesis is that frustration does not always cause aggression; it can also cause other types of behavior. For the little boy trying out for a little league team who does not make it, frustration may merely cause him to quit and withdraw from sport completely. Thus, if frustration does not *necessarily* cause aggression, it cannot be said that all aggression is the result of frustration. Probably the most sensible way to view the frustration-aggression hypothesis is that frustration produces a physiological arousal—with the response to this arousal very definitely a function of past learning (Levin and Fleischmann, 1968). Some psychologists, as Layman (1970) points out, have even taken the position that human aggressive behavior is learned behavior acquired by means of conditioning. This is supported by results from animal studies which have consistently shown that *some* animals *must* be trained to act aggressively.

TYPES OF AGGRESSION

If we consider aggression as behavior whose goal is to intentionally harm someone, or as Scott (1958) states, "precisely, aggression refers to fighting and means the act of initiating an attack," then it is best to consider aggression in two broad categories: *instrumental aggression,* which is concerned with that aggressive behavior whose purpose is to achieve some goal, and in which harm to another person occurs only because it is the most efficient way of achieving the desired goal; and *reactive* or *goal aggression,* which has as its *purpose* (or goal) injury or harm to another person, with both perception of the other person as a threat or noxious stimuli and the emotion of anger being necessary concomitants.

Instrumental aggression is solely concerned with reward. One is aggressive in a football game in order to win the game — or to be recognized as an outstanding player, etc. The primary goal is *not* injury to one's opponent; even though this may be necessary in achieving an objective, the infliction of injury and pain are incidental. Cool objectivity rather than emotional anger is the essence of this type of aggression. Competitive athletics are primarily the domain of instrumental aggression, in which the contestants are concerned with objectives other than the infliction of pain and injury. For some athletes, however, anger is a necessary adjunct to the generation of aggression, and for these individuals, winning probably must be interpreted in terms of psychologically injuring the opponent in order to make them aggressive. When this fails, some coaches resort to convincing their players to harm and physically injure the opposing players — thus increasing, at least, their *goal aggressiveness.*

In goal aggression, on the other hand, the objective is pain, injuring or maiming your opponent, who is perceived, or interpreted, as the "enemy." Sometimes it is easy to condition players to engage in this type of aggression by convincing them that their opponents are frustrating agents (*i.e.,* "they stand between us and our goals"), that they are the source of noxious stimuli (*i.e.,* "it's either us or them"). In goal-aggression, then, anger, hostility and resentment are concomitant catalysts to aggressiveness. It is within goal aggressiveness that some workers have postulated an aggressive *drive.* It seems likely that emotional arousal is connected to frustration (much like fear is connected to pain) and that this arousal is instinctive rather than learned. When aggressive acts, instigated by frustration, are reinforced either by a reduction in tension or by reward (social approval), then the individual slowly acquires a predisposition to aggression; that is, he learns to be aggressive. If such responses are attacks on other people, the learned behavior is goal aggression; if the responses involve reduction in emotion or goal-attainment, the acquired behavior is instrumental aggression. This is an interpretation of aggressiveness as a *habit* rather than as a drive — that aggressive behaviors become a habitual means of goal-attainment or as learned responses to frustration. Such behaviors are easily imitated, so that the circumstances under which imitation occurs are important determinants of how aggressiveness is learned. This can be seen to occur in athletic competition.

AGGRESSION AND SPORT

The relevance of aggression in sport has been traditionally centered around the usefulness of sport in providing an outlet for aggression and, thereby, in part, controlling violence in our society. Lorenz (1966) concisely states this viewpoint by believing that "the main function of sport today lies in the cathartic discharge of (the) aggressive urge." Subjective observation, as well as considerable research, does not bear out this position. Athletes who are aggressive in their sports are rewarded, praised, and reinforced for their aggressiveness, which quite simply makes them *more* rather than less aggressive. Also, as Scott (1971) observes, violence in sport is even institutionally romanticized by the respect and awe directed toward players who are nicknamed "Mad-Dog," "the Purple People Eaters," "Bronco," etc. Some players even, unfortunately, bask in the doubtful glory of being regarded as "animals." Catharsis of aggressive impulses for spectators is also an issue of obvious doubt. The rioting of fans at athletic contests around the world attests to the failure of sport as providing a socially acceptable means for releasing aggression. And the extreme exhortations of "Kill 'em," "murder them," and "fight, fight, fight," from fans at *sporting* contests is not particularly valid evidence that sports-watching reduces aggressive violence in the spectator. Research in play therapy also touches upon the weaknesses of the "catharsis hypothesis" in aggression. Sears, Maccoby and Levin (1957), for example, found that children who have parents high on both permissiveness and punishment of aggression will themselves be aggressive. Mussen and Rutherford (1961) observed increases in aggression after exposing subjects to aggressive films. And it has also been found that if a child is not punished for aggressive actions during doll play, he will become more aggressive across the play sessions (Levin and Wardell, 1962).

It is, however, not the purpose of this section to delve into the issue of whether or not sport efficiently provides an outlet for aggressive impulses or urges. Rather, it is our intention to examine aggression in order that we can better understand the *nature* of aggressiveness in the individual athlete. A better understanding of aggressive behavior will permit both the athlete and the coach to achieve a closer realization of the athlete's potential. Therefore, the following sections would seem to bear more direct relevance to aggression in sport than those hitherto explored.

AGGRESSIVENESS IN THE ATHLETE: INNATE OR ACQUIRED

To argue that aggressiveness is a universal instinct—that everyone possesses it—innate in man, allows us to explain and understand very little about the construct. Though the concept of instinct is initially quite appealing, upon closer inspection it provides us with no new information. When something happens it is ascribed to an instinct; when it doesn't happen, the instinct is said to be lacking. This explains nothing. Intuitively, we can proceed from the basic premise that man, as an animal, has basic aggressive tendencies—how aggressive he becomes, on the other hand, will depend largely on the development of this characteristic throughout his life and the specific situational variables which stimulate the characteristic in him. An instinct or drive theory of aggression is predicated on *periodic outbursts* of aggressiveness, regardless of situational stimuli; a situational theory implies that certain stimuli in a situation must be present to trigger aggression. Moreover, individual experience—the learning or acquiring of aggressiveness—is very important in determining a boy's propensity to be aggressive in athletics. A paradigm briefly describing the main influences on the development of aggressiveness in the individual is shown below (Diagram 15). It is obvious, then, that the above question has no simple answer.

Each person is born with a capacity and a need to move against his environment—to be aggressive. This capacity is developed to a lesser or fuller degree during the remainder of his life, depending largely on a continual series of complex learning experiences. The first aggressive responses of a newborn baby, probably concerned with discomfort and restraint, appear in the form of indiscriminate anger. However, as the child grows older he learns to focus his anger in such a way as to remove the source of his discomfort; this is instrumental aggression. He is already learning that, to achieve certain goals, aggressiveness is successful. With direct reference to the frustration—aggression hypothesis previously described, Dollard and Miller (1950) feel that there are certain critical periods and situations through which the young developing child passes in which

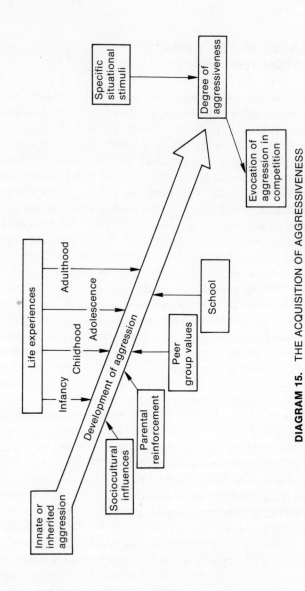

DIAGRAM 15. THE ACQUISITION OF AGGRESSIVENESS

there is a strong likelihood that frustration will occur. These periods, such as feeding, cleanliness, toilet training, and training in controlling emotions, are major sources of frustration for the child because of the conflict between what he wants to do and what his parents say he can do. The child, in most of these situations, reacts to frustration by resorting to aggression. This basic conflict between individual desires and societal, parental, or cultural restrictions is the main source of frustration for the growing youth, and it is probably in this context that he acquires most of his aggressiveness. Although aggression is not the invariable response to frustration, it is nevertheless a response which is encouraged in our society.

The newborn infant probably never engages in *instrumental aggression*—rather, it is something he gradually acquires through his increasing knowledge of the external world. This conditioning is probably closely allied to the *anger* a child manifests and his eventual intent to injure the sources of his frustrations. This acquisition of the knowledge that injuring others is successful in achieving one's objectives leads directly into competition, power, dominance and other motive-incentive systems.

Sears, Maccoby, and Levin (1957) demonstrated in their study that as the child learns to attack the various objects which frustrate him he learns one of his first lessons—punishment usually accompanies aggressive actions directed toward his parents. His next lessons are learned when he directs aggression to his peers. A child's aggressive experiences are usually a matter of chance in that no two situations are ever identical. Different children grow up in different environments, and they all will respond differently to these variable situations. Aggressiveness, then, as a function of socioeconomic background, sex, age, number of siblings, personality characteristics of parents or peers, becomes very much an individual thing. Two children living and maturing in exactly the same environmental milieu, for example, may develop completely different levels of aggressiveness. However, this chance development probably operates within a basic regular schema. This is as follows:

The developing child learns to repeat those responses which are rewarded and not those which are punished. He prefers, naturally, to engage in behavior which leads to his basic instinctual gratifications, and it is here that fundamental conflict first, and for the rest of his life, arises. When frustration occurs as a result of some gratification being blocked, the child, probably accidentally, learns that being aggressive will clear the path to gratification of his desires. When he discovers this, he begins to become quite skilled in using his knowledge to control or manipulate other people aggressively. If he continues to be sucessful in this manner he becomes an aggressive person — if he is unsuccessful, he resorts to behaviors other than aggression to achieve his ends. If a child starts to anticipate punishment each time he acts aggressively he starts to build up an inhibition to aggression — so that, rather than acting aggressively he becomes fearful, or guilty, or anxious about the situation and withdraws or runs away from the frustration. In doing this he becomes dependent upon other people to solve his problems. However, as the child learns to be successfully aggressive he realizes that symbolic or psychological aggression can be just as effective as physical, and the forms his aggression takes become more sophisticated. Where the very young child resorts to screaming and kicking actions, the older child manifests his aggressiveness in whining, sulking, and pouting — in these stages aggression is usually focused on the frustrating agent rather than on the environment in general. Along with this change in aggression is a change in the length of anger behavior. The length of time in which anger is visibly nurtured decreases with age — sullenness, brooding and resentment, however, increase with age.

There is a rapid increase in social awareness during the preschool and early school years on the part of children, with friendly cooperative play being mainly characteristic of these years. Aggression, competition and dominance behaviors appear usually in peer group interactions. The need for aggressiveness a child learns in peer interactions is transmitted quite mercilessly by other children. The quite active child who interacts with a larger number of children probably learns to be more aggressive than one who has less encounters with other children.

Finally, then, it would appear that the athlete who is highly aggressive is one who has had a past history of successful *instrumental* aggression — i.e. he has continually been successful in achieving various goals by being aggressive. The athlete who is low on aggressiveness would appear to be one who in the past has reacted to frustration with successful behaviors other than aggression.

AGGRESSIVENESS AS A REACTION TO FRUSTRATION

Most aggression in sport results from frustration. This frustration is the result of various motives being thwarted or blocked. Those motives, which are predominant in sport and which usually generate aggression when thwarted, revolve around achievement, dominance, power, recognition and prestige, and excellence. If a boy places high incentive value on one or a combination of these motive-incentive systems and is blocked from attaining or satisfying them, he becomes frustrated. If this frustration results in aggression toward the frustrating agent, the coach and the athlete together should identify the frustrating stimuli so that the most beneficial aggressive responses can be made. It is a waste, for example, for the boy to expend aggressive energy in useless temper tantrums. Of particular interest here is a clear-cut study of frustration and aggression by Sargent (1948). Sargent proposes a simple conceptual scheme (Diagram 16) for behavior resulting from frustration and centers it around the thesis that, first and foremost, frustration arouses a "pronounced emotional reaction"—that *emotion* is the core of reaction to frustration. The emotion aroused may be broad and diffused (generalized anger or fear) or specific (hostility, shame, jealousy, etc.) and depends upon *how* the individual interprets the whole precipitating situation. Though the individual's behavior is partly dependent upon the emotion which agitates him, his overt reaction to the frustration will definitely be a function of his habitual adjustive mechanisms and the way he interprets each situation. Sargent's schema, shown in Diagram 16, generally indicates how one reacts to frustration. To attempt a perspective let us use typical examples of situations that occur constantly in athletics. An athlete, thwarted in attaining a particular goal which is important to him—for example, a pass receiver drops a pass in the end zone, a basketball player misses a lay-up, or a hockey player fails to check his man who scores an easy goal—immediately becomes emotional; but how? If his overt behavior can be observed, some indication as to the habit mechanisms he normally uses to handle the emotion can be seen. It is these mechanisms which can tell us how aggressive a boy is going to be in the crucial situations that continually occur in sport. Also, an analysis of these habitual patterns of behavior can aid us in helping the athlete to focus his emotional energy in constructive and beneficial ways. As can be seen in Diagram 16, it is probably the athlete who is least inhibited that will react to frustration by being physically aggressive. This would indicate that boys low on aggressiveness "mask" their reactions to frustration by resorting to psychological mechanisms that do not eventuate in outright physical aggression. Such mechanisms as *regression* (a process by which a person readopts responses characteristic of an earlier phase of development), *displacement*

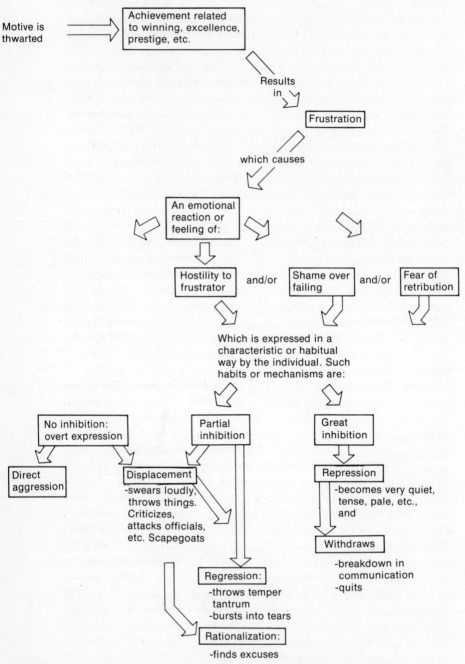

Motive is thwarted

Achievement related to winning, excellence, prestige, etc.

Results in

Frustration

which causes

An emotional reaction or feeling of:

Hostility to frustrator — and/or — Shame over failing — and/or — Fear of retribution

Which is expressed in a characteristic or habitual way by the individual. Such habits or mechanisms are:

No inhibition: overt expression

Partial inhibition

Great inhibition

Direct aggression

Displacement
-swears loudly, throws things. Criticizes, attacks officials, etc. Scapegoats

Repression
-becomes very quiet, tense, pale, etc., and

Regression:
-throws temper tantrum
-bursts into tears

Withdraws
-breakdown in communication
-quits

Rationalization:
-finds excuses

DIAGRAM 16. REACTION TO FRUSTRATION. (MODIFIED FROM SARGENT, 1948.)

(a process by which the discharge of unconscious impulses are shifted from the original object to a substitute) and *repression* (a process in which the boy purposely forgets or excludes from his consciousness impulses associated with objectionable aggressive demands) restrict the individual from overt behavior. If a boy is resorting to such mechanisms his aggressiveness will probably be quite low—simply because he is turning his aggressiveness inward and punishing himself rather than some external object or person. This is normally referred to as an *intra-punitive* reaction—an aggressive reaction directed toward self. Such a reaction is caused by feelings of guilt, humiliation and judgments of self-blame, with the boy regarding himself as unworthy and inferior. In this situation, the coach can help the boy by explaining to him what is probably occurring and by pointing out to him that overt aggressiveness in sport is quite socially acceptable behavior as long as no intent to injure an opponent is present. A strong effort is required here in building up the boy's self-confidence, and convincing him of his worthiness as an individual and as an athlete. A similar reaction to frustration has been termed an *impunitive* reaction: this is an unaggressive reaction. It is due to feelings of embarrassment, shame and judgments manifested as "Oh well, it can't be helped anyway!" Such a reaction is evident in the athlete who turns off or just doesn't care. This reaction is much harder to handle simply because the boy is probably de-emphasizing the importance that sport has for him. A reexamination of his personal objectives with the coach is the first step in correcting this behavior. The boy must be told that considerable aggressive drive is necessary for success in sports, and that if he is not prepared to pay the price he is not only wasting his time but also being unfair to his teammates who are depending on him. Sometimes all that is needed in this kind of situation is to help the boy examine his motives for participating and see if they are genuine or not. The third basic kind of reaction to frustration is the one that is mostly observed in sports—the *extra-punitive* aggressive reaction toward other people. It arises from anger and indignation and from the individual's judgment, which puts the blame on others; "I'll get you!" is its main manifestation. Thus, when frustrated, the extra-punitive reaction is immediate overt aggressive behavior toward other people. Here the athlete must be convinced that such behavior is wasted unless it is channelled into constructive pursuits such as running harder or faster, tackling or body-checking harder, or rebounding more strongly. Expending such energy in temper tantrums is a waste.

It would appear, then, that when a boy seems to be low on aggressiveness his reactions to specific situational frustrations should be examined. If a boy has habitually channelled his re-action to frustration into nonaggressive outlets, a reeducation is necessary. Convincing him that aggressiveness within the real and moral rules of conduct for his sport is all right and socially acceptable is the key to this problem.

INDIVIDUAL DIFFERENCES IN AGGRESSIVENESS

This question deals with the individual differences that exist between people in terms of their dispositions to find attractive incentives for aggression. One point of view considers potential *constitutional* differences as influencing the development of the motive for aggression in individuals. Some children from birth are considered "colicky"—they hyper-react to contact with other people, and they appear to experience a great deal of pain and uncomfortableness. Rage and anger are their usual responses to pain connected with teething and toilet mishaps. Preschool children for whom such occurrences are common tend to develop strong dispositions for aggressiveness. Most children, and adults too, who are quite phlegmatic probably did not experience these situations as infants.

A second viewpoint considers certain family conditions that influence a child's disposition toward aggression. Parents, siblings, and peers can be significant sources of pain in the early life of a child. Such experiences can very definitely contribute to the development of aggressive motives. This motive-state of aggression is usually labeled *resentment* (Birch and Veroff, 1966). A typical example of such a motive-state being developed is portrayed by Dave Meggyesy (1971) in his book on big-time football. Meggyesy's childhood on a run-down, primitive farm in Ohio was constantly punctuated by brutal beatings from his father, using anything from a razor strap to an axe-handle. The resentment generated in Meggyesy from such treatment probably profoundly influenced his eventual aggressive and hustling behavior as a football player. In slightly more general terms though, some children are so thwarted in their actions by other people, and are so often required to repress their aggressive tendencies, that a deep feeling of resentment may remain within them for a lifetime. The prime factor in this background is usually overbearing or dominant parents who induce strong resentment in the child—which he cannot express directly back at his parents for fear of punishment—who then releases or displaces this resentment to other people in his society. Such displacement of resentment in sport, with the opponents as substitute targets, is quite common. It is important to note there that such resentment to parents or siblings is usually not felt consciously by the child—in fact, in most cases, these children idealize their parents.

Children also learn physically aggressive behavior from their parents through imitation. Parents who are aggressive with each other and toward their children usually make available to these children opportunities for them to be aggressive. Constant opportunities for aggressive behavior with constant reinforcement of aggressive responses, via approval and recognition, contribute very heavily toward causing the child to become aggressive. In the past, such aggressiveness has been more verbal in middle-class families and more physical in working-class families, but recent research (Eron *et al.*, 1963) indicates such class differences are becoming less prominent.

SITUATIONAL-SPECIFICITY OF AGGRESSIVENESS

One mistake that is often made in athletics is the attributing of a certain behavior to a general trait or characteristic that the individual is said to possess. This is a particularly tenuous conclusion with respect to aggressive behavior. Boys who are aggressive in sports may *or may not* be aggressive in other, non-athletic situations. The converse is also very true: you cannot evaluate a boy's level of aggressiveness in any situation other than the one which is of concern and expect it to apply generally. Aggressiveness, like any other trait, characteristic or ability, has to be highly *situation-specific*. This is largely a result of the differential reinforcement that the individual receives across the many facets of his life. For example, a boy who is aggressive in football may be quite timid in the classroom or in a social situation where he feels (or knows) his level of competence is inferior to that of other people. Differential reinforcement means that a child may be constantly reinforced for aggressiveness in one particular class of situations (*e.g.*, sports) but not in others (*e.g.*, social interactions with parents and peers). When this happens, the child very quickly learns when it is beneficial to him to be aggressive and when it is not. This apparent lack of aggressiveness in non-sport milieus can be constantly observed in hyper-aggressive athletes. If a boy is aggressive in many different kinds of situations it is because his aggressiveness in each of these situations has been specifically reinforced. Some very young boys when they first begin their competitive sports careers must *learn* how to be aggressive, simply because aggressiveness in their previous experiences was not an important aspect of their behavior. *Expectancy* that aggressive behavior will lead to achieving a particular goal (*e.g.*, being a successful athlete) will predetermine how strong the motive for aggression is in a particular individual. If he has enjoyed success in the past by being aggressive then anticipation of more success will pressure him into being aggressive again. The strength of this expectancy of success through aggressive behavior will be a function of the relative number of times aggressiveness has produced success in the past. A lack of aggressiveness in a boy, therefore, may be only a function of his lack of success in being aggressive in the past. If the boy can be made aware of this causal aspect of his past career, or be convinced that aggressiveness can *now* start to contribute toward success, then one should be able to raise his level of aggressiveness.

DISPLACEMENT OF AGGRESSION

Displacement of aggression occurs when the energy to aggress is directed toward an object or person other than the original object or person who caused the aggression. When a boy, frustrated over missing a basket or striking out, kicks the ground or shoves an official, he is directing his frustration toward a substitute target—he is *displacing* his anger or aggression. Several aspects of aggression displacement are of interest.

First is Freud's speculation that displacement occurs as a result of the original frustrating agent being too remote or dangerous to react against. This blocking causes the person to direct his aggression against someone or something that is immediately available and less dangerous to him. Athletes must learn that when frustrated by something which they have no control (a booing crowd or a bad call by an official), the substitute targets which they direct their anger against should be chosen in such a manner that their aggressive energy is put to constructive use. It should be made clear to a boy that angry resentment is better channelled into playing harder than into wasteful temper tantrums. Second, if the displacement of aggressive energy is to be used constructively, the substitute target should be as similar as possible to the original frustrating agent. If your opponent is frustrating you, then, to make the best use of your aggressiveness, it should be directed against him or one of his teammates. This is consistent with Miller and Dollard's (1941) reasoning that when aggression toward the original object is blocked the tendency to aggress is increased, even to the point where it cannot be contained. At this point, aggression toward substitute, similar objects breaks out and results in a cathartic release of tension. The third aspect now becomes important. Bandura and Walters (1963) have shown that displacement occurs primarily as an outcome of previous discrimination training—children are conditioned into hostility against certain objects, people, or groups of people; racial discrimination is a perfect example of such discrimination training. Thus, if the athlete can be trained to discriminate between those pursuits that are constructive and those that are not, his displaced aggressive energy can be put to some practical use.

Sometimes the criterion of similarity between the original frustrator and the substitute object breaks down when anger is present. Buss (1961) states that anger lowers the threshold of aggressive action regardless of the degree of similarity between the substitute target and the original frustrator.

AGGRESSION MOTIVATION

Birch and Veroff (1966) present a paradigm of motivation within which we can view aggression as a motive-incentive system operating within the individual. Briefly, their thesis is that within any person at any given moment of time a number of tendencies toward relatively independent courses of action are operating. Their *principle of action* states that the *strongest* of these competing tendencies will determine the action a person chooses or takes toward a goal. Four main determinants* influence which tendency is evoked as activity: *availability, expectancy, incentive* and *motive*. Aggression as a basic motivation in athletics can be viewed in terms of these four main sources of effect.

Availability. Availability as a determinant is the extent to which a particular stimulus situation *makes available* a particular course of action. All situations give rise to, or permit, certain activities (Birch and Veroff, 1966)—a basketball court suggests or makes available different actions than does a classroom or laboratory. Aggression or aggressiveness within a boy thus has a better opportunity for expression, for example, in a basketball game than during a lecture or laboratory experiment. Thus, the milieu of a basketball game (the competition, the opponents, the crowd,

---

*In this particular context the discussion refers only to *instrumental* or goal-directed activity, not to what the authors refer to as consummatory activity.

the actual physical movement, etc.) acts as a stimulus to one or more of a variety of responses within the individual, and, in a sense, makes *available* for these responses to be expressed in actual, overt behavior. Thus, in a game, aggressive activity by an individual can be explained simply in terms that the game itself (milieu) made available or *released* the aggressive behavior observed in one or all of the contestants. It is also reasonable to assume that some sports (and their peculiar or specific milieus) have more of a *releasing capacity* for aggression than others. Football, rugby, ice hockey, boxing, wrestling, judo, etc., the so-called physical contact sports, may provide, or make available, aggressive responses more than non-contact sports such as track and field, tennis, golf, swimming, skiing. So the presence of aggressiveness in a boy in the former category of sports, or its absence in the latter category, may simply be a function of the situational aspects of the particular sport. A boy's aggressiveness or lack of it quite possibly may not be connected to any inherent trait whatsoever. Incidentally, this view can be applied to explaining both the situational specificity *and* generality of aggressiveness in sport. If aggressiveness is viewed as specific to the situation, the Birch-Veroff position would indicate that different sports have different releasing capacities for aggression, with differential manifestations of aggression occurring in different people in different sports. On the other hand though, quite possibly there is some factor operating in *all* sport (*i.e.*, some general factor) that causes or elicits aggressiveness in the individual. Maybe a direct connection can be made from the competitive urge or struggle that occurs in practically all sports to aggressiveness, thus making the releasing capacity of sport for aggression quite general in nature. This is an issue that can only be verified through research.

In addition to the situational aspects pertaining to availability are its historical origins. The past history of each individual influences availability basically in two ways (Birch and Veroff, 1966). First, through the habit patterns the person has developed comes the idea that a person will predictably behave in a manner in which he has behaved previously. When a boy has a past history of acting aggressively in his sport, then it is quite likely that he will act aggressively in current, similar situations. The virtual habit of aggressiveness reoccurs. Second, and slightly more indirect, is the fact that certain stimulus situations (such as sports) may suggest certain *goal* activities* rather than

---

*A goal activity, or consummatory activity, is an activity which a person engages *in* rather than activity which is purposely directed *toward* a goal.

instrumental or goal-*directed* activities; these goal activities then suggest available courses of instrumental action which will yield these goals. For example, boys differ according to their past histories in the extent to which they act aggressively in sports situations. A boy who is disposed to anticipate success in sport as an outcome of aggressive behavior will quite naturally think of courses of action that yield success in essentially aggressive terms; he thus will probably automatically behave aggressively in new situations. Another boy, with a different past history of aggressive behavior, will not tend to think of aggressive responses instrumental to athletic success.

Expectancy. Expectancy as a determinant is merely the *anticipation* that engaging in a certain activity will lead to a particular goal. A boy's level of motivation at any point in time is naturally dependent on how well he expects to do in his sport or event. He anticipates how well he will be able to do by speculating as to which courses of action will be most beneficial for him. This is very much a goal-connected determinant—the consequence or outcome of his endeavors influence the kind of action he engages in. So, if a positive outcome is likely through an aggressive course of action, the boy is aggressive—if not, he isn't. The strength of his expectancy of success as a result of aggressive action is dependent on how many times in the past aggressive action has led to success. It is interesting here to note that parents who allow or push their children into ability levels too high for them, risk putting them into certain failure situations. This kind of handling merely weakens the connection between the young athlete, aggressiveness, and success because he constantly experiences failure. His failure is not caused by a lack of aggressiveness but simply because he's too far above his ability level. Lack of aggressiveness can be readily observed in young athletes who have been pushed too fast, too soon.

Expectancy, as a determinant in motivation, then, serves to link an activity to its outcome. A boy's expectancy of success or failure in his event directly determines his level of aggressiveness. This is a function of both past associations and immediate or current perceptions of the situation.

Incentive. The consequences of a particular action—success, failure, or a combination of the two—have specific kinds of incentive value to the individual. Success has a high positive incentive value; failure a high negative incentive value. Incentive, then, as a determinant of motivational level, is rather clearly defined in athletics. If winning or succeeding in sport has high incentive for the boy, then this will enhance his level of aggressiveness; especially instrumental aggression. Aggressiveness, again, is linked to outcomes or consequences. Depending on the boy's past history, then, certain consequences of the aggressive action he takes toward succeeding will have varying amounts of either negative or positive incentive value.

In the athletic world, every effort is made to identify all motivational activity as having high incentive value only when the outcome is winning or success. In such a narrow context aggressiveness is reinforced only when the boy wins. When one considers all of sport, one is forced to realize that, while a few athletes win some of the time, most athletes lose most of the time. Fortunately, of course, most participants place incentive value on factors other than winning and thus are able to maintain their motivational levels in the absence of winning. Coaches, however, who place too much emphasis on winning as the "only thing" will experience tremendous difficulty in maintaining the motivational level of their players; especially their aggressiveness. How can one sensibly expect the young athlete who has played a hard, aggressive game to place any incentive value on aggressiveness if he loses? Many coaches handle their athletes in this manner and then wonder why motivation is low on the team. The sensible course of action to raise levels of aggressiveness, of course, is to place high incentive value on the action itself rather than its outcome.

It is also important for the student of sport to realize which actions and which consequences have positive or negative incentive value for each individual. Generally speaking, achievement, aggressiveness, praise, winning, success, recognition, etc., have positive incentive value, whereas physical injury, isolation, punishment, criticism, and failure have negative incentive value. Whatever their source, and regardless of individual differences, consequences with positive incentive value attached to them function to strengthen motivation; consequences with negative incentive value attached to them function to weaken motivation. Specifically, this holds true for aggressiveness.

Motive. Incentive, as a determinant, acts specifically in terms of consequences to affect motivation. Motive acts more generally to influence motivation. The strength of repulsion or attraction to a general class of consequences is called the *motive* for that class. Athletes then can be said to have a high motive for aggression when they generally feel that aggressiveness is necessary to achieve their particular goals — whatever they may be.

Athletes, like other people, will differ in the strength of a motive such as aggressiveness, in that individuals who have a high motive for aggression instinctively attempt to achieve their goals through predominantly aggressive actions rather than through alternative methods. Some people in athletics, for example, feel that aggressiveness is solely important for success, although athletes low in aggressiveness can easily accomplish their particular goals by being motivated differently. Birch and Veroff (1966) also emphasize that motives modify the incentive value of particular consequences. For example, if outright aggression in football has a high positive incentive value for a player (*i.e.*, being aggressive really appeals to him), then, if he already has a high motive for aggression, the consequences of aggressive performances will be even more attractive to him. Physically injuring an opponent in a sport can have a very high incentive value for an athlete who has a high need for aggression, whereas such a consequence would have far less incentive value for a boy whose need for aggressiveness is low.

Overview

Aggression as a motivational system must, in the final analysis, be directly associated with the intentional injury of another person, with the greater the injury, the greater the incentive. This is not an overstatement if one is aware of the dominant reinforcement directed toward aggressiveness in sport. A boy told to go out and "get" his opponent will do exactly that, and this behavior, constantly reinforced by hysterical fans, will gradually convince him that outright violence is condonable and correct. To rationalize that being aggressive is only a means to an end is to ignore the unfortunate result, that violence becomes an end in itself. In terms of raw energy output, there is little doubt that aggression is the most intense of all primary motivations, and sports competition, by its very nature, aggravates and intensifies aggressive tendencies — one's opponents are out there to frustrate one from reaching one's goals; frustration leads to anger, which leads to aggression, which often results in violence, which is sometimes in the form of brutality. Such a syndrome in sport is, unfortunately, too often encouraged and reinforced.

AFFILIATION IN SPORT

Preface

Man is gregarious, both by instinct and nature. Since his primitive days, when he huddled together with others for warmth and protection, he has sought and enjoyed the company of his contemporaries. Though he hunted with others out of necessity, there is little reason to believe he found this togetherness unenjoyable. However, regardless of whether the need for affiliation is biologically determined or is merely a learned pattern of social behavior, there is little doubt that a strong tendency exists in humans today to *seek, attain,* and *maintain* a social bond with other people. If such a general tendency underlies the motivational structure in man, then there is an immediate implication in terms of its relevance for explaining behavior in play, physical activity, and sport.

INTRODUCTION

Of paramount interest here is the question of whether or not the need for affiliation in an individual has a major influence on his initial and continued participation in physical activity and sport. For some time now there has been the feeling that children participate in sport for affiliative needs just as much as they do for achievement needs — that it is just as important for them to be members of a sports group as it is for them to achieve success in athletic performance. The attractiveness for the young participant just to be chosen to play on a team, or to represent one's school in a sporting event, is only now being realized as a major motivational component in athletics. In fact, for many children, mere *membership* on a team is enough to satisfy their basic needs in playing a sport. So much so, that it exists as a problem for many coaches. Children who are satisfied in *only* making the team tend to fall off in their performance, or to not improve any farther, simply because they have achieved their main objective of affiliative membership in a high status group.

Three major dimensions probably operate to cause the affiliative tendency in people and all three have immediate relevance for behavior in physical activity and sport. These dimensions, though they will be covered in detail shortly, can be operationalized as: 1) the fear of isolation or separation from the group, 2) the need for self-evaluation, and 3) the availability of gaining self-esteem through affiliation with other people. The common root of these dimensions is characterized by Birch and Veroff (1966), when they suggest that the affiliation incentive is *"the attraction to another organism in order to feel reassured from the other that the self is acceptable."* A pictorial representation of these dimensions can be seen in Diagram 17.

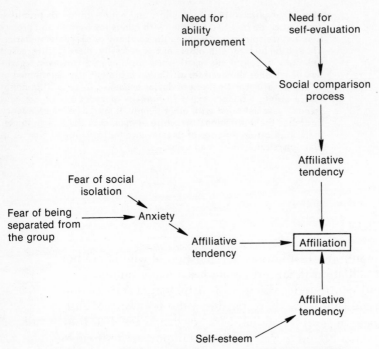

DIAGRAM 17. MAJOR AFFILIATIVE DIMENSIONS IN SPORT

DEFINITION AND TYPES OF AFFILIATION

Affiliation can be generally characterized by:

The desire to seek, attain, and maintain a close social bond or association with other people.

Schacter (1959) divides the need for affiliation into two broad categories:

1. *Asocial* Affiliation.   Affiliative needs for which other people are only *incidental* to need satisfaction.

2. *Social* Affiliation.   Affiliative needs which can only
                                be satisfied by some sort of con-
                                tact with other people who are
                                essential for need satisfaction.

Examples of the first type are those needs concerned with
recreation, excitement, and diversion that one can satisfy, for
example, by going to a football game; other people, while present, are only incidental to one's enjoyment. This kind of *asocial*
affiliative behavior in which other people are useful, but not
essential, accounts for most affiliative tendencies in people.
Social affiliative behavior, on the other hand, which concerns
people wanting membership in groups for reasons of acceptance,
recognition, status, etc., probably has more psychological significance and relevance for behavior in physical activity and
sport. The little boy who wants to play on his local little league
baseball team because of the feelings of belongingness that it
gives him, or the men and women who enjoy their membership
in a golf club because of the warm companionship that exists, are
probably functioning, at least partially, within a *social* affiliation
framework.

Common sense tells us that people will associate with each
other simply because it is necessary in order for them to achieve
their own particular goals. One can't really play any of the so-
called "team" sports such as baseball or football, without at least
several other people. We know that playing hockey, for example,
has little satisfaction or fun connected to it if one is forced to play
alone, and we know that a great deal of the enjoyment playing a
game with a group of friends results from the companionship.
Supporting this contention is evidence indicating that belonging
to a group is even more attractive to an individual if there is some
guarantee that his own particular needs or motives will be satisfied (Gilchrist, 1952, and Thibault, 1950). *People* also represent
goals to people, in that certain needs can only be satisfied through
interpersonal relationships. Recognition, approval, support, and
friendship exemplify such needs, with the association *itself* providing the satisfaction, not some indirectly related individual
achievement.

SOCIAL ISOLATION, ANXIETY, AND AFFILIATION IN SPORT

Considerable evidence comes from the developmental literature dealing not only with institutionalized children but also
with normal adult subjects and college students that even tem-

porary *social isolation* is anxiety producing, and that individuals respond to this anxiety by seeking affiliation with other people. Thus, it is anxiety that causes the affiliative tendencies, not the isolation *per se*. Walters and Ray (1960), for example, tested four groups of subjects in terms of how they responded to social reinforcement (*i.e.,* affiliation with each other). The groups were structured in the following manner: 1) subjects isolated and made anxious, 2) isolated but not made anxious, 3) not isolated and made anxious, and 4) neither isolated nor anxious. Results indicated that, whether or not there was isolation, subjects made anxious chose the social reinforcement; if not made anxious, they did not. Schacter's (1959) findings were in agreement with this conclusion: he found that girls suffering high anxiety prior to receiving electric shocks in an experiment preferred waiting with other girls to waiting alone. Schacter also found that restricting conversation among the girls waiting together made no difference, they still chose social reinforcement over isolation.

Implicit in these findings is the indication that generally high levels of anxiety are generated in people, and especially children, when they are forced into social isolation. One of the most prevalent responses to this anxiety is an affiliative tendency. This partially explains why young children would rather play with friends than alone. It may also have strong implications for explaining why the large-group sports or team sports are more attractive to children than the relatively lonely or socially isolated individual sports. It certainly is consistent with Kenyon's (1968b) findings on the attitudes toward physical activity of secondary high school students who rate physical activity as a social experience having the strongest meaning for them of all the six subdomains of physical activity characterized by Kenyon. Children are aware of the importance of belonging to the various peer social groups operating in their teen-age society, and undoubtedly have real feelings of anxiety if for some reason they are isolated from these groups. Participation in athletics offers them the opportunity of alleviating such anxiety, so they "turn out for the team." Byrne (1961), for example, has shown that people with high need affiliation (as measured by the Thematic Apperception Test) are significantly more anxious than those with low need affiliation. Thus, if a child is participating in athletics in order to reduce anxiety arising from a strong need for affiliation (or because he is a social isolate), then his motivation to be part of a particular athletic group will be extremely high. And unless this desire is redirected toward other objectives once he has "made the team," then it will fall off quite significantly.

Why should a person be highly anxious about social isolation? What is it in man that causes him to affiliate? The major viewpoint concerning this is that a "dependency drive" grows out of the nurturance, succorance, and positive reinforcement of the child by his parents, in particular his mother. Such a dependency "drive" is deeply rooted in any animal species — survival of the species depends on the performance of appropriate responses between members of that species. To learn how to survive, the young organism learns first from his parents, on whom he is dependent. Harlow (1959) feels that the affectionate bond between mother and child has its antecedents in the comfort caused by the physical contact between them. Via stimulus generalization, the comfort emanating from contact is transferred to other stimuli and takes on secondary reinforcing properties for the child. Thus, under conditions of stress, the person exhibits dependent behavior, which, in turn, if reinforced causes repetition of that behavior. Dependency, thus, is a set of responses having its origins in the affectionate relationships between mother and child. With experience, dependency behavior is learned as an escape response from anxiety, and thus is initiated *by* anxiety.

Quite possibly the above explanation partially accounts for the presence of strong *sensory incentives* which probably operate in affiliative settings. That is, the strong attraction of affectionate relationships between athletes on a team has its origins in the dependency drive common to the human species. This is part of the affiliative tendency in people — to have warm friendly relationships with one's teammates, especially in terms of physical contact — a strong incentive operating in stressful athletic situations. Explicit here is the obvious importance attached to, and the enjoyment of, clapping teammates on the shoulders when a good play is made, a touchdown is scored, a game is won, or a goal is scored. These occurrences are immediately followed by teammates hugging each other and, in some periods of extreme excitement, actually kissing each other. It is all part and parcel of the strong affiliative tendencies operating in athletes participating in competitive sport.

One other strong implication for sport is of interest here. Janis (1963), in a study concerned with group identification under conditions of external danger, proposed that dependency on a leader may constitute a motive for affiliation. He hypothesized that much of the motivation for group solidarity comes from the strong emotional bonds established between each member and the leader. This view is based on the occurrence of "transference" reactions toward the idealized leader who, as a parent surrogate, provides the main impetus to a group sharing common ideals and standards of conduct. (Such a transference reaction is implicit in the writings and statements of those athletes who played for the late Vince Lombardi.) One construct which seems useful in accounting for the expression of those dependency reactions is the *reactivation of separation anxiety, i.e.,* fears of separation from one's parents in childhood. Janis feels that these fears persist in latent form into adulthood and underlie the characteristic changes in the social behavior of people exposed to danger stress, pressure, or extreme anxiety producing situations. This fear-ridden type of dependency is likely to develop toward authority figures, who are perceived as being responsible for controlling the danger. Considerable amounts of faith, thus, are loaded onto authority figures, such as coaches, because of their supposed ability to pull the group or team through periods of crises. Thus, strong identifications with coaches and, in some instances, other players on the team occur because they are seen as being able to handle or control the danger to which the team is exposed. In some cases, a coach can completely destroy the morale of his team by "cutting" a player who many of the players have identified with as a parent surrogate.

SELF EVALUATION, SOCIAL COMPARISON, AND AFFILIATION IN SPORT

The Drive for Self-Evaluation.   A great deal of affiliative behavior is prompted by needs for self-evaluation. This proposition is covered partially by Festinger's (1954) theory of social comparison processes. Festinger first postulated that "*there exists in the human organism a drive to evaluate his opinions, abilities and (emotions).*" That is, people desire an accurate appraisal of their abilities; how well their opinions coincide with those of others, and how appropriate their emotional reactions are to various events and circumstances. In athletics, for example, there exist certain objective, physical standards with which an athlete can compare and evaluate quite easily his own abilities (*e.g.,* the height or distance which he can jump can be evaluated by comparing with local or world records in the high and long jumps). However, when objective standards are nonexistent, comparison for purposes of evaluation is sometimes impossible, and it is in this kind of situation that one is usually required to compare one's abilities, attitudes, opinions, and emotional reactions with those of other participants or athletes. The small boy playing hockey on the local pond in a remote rural community, for example, has little opportunity to eveluate his performance realistically or to know what kind of behavior is appropriate for his particular objectives. By being a member of a team or minor hockey association, and playing and interacting with boys his own age, relative standards of performance and conduct are made available to him for evaluation. According to Festinger (1954) and Schacter (1959), such evaluation is termed *social comparison* and the information provided is called *social reality*.

When young children play they are engaging in social comparison, because no objective standards of how competent they are are available to them. They can, by accurately judging the reactions of their playmates to their own performances and behavior, receive external feedback as to whether they are doing the right or wrong thing, and to what degree. Such feedback establishes for them a framework of reference within which they can evaluate how competent they are in the "real" world. Similarly, this drive can be visualized as existing in older children as they participate in athletics; under the pressures of competition, the evaluation a boy receives of his abilities and emotions, both internally and externally, has a very real emphasis. It is quite probable that this need for evaluation is a prominent reason for why children participate in sport.

Relevant evaluation through social comparison is only adequate when the comparison people are similar to the person receiving the evaluation. Comparison with athletes his own age and ability level is much more valid for a boy than if he were to compare himself with older, college or professional players. This kind of comparison is becoming increasingly more obvious with the contemporary young athlete whose evaluation by his teammates is more important to him than evaluation by various authority figures such as the coach. This is, and always has been, a predominant aspect of adolescent society; in particular, where status with the peer group becomes as important, if not more important, than status in the family group.

The Unidirectionality of Ability Self-Evaluation. One distinction is relevant at this point. Festinger (1954) states that, with respect to abilities, there is upward drive to improve or change (see Diagram 17). That is, in the Western world a high value is set on doing better and better and/or becoming a success. When a boy, seeking evaluation of his athletic ability from boys similar to him, discovers that he is below or at the group average, he will engage in unidirectional behavior upward to improve his ability (he feels a "pressure" on him to do so). However, with respect to opinions, in the absence of social comparison with others, no such force to change exists. No one opinion is necessarily preferable or "better" than another. The value or validity of one's opinion on something comes from a subjective feeling that it is true. So, for example, a boy participating in sports, in the absence of any social comparison, will feel it necessary to improve his athletic performance, but not his opinions on, for example, the importance of winning. His opinions will only change if he finds, in the presence of social comparison, that they are quite divergent from those held by his reference group. This action to change his opinion in order to reduce the discrepancy between him and the group results in a more comfortable uniformity within the group and is generally called *social quiescence*.

When a discrepancy in opinion exists within a group, there is an action on the part of the group members to reduce that discrepancy. This is quite evident in athletics. Teams which have a high degree of pride or discipline, for example, tend to have within themselves a strong pressure on each individual team member to conform or be uniform with the group opinion. This pressure is much stronger and more effective than any influences from the outside, such as the coach, the fans, or the spectators, even though it is recognized that a good coach can foster and aid the development of such opinions. Pride and discipline, however, exist within any group if, in terms of social comparison theory, there is no discrepancy in opinion within the group. Also, the more attractive the group is to the individual, the more important the group is as a comparison group to him. For the young child participating in athletics this is highly prevalent. If he wants to play on the local little league team badly enough, he will be more than prepared to change his opinions if, on comparison with the opinions of the other boys on the team, he discovers a discrepancy.

The Instability of Subjective Evaluations. In the absence of either physical or objective standards, or of social comparison with others, evidence indicates that one's own subjective evaluation of abilities and opinions is usually unstable. This premise is clearly seen in "level of aspiration"[*] experiments. If a person scores as well on a task as he said he expected to do, he feels success and if he scores less than his aspirations, he experiences failure. However, if the person is performing this task in the absence of comparison with other people's performances, or in the absence of comparison with objective standards, his level of aspiration (*i.e.*, how well he expects or hopes to do) will become completely a function of his own performance, the former fluctuating as a result of the latter. For the young athlete or sports par-

---

[*]The paradigm of "level of aspiration" experiments is outlined in Chapter 9, Achievement in Sport.

ticipant such a situation becomes confusing and uncomfortable. Not "knowing" how well he is performing will cause a marked negative effect on his subconscious levels of aspiration (his motivation), which, if continued for any length of time, will ultimately cause a deterioration of his performance. Young athletes require frameworks within which they can evaluate their performances and behavior and this, in many cases, leads to a desire for affiliation.

Social Comparison. To the extent that self-evaluation can only be accomplished through social comparison, the self-evaluatory drive causes people to join and belong to certain appropriate reference groups, to *affiliate*. Such a drive also causes people to be pressured toward a uniformity of opinions and emotions consistent with the group opinions and emotions. Social comparison is normally made through observation of and conversation with others, although it can also be achieved through reading, watching TV, and other quasi means. The need one has for accurate evaluation will determine the types of groups with which he affiliates, and normally he will tend to affiliate with people similar to him in abilities and opinions. Conversely, he will tend to avoid or to leave groups which do not provide him with accurate evaluations of his abilities, opinions, and emotions. The pressure toward group uniformity will cause the person to change himself in the direction of the group norm, to recruit others from outside who have the same opinions, and to reject those who have divergent views.

Though social comparison is not the only reason people associate with one another, it is a strong reason for people associating with each other when other people are essential for evaluation. Also, it is important to realize that not all abilities and opinions subject to evaluation by social comparison arouse the tendency to affiliate. Only when the evaluation of abilities and opinions is important to the person, or when intense emotional reactions exist, does the drive to affiliate occur. Vast individual differences obviously exist in the need to affiliate, and nowhere is this more evident than in sport. Only by being a member of a sport group (whether it is a team or not) can one estimate the adequacy of his ability or achieve a feeling of correctness in his opinions of the way athletes should behave. This is especially true for young participants and probably has an important socializing effect on them. How strong this drive for self-evaluation in sports is when compared to the other needs which an individual satisfies in group membership is difficult to say, but it would seem quite clear that such a drive does contribute considerably to the desirability of better performance.

Especially in sports groups, we will find people of relatively similar abilities and opinions; in particular those which possess a high degree of relevance or importance for the individual. People who play golf, for example, have relatively the same attitude toward golf and attach much the same degree of importance to it. The ability to play golf and a positive opinion of the relative importance of golf thus become crucial requirements in the formation of a group of golfers.

Thus, in humans, there exists a need to evaluate one's opinions, abilities, and emotional behavior. In the absence of external, physical, and objective standards, one will compare these aspects of one's psychological structure with those of other people in order to derive self-evaluation. This process is called *social comparison,* and the information derived is termed *social reality.* Adequate evaluation requires that the comparison people be similar to the evaluator, that the emotional reactions of other people be appropriate to those of the evaluator, and that the range of abilities, opinions, or emotional reactions in the reference group be non-divergent enough to enable the evaluator to make a realistic comparison.

SELF ESTEEM THROUGH AFFILIATION IN SPORT

Probably one of the most significant group of needs facilitated through association with other people in sports and physical activity settings are those involving self-esteem and the esteem of others for oneself. Such needs can be seen as revolving around the necessity of having a high evaluation of oneself that is stable and enduring. Maslow (1970) suggests that these esteem needs can be divided into two types:

1. Those involved with needs for achievement, mastery, and competence which lead to self-confidence; and
2. Those involved with prestige, status, recognition and reputation which lead to feelings of self-worth.

The satisfaction of such needs is seen as leading to convincing the person of his adequacy and capability in the world; the thwarting or blocking of them to feelings of inferiority and weakness. It is also fairly well accepted that the most stable, and most healthy, kind of self-esteem is that which is based on *deserved* respect from others, rather than on the temporary or semi-valid adulation derived from non-informed others. That is to say, self-esteem tends to be valid only when it is based on *real* competence, capacity, or adequacy for particular tasks and when this competence is judged by informed people. For example, when a boy's teammates judge his worth highly, on the basis of his real or actual competence on the team, his self-esteem will be reinforced much more significantly than if the approval comes from the media or spectators, who are relatively uninformed as to his true worth to the team.

It is highly unlikely that the need for self-esteem can be satisfied in a vacuum, in the absence of information feedback from other people. As Schacter (1959) has suggested, *"People do mediate goals for one another . . . and that it is (probably) necessary to associate with other people or belong to particular groups in order to gain specifiable individual goals."* This is obvious in sport. To gain recognition, to achieve, or to master certain skills in sport, one must perforce have some degree of association with other people. When one is attempting to attain such goals as self-esteem through participation in sport and other people are only *incidental* to the satisfaction of such needs, the affiliation is termed *asocial.* Affiliation is only a means to an end. However, when *people* represent the goals for which one is striving, the affiliative tendency is termed *social.* Here, the reference is to those particular kinds of needs which can be satisfied *only* in social interpersonal relationships with other people. Needs such as recognition, approval, support, and prestige can only be satisfied through a social type of affiliation. When a boy desires an enhancement of his self-esteem through the approval or recognition of other people, then he is forced to affiliate with them. When he realizes this acceptance of self can only be generated through other people, then the affiliative tendency within him begins to function very strongly. And when this affiliative urge starts to function, he becomes aware that various alternatives are open to him which can satisfy this need for self-esteem. One of the alternatives is affiliating with sports groups. Thus, one of the strong motivating influences involved with sports participation can be interpreted as a need for affiliation. If the need for self-esteem is met through affiliating with sports groups, the boy continues to participate; if it is not, he drops out. Some children, as we have already noted, have as their main goals in sports participation the enhancement of self-worth, and in many cases these are met through simple affiliation. For some children mere membership in a sports group is more than sufficient. When a child has some doubts about himself, there is a strong tendency generated within him to affiliate. When the discrepancy between the ideal and realistic conceptions of himself widens, a great deal of anxiety occurs, and he is forced into affiliating with other children to restore his self-image. The greater this discrepancy, the lower his self-esteem. The lower the self-esteem, the greater the feelings of inadequacy and inferiority, and, consequently, the greater reliance that is placed on supportive feedback from other people.

When, by participating in sport, a child enhances his self-esteem, immediately feelings of pride, self-worth, and adequacy accrue. This, in turn, causes an improvement in both general behavior and specific athletic performances. Considerable evidence exists which indicates that strong self-concepts are highly correlated to success in achievement-oriented activities such as athletics. The affiliative tendency in sport, thus, becomes of particular relevance for understanding why children participate in sport and why some children are more successful than others.

Overview

Intuitively, one must accept that in today's society of increasing urbanization and technology, with the obvious breakdown of the traditional family group, and with the depersonalization of our daily life caused by greater numbers of people crowded together (but still relatively isolated from each other), there is operating within us a strong need for relevant affiliation with people of similar attitudes, interests, and ideas. Maslow (1970), for example, feels that the recent increase in interest shown toward communal living, T-groups, and related activities are probably manifestations of this need for personal contact and affiliation. In particular, feelings of alienation toward society have become widespread among our younger people. They sense, and can identify in many cases, a lack of control over the goals toward which our society is moving. This dissatisfaction expresses itself in many ways, of course, one of which is the grouping together of "kindred spirits." This tendency to seek out and affiliate with similar others is, naturally, not just a recent thing; it has been with us since we first huddled together in caves for warmth and protection. It seems, nevertheless, to be particularly prevalent nowadays, and it is our contention that this tendency permeates strongly down into the behavioral patterns of people involved in sport.

The love and affection people have for each other, and the feelings of belonging to an important group, tend to be emphasized when the group faces a common external threat. Nowhere can this be seen as well as in the strong camaraderie and friend-ship developed in competitive sports teams. When one trains, practices, sacrifices, and dedicates oneself, day in and day out, alongside close friends who are doing the same thing, a strong bond is forged. This becomes a significant motivational drive in the behavior and performance of these people. In order to gain insight into athletic behavior, then, it is obviously necessary to take into account the strong affiliative tendency operating in sport and physical activity.

BIBLIOGRAPHY

Adler, A. (1927): *The Practice and Theory of Individual Psychology.* New York, Harcourt Brace & World.

Adler, A. (1930): Individual Psychology. *In* C. Murchinson (ed.): *Psychologies of 1930.* Worcester, Mass., Clark University Press.

Allport, F. (1924): *Social Psychology.* New York, Houghton Mifflin.

Allport, G. W. (1937): *Personality: A Psychological Interpretation.* New York, Holt.

Allport, G. W. (1961): *Pattern and Growth in Personality.* New York, Holt, Rinehart and Winston.

Appleton, L. E. (1910): *A Comparative Study of the Play of Adult Savages and Civilized Children.* Chicago, University of Chicago Press.

Ardrey, R. (1966): *The Territorial Imperative.* New York, Atheneum.

Asch, S. E. (1952): *Social Psychology.* New York, Prentice-Hall.

Atkinson, J. W. (1957): Motivational Determinants of Risk Taking Behavior. *Psychol. Rev.* 64:359–372.

Atkinson, J. W. (ed.) (1958): *Motives in Fantasy, Action and Society.* Princeton, D. Van Nostrand.

Atkinson, J. W. (1964): *An Introduction to Motivation.* Princeton, D. Van Nostrand.

Avedon, E. M., and Sutton-Smith, B. (1971): *The Study of Games.* New York, John Wiley & Sons.

Baldwin, J. M. (1895): *Mental Development in the Child and the Race.* New York, MacMillan.

Bandura, A. and Walters, R. H. (1963): *Social Learning and Personality Development.* New York, Holt, Rinehart and Winston.

Behrman, R. M. (1967): Personality Differences Between Swimmers and Non-Swimmers. *Res. Quart.* 38:163–171 (May).

Berkowitz, L. (1962): *Aggression: A Social Psychological Analysis.* New York, McGraw-Hill.

Berlyne, D. E. (1960): *Conflict, Arousal and Curiosity.* New York, McGraw-Hill.

Berlyne, D. E. (1968): Laughter Humor and Play. *In* Lindzey, G., and Aronson, E. (eds.) *Handbook of Social Psychology.* Reading, Mass., Addison-Wesley.

Biddulph, L. C. (1954): Athletic Achievement and the Personal and Social Adjustment of High School Boys. *Res. Quart.* 25:1–7 (March).

Birch, D. and Veroff, J. (1966): *Motivation: A Study of Action.* Belmont, Calif., Brooks/Cole.

Booth, E. G. (1958): Personality Traits of Athletes as Measured by the MMPI. *Res. Quart.* 29:127–138 (May).

Brehm, J. W., and Cohen, A. R. (1962): *Explorations in Cognitive Dissonance.* New York: John Wiley & Sons.

Brunner, B. C. (1969): Personality and Motivating Factors Influencing Adult Participation in Vigorous Physical Activity. *Res. Quart.* 40:464–469 (October).

Buhler, C. (1935): *From Birth to Maturity: An Outline of the Psychological Development of the Child.* London, Kegan Paul.

Buss, A. (1961): *The Psychology of Aggression.* New York, Wiley & Sons.

Buytendijk, F. J. J. (1933): *Weser und Sinn des Spiels: Das Spielen des Menschen und der Tiere als Erscheinungsform der Lebenstriebe.* Berlin, Wolff.

Byrne, D. (1961): Anxiety and Experimental Arousal of Affiliation. *J. Abnorm. Soc. Psychol.* 63:660–662.

Callois, R. (1955): The Structure and Classification of Games. *In* Loy, J., and Kenyon, G. (eds.): *Sport, Culture, and Society.* New York, Macmillan.

Callois, R. (1961): *Man Play and Games.* New York, Free Press.

Caplow, T. (1964) *Principles of Organization.* New York, Harcourt, Brace and World.

Carr, H. A. (1902): The Survival of Play. *An Investigation of the Department of Psychology and Education.* Boulder, Colo., University of Colorado Press.

Carter, G. S., and Shannon, J. R. (1940): Adjustment and Character Traits of Athletes and Non-athletes. *School Review,* 46:127–130.

Cattell, R. B. (1948): Concepts and Methods in the Measurement of Group Syntality. *Psychol. Rev.* 55:48–63.

Cattell, R. B. (1950): *Personality: A Systematic, Theoretical, and Factual Study.* New York, McGraw-Hill.

Cattell, R. B. (1957): *Personality and Motivation: Structure and Measurement.* New York, World Book.

Cattell, R. B. (1966): *The Scientific Analysis of Personality.* Chicago, Aldine.

Cattell, R. B., Blewett, D. B., and Beloff, J. R. (1955): The Inheritance of Personality. A Multiple Variance Analysis Determination of Approximate Nature-Nurture Ratios for Primary Personality Factors in Q Data. *Amer. J. Hum. Genetics.* 7:122–146.

Cattell, R. B., and Eber, H. W. (1964): *Handbook for the 16 PF Questionaire.* Champaign, Ill., IPAT.

Church, R. (1968): Applications of Behavior Theory to Social Psychology. In Samuels, R. A., *et al.* (eds.): *Social Facilitation and Imitative Behavior.* Boston, Allyn and Bacon.

Cofer, C., and Johnson, W. (1960): Personality Dynamics in Relation to Exercise and Sport. In Johnson, W. (ed): *Science and Medicine of Exercise and Sports.* New York, Harper Bros.

Cooper, L. (1969): Athletics, Activity and Personality: A Review of the Literature. *Res. Quart.* 40:17–22 (March).

Cottrell, N. B. (1968): Performance in the Presence of Other Human Beings: Mere Presence, Audience, and Affiliation Effects. In Samuels, R. A., *et al.* (eds.): *Social Facilitation and Imitative Behavior.* Boston, Allyn and Bacon.

Cox, F. N. (1966): Some Effects of Test Anxiety and Presence or Absence of Other Persons on Boys' Performance on a Repetitive Motor Task. *J. Extl. Child Psychol.* 3:100–112.

Cox, F. N. (1968): Some Relationships Between Test Anxiety, Presence or Absence of Male Persons, and Boys' Performance on a Repetitive Motor Task. *J. Exptl. Child Psychol.* 3:1–12.

Cratty, B. J. (1964): *Movement Behavior and Motor Learning.* Philadelphia, Lea & Febiger.

Cratty, B. J. (1968): *Psychology and Physical Activity.* Englewood Cliffs, N.J., Prentice-Hall.

Davey, C. (1972): *Exertion, Arousal, Personality and Mental Performance.* Ph.D Dissertation. University of Alberta, Edmonton, Canada.

Dember, W. N., and Earl, R. W. (1957): Analysis of Exploratory, Manipulatory and Curiosity Behavior. *Psychol. Rev.* 66:297–333.

Dembo, T. (1931): Der arger als Dynamisches Problem. *Psychol. Forsch.* 15:1–44.

Deutsch, M. (1949): A Theory of Cooperation and Competition. *Hum. Relations.* 2:129–152.

Dollard, J., and Miller, N. E. (1950): *Personality and Psychotherapy: An Analysis in terms of Learning, Thinking and Culture.* New York, McGraw-Hill.

Dollard, J., Miller, N. E., Doob, L. W., Mowrer, O. H., and Sears, R. R. (1939): *Frustration and Aggression.* New Haven, Conn., Yale University Press. Reprinted 1961.

Duffy, E. (1949): A Systematic Framework for the Description of Personality. *J. Abnorm. Soc. Psychol.* 44:175–190.

Duffy, E. (1951): The Concept of Energy Mobilization. *Psychol. Rev.* 58:30–40.

Duffy, E. (1957): Psychological Significance of the Concept of Arousal or Activation. *Psychol. Rev.* 64:265–275.

Duffy, E. (1962): *Activation and Behavior.* New York, John Wiley and Sons.

Easterbrook, J. A. (1959): The Effect of Emotion on Cue Utilization and the Organization of Behavior. *Psychol. Rev.* 66:183–201.

Erikson, E. H. (1950): *Childhood and Society*. New York, Norton.

Eron, L. D., Walden, L. O., Toigo, R., and Lefkowitz, M. M. (1963): Social Class, Parental Punishment for Aggression, and Child Aggression. *Child Develop.* 34:849–868.

Escalona, S. V. (1940): The Effect of Success and Failure upon the Level of Aspiration and Behavior in Manic-Depressive Psychoses. *University of Iowa Studies on Child Welfare*. University of Iowa.

Eysenck, H. (1947): *Dimensions of Personality*. London, Routledge.

Eysenck, H. (1960): *The Structure of Human Personality*. London, Methuen.

Eysenck, H. (1964): *Experiments in Motivation*. New York, Macmillan.

Eysenck, H. (1967): *The Biological Basis of Personality*. Springfield, Ill., Thomas.

Eysenck, H. (1968): *Manual for the Eysenck Personality Inventory*. San Diego, Calif., Educational & Industrial Testing Service.

Festinger, L. (1942): A Theoretical Interpretation of Shifts in Level of Aspiration. *Psychol. Rev.* 49:235–250.

Festinger, L. (1954): A Theory of Social Comparison Processes. *Hum. Relat.* 7: 117–140.

Festinger, L. (1954b): Motivations Leading to Social Behavior. In Jones, M. R. (ed.): *Nebraska Symposium on Motivation*. Lincoln, University of Nebraska Press.

Fiske, D. W., and Maddi, S. R. (eds.) (1961): *Functions of Varied Experience*. Homewood, Illinois, Dorsey Press.

Fitts, P. and Posner, M. (1967): *Human Performance*. Belmont, Calif., Brooks/ Cole.

Fleishman, E. (1964): *The Structure and Measurement of Physical Fitness*. Englewood Cliffs, N.J., Prentice-Hall.

Frank, J. D. (1935): Individual Differences in Certain Aspects of the Level of Aspiration. *Amer. J. Psychol.* 47:119–128.

Frank, L. K. (1963): Human Development: An Emerging Scientific Discipline. In Solnitand, A., and Provence, S. A., (eds.): *Modern Perspectives in Child Development*. New York, Int. Univ. Press Inc.

Frankenburg, R. (1957): *Village on the Border*. London, Cohen & West.

Freud, S. (1908): Creative Writers and Daydreaming. *In* Strachey, J. (ed.): *The Standard Edition of the Complete Psychological Works of Sigmund Freud*. London, Hogarth. Reprinted in 1959.

Freud, S. (1913): *Totem and Taboo*. London, Routledge & Kegan. Reprinted in 1960.

Freud, S. (1920): Beyond the Pleasure Principle. *In* Strachey, J. (ed.): *The Standard Edition of the Complete Psychological Works of Sigmund Freud*. London, Hogarth. Reprinted in 1959.

Freud, S. (1930): *Civilization and Its Discontents*. Reprinted London, Hogarth Press 1957.

Freud, S. (1943): *A General Introduction to Psychology*. New York, Garden City.

Ganzer, V. J. (1968): Effects of Audience Presence and Test Anxiety on Learning and Retention in Serial Learning Situation. *J. Pers. Soc. Psychol.* 8:194–199.

Gilchrist, J. C. (1952): The Formation of Social Groups Under Conditions of Success and Failure. *J. Abnorm. Soc. Psychol.* 47:174–187.

Gilmore, J. B. (1966): Play: A Special Behavior. In Haber, R. N. (ed.): *Current Research in Motivation*. New York, Holt, Rinehart and Winston.

Goffman, I. (1961): *Encounters*. Indianapolis, The Bobbs-Merrill Co.

Gray, J. A. (1964): *Pavlov's Typology*. New York, Pergamon.

Groos, K. (1898): *The Play of Animals*. New York, D. Appleton.

Groos, K. (1901): *The Play of Man*. New York, D. Appleton.

Groves, B. R. (1966): An Investigation of Personality Changes Resulting from Participating in a College Intra-Mural Program for Men. *Dissertation Abstracts* 26:7145 (June).

Guilford, J. P. (1959): *Personality*. New York, McGraw-Hill.

Hall, C. S., and Lindzey, G. (1970): *Theories of Personality*. 2nd ed. New York, John Wiley and Sons.

Hall, G. S. (1906): *Youth*. New York, Appleton.

Hanawalt, N. G., Hamilton, C. E., and Morris, M. L. (1943): Level of Aspiration in College Leaders and Non-Leaders. *J. Abnorm. Soc. Psychol.* 38:545–548.

Harlow, H. F. (1959): Love in Infant Monkeys. *Sci. Amer.* 200:68–74.

Hebb, D. O. (1955): Drives and the Conceptual Nervous System. *Psychol. Rev.* 62:243–253.

Heckhausen, H. (1964): Entwurf einer Psychologie des Spielens. *Psychol. Forsch.* 27:225–243.

Hoppe, F. (1930): Erfolg und Musserfolg. *Psychol. Forsch.* 14:1–63.

Horn, J. L. (1966): Motivation and the Dynamic Calculus Concepts from Multivariate Experiments. *In* Cattell, R. B. (ed.): *Handbook of Multivariate Psychology.* Chicago, Rand McNally.

Huizinga, J. (1955): *HomoLudens.* Boston, Beacon.

Hull, C. L. (1943): *Principles of Behavior.* New York, Appleton-Century-Crofts.

Ikegami, K. (1970): Character and Personality Changes in the Athlete. *Contemp. Psychol. Sport.* Chicago, Athletic Institute.

James, W. (1890): *The Principles of Psychology.* New York, Henry Holt.

Janis, L. L. (1963): Group Identification Under Conditions of External Danger. *Brit. J. Med. Psychol.* 36:227–238.

Johnson, C. J. (1966): Personality Traits Affected by High School Football as Measured by the Guilford-Zimmerman Temperament Survey. *Dissertation Abstracts.* 27:658A (September).

Johnson, W. R., Hutton, D. C., and Johnson, B. J. (1954): Personality Traits of Some Champion Athletes as Measured by Two Projective Tests: Rorschach and H-T-P. *Res. Quart.* 25:484–485 (December).

Jones, E. E., and Gerard, H. B.: *Foundations of Social Psychology.* New York, John Wiley and Sons, 1967.

Jung, C. G. (1929): *The Significance and Constitution of Heredity in Psychology. In* Collected works. Princeton, Princeton University Press 1960.

Jung, C. G. (1933): *Psychological Types.* New York, Harcourt, Brace and World.

Kane, J. E. (1964): Personality and Physical Ability. *Int. Congr. Sport Sci. Proc.* Tokyo, Japan.

Kane, J. E. (1965): Personality Profiles of Physical Education Students Compared with Others. *1st Int. Congr. Sports Psychol. Proc.*

Kane, J. E. (1970): Personality and Physical Abilities. *Contemp. Psychol. Sport.* Chicago, Athletic Inst.

Kenyon, G. S. (1968a): A Conceptual Model for Characterizing Physical Activity. *Res. Quart.* 39:96–105 (March).

Kenyon, G. S. (1968b): *Values Held for Physical Activity by Selected Urban Secondary School Students in Canada, Australia, England, and the United States.* United States Office of Education Contract S-376. University of Wisconsin (February).

Klein, M., and Christianson, G. (1966): Gruppenkomposition, Gruppenstruktur, und Effectivität von Basketballmannschaften. *In* Luschen, G. (ed.): *Kleingruppenforschung und Gruppe im Sport, Kolner Zeitschrift fur Soziologie und Sozialpsychologie.* 10:180–191.

Kohler, W. (1921): *The Mentality of Apes.* New York, Harcourt, Brace.

Kroll, W. (1967): Sixteen Personality Factor Profiles of Collegiate Wrestlers. *Res. Quart.* 38:49–57 (March).

Kroll, W., and Crenshaw, P. (1970): Multivariate Analysis Personality Profiles of Four Athletic Groups. *Contemp. Psychol. Sport.* Chicago, Athletic Institute.

Lakie, W. L. (1962): Personality Characteristics of Certain Groups of Intercollegiate Athletes. *Res. Quart.* 33:566–573.

Layman, E. (1970): Aggression in Relation to Play and Sports. *Contemp. Psychol. Sport.* Chicago, Athletic Institute.

Lazarus, M. (1883): *Uber die Reize des Spiels.* Berlin, F. Dummler.

Leach, E. R.: Ritual. *In* Gould, J. and Kolb, W. L. (eds.) (1964): *A Dictionary of the Social Sciences.* New York, The Free Press.

Lenck, H. (1964): Konflikt und Leistung in Spitzensportsmannachschaften. *Soziale Welt.* 15:307–343.

Levin, H., and Wardwell, E. (1962): The Research Uses of Doll Play. *Psychol. Bull.* 59:27–56.

Levin, H., and Fleischmann, B. (1968): Childhood Socialization. *In* Borgatta, E. F., and Lamberts, W. W. (eds.): *Handbook of Personality: Theory and Research.* Chicago, Rand McNally.

Lewin, K. (1933): Environmental Forces. *In* Murchinson, C., (ed.): *A Handbook of Child Psychology.* Worcester, Mass., Clark University Press.

Lewin, K., Dembo, T., Festinger, L., and Sears, P. S. (1944): Levels of Aspiration. *In* Hunt, J. McV. (ed.): *Personality and Behavior Disorders.* New York, Ronald Press.

Lorenz, K. (1964): *Ritualized Fighting. In* Carthy, J. D., and Ebling, F. J. (eds.): *The Natural History of Aggression.* New York, Academic Press.

Lorenz, K. (1966): *On Aggression.* New York, Bantam Books.

Loy, J. (1968): The Nature of Sport: A Definitional Effort. *Quest. Mongr.* X. 1–15 (May).

Loy, J. W. Jr., and Kenyon, G. S. (eds.) (1969): *Sport, Culture and Society.* New York, The Macmillan Co.,

Luschen, G. (1970): Cooperation, Association and Contest. *J. Confl. Resol.* 14: 21–34.

Maddi, S., and Propst, B. (1963): *Activation and Personality.* Unpublished Manuscript.

Maddi, S. (1968): *Personality Theories: A Comparative Analysis.* Homewood, Ill.: Dorsey Press.

Malpass, L. (1962): Competition, Conflict, and Cooperation as Social Values. *In: Values in Sport.* AAHPER National Conference, Washington, D.C., AAHPER.

Mandler, G., and Sarason, S. B. (1952): A Study of Anxiety and Learning. *J. Abnorm. Soc. Psychol.* 47:166–173.

Marks, J. B. (1954): Interests, Leadership, and Sociometric Status Among Adolescents. *Sociometry* 17:340–349.

Martens, R. (1969): Effects of an Audience on Learning and Performance of a Complex Motor Skill. *J. pers. soc. Psychol.* 12:252–260.

Martens, R. and Landers, D. M. (1969): Effects of Anxiety, Competition, and Failure on Performance on a Complex Motor Task. *J. Motor Behavior* 1:1–10.

Maslow, A. (1968): *Toward a Psychology of Being.* New York, D. Van Nostrand, Reinhold.

Maslow, A. (1970): *Motivation and Personality.* New York, Harper.

McClelland, D. C. (1951): *Personality.* New York, Dryden.

McClelland, D. C. (1955) (ed.): *Studies in Motivation.* New York, Appleton-Century-Crofts.

McClelland, D. C. (1961): *The Achieving Society.* Princeton, D. Van Nostrand.

McClelland, D. C., Atkinson, J. W., Clark, R. A., and Lowell, E. L. (1953): *The Achievement Motive.* New York, Appleton-Century-Crofts.

McClintock and Nuttin (1969): Development of Competitive Games: Behavior in Children Across Two Cultures. *J. Exp. Psych.,* 5:203–218.

McCloy, C. H. (1940): A Preliminary Study of Factors in Motor Educability. *Res. Quart.* 11:28–39 (March).

McDougall, W. (1908): *An Introduction to Social Psychology.* London, Methuen.

McDougall, W. (1917): *Social Psychology.* Boston, Luce.

McPhee, J. (1970): *Levels of the Game.* New York, Bantam Books.

Mead, G. H. (1934): *Mind, Self, and Society.* Chicago, University of Chicago Press.

Mead, M. (1961): *Cooperation and Competition Among Primitive Peoples.* New York, McGraw-Hill.

Meggyesy, D. (1971): *Out of Their League.* New York, Paperback Library.

Menninger, K. (1942): *Love Against Hate.* New York, Harcourt, Brace.

Merriman, B. J. (1960): Relationships of Personality Traits to Motor Ability. *Res. Quart.* 31:163–173 (May).

Metheny, E. (1965): *Connotations of Movement in Sport and Dance.* Dubuque, Iowa, Wm. C. Brown.

Millar, S. (1968): *The Psychology of Play.* Middlesex, England, Penguin Books.

Miller, N. E., and Dollard, J. (1941): *Social Learning and Imitation.* New Haven, Yale University Press.

Mogar, R. E. (1962): Competition Achievement and Personality. *J. Consult. Psychol.* 9:168–172.

Montagu, A. (1960): *The Humanization of Man.* New York, Grove Press.

Morehouse, L. E. (1965): Neuropsychology of Strength. *In* Antonelli, F. (ed.): *1st Int. Congr. Psychol. Sport Proc.,* Rome.

Mosston, M. (1966): *Teaching Physical Education: From Command to Discovery.* Columbus, Ohio, Charles Merrill.

Murray, H. A. (1938): *Explorations in Psychology.* New York, Oxford University Press.

Mussen, P. H., and Rutherford, E. (1961): Effects of Aggressive Cartoons on Children's Aggressive Play. *J. Abnorm. Soc. Psychol.* 62:461–465.

Neal, P. (1969): *Coaching Methods for Women.* Menlo Park, Calif., Addison-Wesley.

Nelson, L. L. and Kagan, S. (1972): Competition: The Star Spangled Scramble. *Psychology Today.* 6:53–58 (September).

Newman, E. N. (1968): Personality Traits of Faster and Slower Swimmers. *Research Quart.* 39:1049–1053 (December).

Ogilvie, B. and Tutko, T. (1966): *Problem Athletes and How To Handle Them.* London, Pelham Books.

Paddick, R. J. (1967): *The Nature and Place of a Field of Knowledge in Physical Education.* Unpublished M.A. Thesis. University of Alberta, Edmonton, Canada.

Pavlov, I. (1927): *Conditioned Reflexes.* London, Oxford University Press.

Piaget, J. (1932): *The Moral Judgment of Child.* London, Kegan Paul.

Piaget, J. (1945): *Play, Dreams, and Imitation in Childhood.* New York, Norton.

Porter, R. T. (1967): Sports and Adolescence. *In* Slovenko, R., and Knight, J. A. (eds.): *Motivations in Play, Games, and Sports.* Springfield, Charles C Thomas.

Quarter, J., and Marcus, A. (1971): Drive Level and the Audience Effect: A Test of Zajonc's Theory. *J. Soc. Psychol.* 83:99–105.

Raphelson, A. C. (1957): The Relationship Between Imaginative, Direct, Verbal, and Physiological Measures of Anxiety in an Achievement Situation. *J. Abnorm. Soc. Psychol.* 54:13–18.

Reider, N. (1967): Preanalytic and Psychoanalytic Theories of Play and Games. *In* Slovenko, R., and Knight, J. A. (eds.): *Motivations in Play, Games and Sports.* Springfield, Charles C Thomas.

Rentz, R. R., and White, W. F. (1967): Congruence of the Dimensions of the Self as Object and Self as Process. *J. Psychol.* 67:277–285.

Roberts, J. M., and Sutton-Smith, B. (1962): Child Training and Game Involvement. *Ethnology* 1:166–185.

Robinson, W. P. (1964): The Achievement Motive, Academic Success, and Intelligence Test Score. *Brit. J. Soc. Clin. Psychol.* 4:98–103.

Rose, A. (1956): Voluntary Associations Under Conditions of Competition and Conflict. *Soc. Forces* 34:159–163.

Ross, E. A. (1908): *Social Psychology: An Outline and Source Book.* New York, Macmillan.

Ross, R. C., and Van der Haag, E. (1957): *The Fabric of Society.* New York, Harcourt, Brace.

Ruffer, W. A. (1965): A Study of Extreme Physical Activity Groups of Young Men. *Res. Quart.* 36:183–195.

Ryan, D. (1962): Relationships Between Motor Performance and Arousal. *Res. Quart.* 33:279–287.

Sarason, S. B., and Mandler, G. (1952): Some Correlates of Test Anxiety. *J. Abnorm. Soc. Psychol.* 47:810–817.

Sargent, D. A. (1887): The Physical Characteristics of the Athlete. *Scribner's Magazine.* II:541–561 (July–December).

Sargent, S. S. (1948): Reaction to Frustration: A Critique and Hypothesis. Abridged from *Psychol. Rev.* 55:108–114.

Schacter, S. (1959): *The Psychology of Affiliation.* Stanford, Stanford University Press.

Schendel, J. (1965): Psychological Differences Between Athletes and Non-Participants in Athletics at Three Educational Levels. *Res. Quart.* 36:52–67 (March).

Schendel, J. (1970): The Psychological Characteristics of High School Athletes and Non-Participants in Athletics: A Three Year Longitudinal Study. *Contemp. Psychol. Sport.* Chicago, Athletic Institute.

Schiller, F. von (1875): *Essays Aesthetical and Philosophical.* London, George Bell.

Schlosberg, H. (1947): The Concept of Play. *Psychol. Rev.* 54:229–231.

Scott, J. (1971): *The Athletic Revolution.* New York, Free Press.

Scott, J. P. (1958): *Aggression.* Chicago, University of Chicago Press.

Sears, R. R., MacCoby, E. E., and Levin, H. (1957): *Patterns of Child Rearing.* Evanston, Ill., Row, Peterson.

Sheldon, W. H. (In collaboration with S. S. Stevens.) (1942): *The Varieties of Temperament: A Psychology of Constitutional Differences.* New York, Harper.

Singer, R. N. (1969): Personality Differences Between and Within Baseball and Tennis Players. *Res. Quart.* 40:582–588 (October).

Singer, R. N. (1972): *Coaching, Athletics and Psychology.* New York, McGraw-Hill.

Skinner, B. F. (1935): Two Types of Conditioned Reflexes and A Pseudo Type. *J. Genet. Psychol.* 12:66–77.

Skinner, B. F. (1953): *Science and Human Behavior.* New York, Macmillan.

Skinner, B. F. (1969): *Contingencies of Reinforcement: A Theoretical Analysis.* New York, Appleton-Century-Crofts.

Slovenko, R. and Knight, J. A. (eds.): *Motivations in Play, Games, and Sports.* Springfield, Ill., Charles C Thomas.

Spence, K. W. (1956): *Behavior Theory and Conditioning.* New Haven, Yale University Press.

Spence, J. T. and Spence, K. W.: The Motivational Components of Manifest Anxiety: Drive and Drive Stimuli. *In* Spielberger, C. C. (ed.): *Anxiety and Behavior.* New York, Academic Press.

Spencer, H. (1873): *Principles of Psychology.* New York, D. Appleton.

Sperling, A. P. (1942): The Relationship Between Personality Adjustment and Achievement in Physical Education Activities. *Res. Quart.* 13:351–363.

Starr, H. M. (1961): The Purposes of Competitive Athletics in American Education. *Amer. Acad. Phys. Educ. Proc.* Professional Contributions.

Stone, G. (1962): Appearance and the Self-Concept. *In* Rose, A. (ed.): *Human Behavior and Social Processes.* London, Kegan Paul.

Stone, G. P. (1955): American Sports: Play and Display. *Chicago Review,* 9:83–100.

Strong, C. H. (1963): Motivation Related to Performance of Physical Fitness Tests. *Res. Quart.* 34:497–507.

Sullivan, H. S. (1947): *Conceptions of Modern Psychiatry.* Washington, D.C.: William Allanson White Psychiatric Foundation.

Sutton-Smith, B. (1968): Novel Responses to Toys. *Merrill-Palmer Quart.* 14:151–158.

Symonds, P. M. (1951): *The Ego and the Self.* New York: Appleton-Century-Crofts.

Thibault, J. (1950): An Experimental Study of the Cohesiveness of Underprivileged Groups. *Hum. Relat.* 3:251–278.

Thomas, W. I. (1907): *Sex and Society.* Chicago, University of Chicago Press.

Thorndike, E. L. (1932): *The Fundamentals of Learning.* New York, Teacher's College, Columbia University.

Tillman, K. G. (1964): The Relationship Between Physical Fitness and Selected Personality Traits. *Dissertation Abstract* 25:276–277 (July).

Tutko, T., and Richards, J. (1970): *Psychology of Coaching.* Boston, Allyn and Bacon.

Tutko, T., Lyon, L. P., and Ogilvie, B. (1969): *The Athletic Motivational Inventory.* San Jose, Calif., Institute for the Study of Athletic Motivation.

Ulrich, C. (1968): *The Social Matrix of Physical Education.* Englewood Cliffs, N.J., Prentice-Hall.

Vaught, G. M. and Newman, S. E. (1966): The Effects of Anxiety on Motor Steadiness in Competitive and Non-Competitive Conditions. *Psychol. Sci.* 6:519–520.

Waelder, R. (1933): The Psychoanalytic Theory of Play. *Psychoanal. Quart.* 2:208–224.

Wankel, L. (1971): *A Self-Actualizing Theory of Play.* (Paper presented at the

2nd World Symposium on the History of Sport and Physical Education. Banff, Alberta, Canada, May 1971.)

Walters, R. H., and Ray, E. (1960): Anxiety, Social Isolation, and Reinforcer Effectiveness. *J. Pers.* 28:358–367.

Watson, J. B. (1919): *Psychology From the Standpoint of a Behaviorist.* Philadelphia, Lippincott.

Watson, J. B. (1925): *Behaviorism.* New York, Norton.

Weiss, P. (1969): *Sport, A Philosophic Inquiry.* Carbondale, Ill., Southern Illinois University Press.

Welford, A. T. (1968): *Fundamentals of Skill.* London: Methuen.

Werner, A. C. (1960): Physical Education and the Development of Leadership Characteristics of Cadets at the U.S. Military Academy. *Microcard Psy. 132. Ph.D Thesis.* Springfield College.

Werner, A. C., and Gottheil, E. (1966): Personality Development and Participation in Collegiate Athletics. *Res. Quart.* 37:126–131 (March).

White, R. W. (1959): Motivation Reconsidered: The Concept of Competence. *Psychol. Rev.* 66:297–333.

Whiting, H. T., and Stembridge, D. E. (1965): Personality and the Persistent Swimmer. *Res. Quart.* 36:348–356 (October).

Willis, J. D., and Bethe, D. R. (1970): Achievement Motivation: Implications for Physical Activity." *Quest* XIII: 18–22 (January).

Winterbottom, M. R. (1958): The Relation of Need for Achievement to Learning Experiences in Independence and Mastery. *In* Atkinson, J. W. (ed.): *Motives in Fantasy, Action, and Society.* Princeton: D. Van Nostrand.

Woodworth, R. S. (1918): *Dynamic Psychology.* New York, Columbia University Press.

Yerkes, R. M. and Dodson, J. D. (1908): The Relation of Strength of Stimulus to Rigidity of Habit Formation. *J. Comp. Neurol. Psychol.* 18:459–482.

Zajonc, R. B. (1965): Social Facilitation. *Sci.* 149:269–274.

INDEX